Writing Smarter!

Over 100 Step-by-Step Lessons with Reproducible Activity Sheets to Build Writing Proficiency in Grades 7-12

Keith Manos

**THE CENTER FOR APPLIED
RESEARCH IN EDUCATION**
West Nyack, New York 10994

Library of Congress Cataloging-in-Publication Data

Manos, Keith T.
  Writing smarter! : over 100 step-by-step lessons with reproducible
activity sheets to build writing proficiency in grades 7–12 / by
Keith Manos.
    p. cm.
  ISBN 0-87628-435-7
  1. English language—Composition and exercises—Study and teaching
(Secondary)—Handbooks, manuals, etc.   I. Title.
LB1631.M385   1998
808′.042′0712—dc21   98-33700
                                                                CIP

Printed in the United States of America

10   9   8   7   6   5   4   3   2   1

ISBN 0-87628-435-7

> **ATTENTION: CORPORATIONS AND SCHOOLS**
>
> The Center for Applied Research in Education books are available at quantity
> discounts with bulk purchase for educational, business, or sales promotional use.
> For information, please write to: Prentice Hall Special Sales, 240 Frisch Court,
> Paramus, New Jersey 07652. Please supply: title of book, ISBN number, quanti-
> ty, how the book will be used, date needed.

**THE CENTER FOR APPLIED RESEARCH
IN EDUCATION**
West Nyack, NY 10994
A Simon & Schuster Company

On the World Wide Web at http://www.phdirect.com

Prentice Hall International (UK) Limited, *London*
Prentice Hall of Australia Pty. Limited, *Sydney*
Prentice Hall Canada Inc., *Toronto*
Prentice Hall Hispanoamericana, S.A., *Mexico*
Prentice Hall of India Private Limited, *New Delhi*
Prentice Hall of Japan, Inc., *Tokyo*
Simon & Schuster Asia Pte. Ltd., *Singapore*
Editora Prentice Hall do Brasil, Ltda., *Rio de Janeiro*

Dedication

For my family—Cheryl, Brittny, John Morgan, and Christian—whose inspiration and support keep me teaching and writing.

About the Author

Keith Manos is currently an English teacher at Richmond Heights (OH) High School and has taught writing to grades 7 through 12 for twenty years at four different high schools. His students' poetry, fiction, and essays have earned them awards and recognition after being accepted for publication in local and national magazines.

In 1993 Keith earned a Master's Degree in English (Creative Writing) from Cleveland State University. His skill as a teacher of writing has enabled him to serve as an editior of various educational newsletters, student publications, and local magazines. He has also conducted many in-service seminars for teachers, coaches, and college students.

Keith is a licensed TESA (Teacher Expectations/Student Achievement) trainer, a member of the Ohio Council of Teachers of English, and a North Central Evaluation Team Committee participant. At Richmond Heights High School, he serves as chairperson for the Recognition Committee, School Curriculum Committee, and Athletic Council.

He is the author of many teaching and coaching articles which have appeared in national publications like *Scholastic Coach, School Library Journal, Strategies, Athletic Management, Hicall, Ohio ASCD Journal, Wrestling USA, Athletic Business*, and the Cleveland *Plain Dealer*. He has had fiction and poetry published in *Ohio Teachers Write, Visions, Lutheran Journal, New Earth Review*, and other literary journals. His resource, *Wrestling Coaches Survival Guide* (1995), was published by Parker Publishing, a Prentice Hall imprint. Currently, Keith is marketing two young adult novels while he continues to do freelance writing.

Keith is also a well-known motivational speaker for civic organizations, athletic teams, and awards programs in the Cleveland area when he isn't spending time with his wife and children Brittny, John Morgan, and Christian.

Acknowledgments

- Thanks to Conrad Hilberry for giving permission to reprint his poem "Instruction" which appeared in *Scholastic Scope*, April 3, 1992.
- Thanks to Connie Kallback, editor at Prentice Hall, whose persistence and insights contributed in a great way to the completion of this book.
- To my colleagues at Richmond Heights High School who reviewed my manuscript and offered advice.
- To my students who each day make my classroom experiences both challenging and rewarding.

About This Resource

Writing Smarter! is directed to junior high school and senior high school teachers who want to help their students improve their writing skills. It contains over one hundred practical and interesting lessons in the areas of writing, editing, and analyzing that appeal to all learning styles and intelligences. Teachers can follow step-by-step and day-by-day approximately 25 weeks of lesson plans, with assignments that keep students motivated and on track for success. Even the most veteran teachers can find fresh advice and innovative methods to enhance students' academic success and achieve curriculum goals at the same time.

Designed for flexibility, these lesson plans can be used in sequence as part of general thematic units or as individual lessons on one subject. The plan for each lesson includes an objective, discussion questions and answers, interactive learning activities, reproducibles or writing examples, and homework suggestions to help students carry out writing assignments. The activities build on each student's own cultural background, dominant learning style, and current interests.

Writing Smarter! also includes ready-to-use evaluation instruments that cater to students' strengths, encourage them to become self-directed writers and learners, and spark, at times, their natural competitiveness.

The resource is organized into 12 sections, focusing on different areas in writing, followed by a final section on peer editing that elaborates on the peer editing lesson that concludes most units.

The first section, *Orientation*, establishes evaluation and grading policies and introduces thinking skills (how these relate to writing), a writing portfolio, and cooperative learning. Also available are reproducibles that assist revision, such as the Writing Chart.

Section 2, *Description*, begins with identifying both Standard and Nonstandard English and then introduces the parts of speech, concrete words, and sensory language for a descriptive essay.

Section 3, the *Character Sketch,* continues the work on description and develops skills on writing characterization, developing a caricature, employing figurative language and appositives, and recognizing proper paragraphing skills.

Sentence Structure, Section 4, focuses on understanding effective sentence structure before learning sentence expansion, the various types of sentences, and emphasis and variety in sentences. How to avoid run-ons, fragments, and wordiness in sentences is also covered.

Students are encouraged to write personal narratives in Section 5 with activities such as "When and How and Why?" and "Events and Emotions."

Nine lessons in *Persuasion*, Section 6, give students practice in recognizing precise language as well as dangerous language, supporting opinions, developing a thesis, writing an introduction and conclusion, and more.

The research process from "Facts and Sources" and "Topic and Audience" to "Bibliography" and "Notes and Numbers" is covered in Section 7, packed with activities and reproducibles.

Students are guided through the interview process in Section 8 with lessons like "Celebrities, Idols, and Heroes," "Talk Show," and "Direct Quote vs. Paraphrase."

The News, Section 9, provides eight lessons in journalism basics and concludes with ideas for developing a class magazine or newspaper.

Parts of a letter, consumer mail, letters to the editor, and letters of application are among the topics covered in Section 10, *Writing Letters*.

Short fiction and *Poetry* round out the offerings of section topics in 11 and 12 with lessons in different aspects of each form accompanied by examples of good writing. Both sections contain lists of places students can submit their work for publication.

Although many of the sections conclude with peer editing activities, the final section focuses completely on how to introduce and use peer editing in the writing classroom. It offers five-minute prompts (energizers) for peer editing and time-saving reproducibles such as "Peer Editing Guidelines," three different peer editing checklists, and a peer editing model.

The appendix contains answer keys for activities that aren't in the to-the-teacher portions of the lessons as well as reproducibles—Guidelines for Writing Compositions and Teacher's Checklist for Writing Assignments.

The suggestions and activities in **Writing Smarter!** have been successful in my classes. I trust they will meet with the same success in yours.

Keith Manos

Table of Contents

Section 3   Character Sketch   71

Section 4   Sentence Structure   91

Section 5   Personal Narrative   133

Section 6   Persuasion   147

Section 7   Research   181

Section 8   Interviews   225

Section 9   The News   253

Section 10   Writing Letters   279

Section 11   Short Fiction   309

Section 12   Poetry   341

Section 13   Peer Editing   375

Appendix   387

Section 1 : ORIENTATION

"Public instruction should be the first
objective of government." (*Napoleon*)

Objectives: Establish credibility, classroom management, and rapport
Introduce basic thinking skills and the writing portfolio
Create a classroom environment that nurtures writing

Length: Four Lessons

Introduction:

Try to be unique from the very beginning to make students see your class as different from the five, six, or seven others they have during the day. You have to do this because in today's classrooms more is demanded from the teacher than ever before. You need to be cookbook-organized, rock 'n' roll-dynamic, and Ann Landers-sensitive. To become salespersons for learning, begin that first week. This is your first opportunity to convince students to forget the argument they had that morning with Mom, or the ache in their shoulder from yesterday's football practice, or the muggy heat in the classroom.

They have to realize this class is going to be different; it's not going to be like anything they've experienced before. The first day you plan to start them writing, establish credibility as their writing teacher.

During that first week students should become familiar with your teaching style and expectations. They need to see your classroom as a comfortable, yet challenging environment. Accomplish this by:

1. Opening with a *hook*—a survey, a controversial question, a scene from a video.

2. Using a *variety* of activities—a panel discussion, a class discussion, group work (a fun competition, if necessary), freewriting, etc.

3. Being sure students recognize the reasons for each activity. Most often, a quick explanation—"You need to do it this way because . . ." or "Here's why it's important to do it this way . . ."—can accomplish that.

4. Ending with some sort of *evaluation*—a quiz or test, a writing assignment—or a *debriefing*—an assessment of the lesson by students or a colleague.

1

Lesson 1 GRADING AND EVALUATION

Objective: Establish a teacher-student partnership and an evaluation policy

Activities:

1. **Discussion:** Request one student to take notes on the responses.

    What are your expectations of this course?

    What are your expectations of the teacher?

This discussion involves students in selecting the activities that encourage better performances. They may not know how to respond at first (How often are students asked to participate in the planning of a course?).

---

2. **Announce:** You, the teacher, are the audience. Have them respond to one or more of the folowing **in writing**:

    A. How do you learn best? What is the method or activity that helps you learn most productively?

        Sample responses:

        "I came to the United States about one year ago. still have a little bit problems with vocabulary. I learn best by reading."

        "I learn best when information is presented through lectures or assigned reading. I work best on my own. It gives me a chance to learn at a quicker pace."

        "The way I learn best is by visual aids. When I see a picture, chart, table, etc. I usually can remember it."

        "The way I like to learn best is in a group because we get to share ideas."

    B. What is it that you care most about in this world? Why?

    C. If you could change your name, what would it be and why?

    D. What are your dreams, hopes, and ambitions for the future?

This information helps you organize learning activities, individualize lessons, and discover some useful background on each student to refer to later for possible writing topics.

---

3. Students clarify their thinking better when they write their answers to questions first. Use **Activity 1-1** (Positive/Negative Reactions) to discover their attitudes toward evaluation and grading.

   Follow up with a **discussion** that establishes the connection between thinking, writing, and debating. Permit students to voice their opinions on one or more of these ideas afterwards.

   Collect this paper and check it only for the student's thoroughness in responding.

4. **Distribute:** Give students the **Evaluation/Grading Policy (Form 1-2). Explain** how that policy relates back to the points brought out during the debate and to their writing efforts.

5. **Explain:** Students should now see the connection between their expectations and understand the specific guidelines that will be used for grading their written work. Nevertheless, make clear to them the obstacles which can hinder positive results.

6. **Chart:** List those things that both help and hurt effective writing. Make a chart on the board using **Help** and **Hurt** as titles. Ask students about the habits they have observed in themselves or others that assist or ruin effective writing.

   [Typical answers are laziness, not taking notes, not writing enough, getting distracted, not listening. The obvious conclusion is to avoid these habits.]

7. **Explain:** Note-taking skills. Distribute **Form 1-3**—which shows abbreviations, illustrations, numbering, etc.

   • Show them a model of an effective notebook (some students' notebooks from previous school years).

   • Send students to the board to model their own ways of taking notes.

   • Have them listen to a tape and record key points. This usually creates some difficulty (students will ask, for example, to rewind the tape, to increase the volume, etc.). However, it is an excellent method of pointing out the best ways to extract the key points during a lecture or discussion: asking the speaker to repeat information, asking questions, using a shorthand note-taking technique, etc.

8. **Brainstorm:** As a student volunteer takes notes have students talk about class activities or projects they have enjoyed in the past.

Homework:

Ask students to **make lists** of 5-6 goals they may have for themselves as writers, for example, improving word selections. They should list 5-6 characteristics of books they enjoy reading (for example, authors presenting teenage characters). Explain that this list enables them to give input about the books, activities, and projects assigned during the school year. They should also return the next day with a notebook and folder just for English class.

> **Keep in mind that in many high school classes, students are more likely to be passive consumers of facts rather than active participants in a community of learners. To prompt more active learning, we teachers need to set up activities where students can learn by *doing*, not just by listening. Have them build on what they already know instead of being told what they should know.**

Name _____

Positive/Negative Reactions

Directions: Consider your reaction to each of the ideas below. Then write the positive and negative aspects for each if this school should choose to adopt that proposal.

1. Interscholastic athletics should be considered a specific class in the curriculum.

     Positive

     Negative

2. If a student doesn't want to learn, he or she should be allowed to leave class.

     Positive

     Negative

3. There should be no grades (A, B, C, D, F) in school.

     Positive

     Negative

Grading/Evaluation Policy

Your evaluation will be based on overall work done both in class and out of class. A cumulative point system of grading will determine your progress. The overall quarter and semester grades will be based on the following:

1. **Test and quiz results** (points earned).

2. **Effort**—as exhibited in the thoroughness of the writing assignments for both classwork and homework.

3. **Participation**—in class discussions and group work (peer editing) in terms of your contribution of ideas. The respect and courtesy you show to all classmates and adults, especially substitutes, counts as well.

   This requires that you do not interrupt others, curse, toss paper or other objects, or touch others or their property. Inappropriate behavior like this ruins positive relations with others.

4. **Projects**—You are responsible for completing all essays on regulation-sized, white paper. This makes your work easier to read and evaluate. Any work that does not comply will be returned. All assignments are due by the due date, unless a prior arrangement is made. If you are absent, you have the number of days missed to make up the work. (For example, if you are absent two days then two days are allotted to make up the work). No late work is accepted!

5. **Critical thinking**—as seen in your asking questions, offering new ideas and insights, and making effective inferences, especially in your essays.

6. **Preparation for class**—Have pen and pencil, notebook, textbook, and any supplementary material required in class each day. Your successful participation in class depends on having all the required materials and demonstrating this kind of commitment. Attentiveness is also important here.

7. **Group work**—You are expected to be cooperative and productive whenever we do group work (peer editing).

8. **Integrity**—Cheating or plagiarizing on any assignment will result in an automatic failure for that assignment.

Form 1-3

Sample Note-taking

Sept. 6

Writing Portfolio

1. Work in progress (Prewriting/Drafts)

   Refers to problem solving/ask questions/trial and error

2. Work completed (Final Copies)

   Reports, Poems, Essays, Stories—on various topics

   (Ex) Best athlete in school

3. Charts—example:

Synthesis	*Creativity*
Using technical information for a new plan/product	Based on imagination, uniqueness
(Ex) A new beverage?	(Ex) First visitors to our planet?

4. Lists

5. Webs

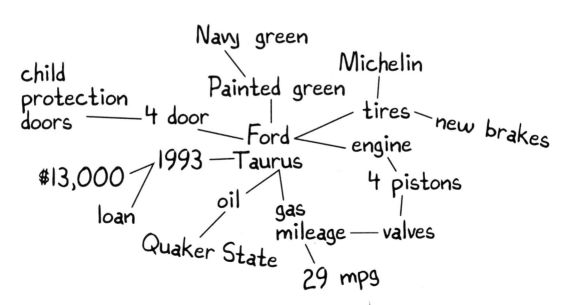

6. Notes from conferences

Lesson 2 TEAMWORK AND WRITING

Objective: Work effectively and cooperatively with two or more classmates (teamwork in writing)

Activities:

1. **Review:** Check students' homework. Review proper note-taking methods and class procedures if needed.

> **For cooperative learning, arrange individual groups of 4-5 students considering racial and ethnic diversity. Also, mix students of various academic and social backgrounds. Be sure to break up friends and any romantic relationships. Try for a balance of males and females.**
>
> **It can be effective here to refer to the ways groups form—those that form spontaneously like a rural community that piles sandbags ahead of a flooding river, those that are assigned like their writing group, and those that base a long career on a group effort like the Grateful Dead. Tell students they will be a part of some group all their lives, and therefore these skills are essential.**

2. **Freewriting:** Write the most common (and humorous) reasons for failing to get homework completed—obviously mistakes that are to be avoided. Use this later in the class.

3. **Explain:** Make **preliminary announcements** (homework, proper materials, the day's objective, etc.). Distribute Form 2-1 **Keys to Cooperative Learning**. For any group learning it is best for the teacher to serve as a facilitator, rather than an instructor, while the groups are in session. Your job here is to listen and guide, not lecture and explain.

4. **Student Interviews:** Students **interview** each other (**Activity 2-2**). When each person is finished, they share results of their interviews and introduce their interviewee to the other group members.

5. **Teacher Interview:** For fun, each group devises 1-2 interview questions to ask you (these answers need not be written down). Be ready for questions about your age, personal life, or family.

6. **Group activities:** Some techniques to promote group rapport and listening skills are:

    *   **"Whisper"**—Here, one student whispers a detailed "secret message" to the person on his/her right. The message continues around the group until it returns to the originator who reveals how the message changed.

- **"Echo"**—Each member, in turn, talks about himself/herself for 30-45 seconds. The others must then echo exactly that monologue in its entirety.

- **"Share and Compare"**—Students share and compare the results of their writing assignment from the beginning of class (failing to complete homework). They can also come up with a name for their group, hopefully a moniker that is English related, like The Poets, The Spellers, or The Sentence Run-ons.

- **"Time Capsule"**—This is a wonderful way to discover students' insights and values. Each group must make a list of the most important items they feel should be in the capsule.

  They should also decide what the time capsule should look like and where it should be buried. Finally, each group could describe the reactions of the people who eventually find the time capsule in the future.

7. **Brainstorm:** Students list the rules necessary for effective group work (to be reviewed later).

Homework:

Students must transform the answers from their interview into a 1-2 paragraph article that eventually will be typed and grouped with the other paragraphs and copied off for the entire class to read the following week. The publication of these mini-biographies serves to build a sense of class unity and to promote students' interest in having their writing read by others. (Give a copy to the principal, too.)

For students who demonstrate hostility towards group work or simply avoid being cooperative, some special intervention is needed. These students may do other work during group work or refuse to participate in any discussion. They might have poor attendance, lack the skills to function with others, or simply be tremendously shy or insecure individuals. For these kids it is best to give them very specific tasks, such as serving as the Recorder of all comments or the Reference Person who is in charge of the dictionary or other reference books needed by the group. Praise any effort on their part towards group work, and try to devise a group activity that appeals especially to their personal interests.

Keys to Cooperative Learning

1. Equal participation.

2. Only one person speaks at a time.

3. Respect others' ideas and proposals.

4. Eliminate socializing (stay on task).

5. No talking to other groups.

6. Work toward a common goal, but do not be afraid to challenge another member's idea. Just be sure it is the idea, not the person, you are challenging.

7. Listen carefully to group mates (take notes if need be) and ask questions when confused.

8. Take turns being the group reporter.

9. Get organized quickly and function as a team.

10. Groups who finish early can work on an enrichment activity, assess the progress of their group or another group, or review for an upcoming test by developing possible test questions.

11. Stages of effective cooperative learning:

    Stage 1   Members are unclear about purpose or direction of the group. Ask the teacher.

    Stage 2   Members find it difficult to get along or reach agreements with others. There are conflicts and some frustration. Differences resolve through compromise.

    Stage 3   Members develop harmony by listening and avoiding conflicts. They become more comfortable.

    Stage 4   Members cooperate more closely and become more productive. Efficient work begins.

Name _____

Teammate Interview

I am interviewing *(full name)* _____

1. WHERE WERE YOU BORN?

2. WHAT IS YOUR FAVORITE FOOD?

3. WHAT IS YOUR USUAL AFTER SCHOOL ACTIVITY?

4. WHO IS THE MOST FAMOUS PERSON YOU EVER MET?

5. WHO ARE YOUR BROTHERS AND/OR SISTERS?

6. WHAT IS YOUR ALL TIME FAVORITE MOVIE?

7. WHAT IS YOUR FAVORITE TELEVISION PROGRAM?

8. WHAT IS THE MOST INTERESTING BIRTHDAY PRESENT YOU EVER RECEIVED?

9. WHAT KIND OF MUSIC DO YOU LIKE?

10. WHAT TYPE OF WRITING DO YOU LIKE TO DO?

Lesson 3 THINKING SKILLS AND WRITING

Objective: Identify the basic thinking skills

> **Thinking is hard work, especially in an English class. Most students have never considered thinking itself to be a skill, nor have they been given strategies for improving their ability to recall, analyze, evaluate, synthesize, or create. Clearly, there is a strong connection between effective thinking and successful writing.**

Activities:

1. **Discuss:** Introduce thinking skills by having students first recognize the difference between *thinking* and just *having thoughts*. Ask:

    "What will be the day after the day after tomorrow, if the day before the day before yesterday was Wednesday?"

    [The correct answer is Tuesday. As they offer answers they've formulated (through trial and error) they soon realize they've been really *thinking,* and not *daydreaming.*]

2. **Explain:** Give an anecdotal lecture about the basic thinking skills. Students should take notes on these fundamental thinking skills:

    *   Recall: Refers to rote learning and memorization of facts.

        (ex) What is your best friend's phone number?

    *   Analysis: Refers to problem solving where one has to ask questions or gain a solution through trial and error.

        (ex) How can we solve the homeless problem?

    *   Evaluation: Refers to making comparisons, selections, or judgments (conclusions).

        (ex) Who is the best athlete in this class?

    *   Synthesis: Refers to using technical information to devise a new plan or product.

        (ex) What could be a new beverage to put on the market?

    *   Creativity: Refers to the most difficult thinking skill that is based on the use of the imagination. Uniqueness is the key quality here.

        (ex) What will the first visitors to our planet be like?

    [Most students quickly grasp the concept of recall, the easiest thinking skill, but the rest can prompt some difficulty.]

3. **"What's in the bag?":** Before students enter class, put a Mr. Potato Head toy (any small object is useful) inside a brown grocery bag, folding and sealing the top. Set it on a table or podium at the front of the classroom and make no reference to it until the discussion of *Analysis*. Direct students to observe the bag and ask: "What's in the bag?"

    Students must discover what is in the bag by asking questions (other than "What is in the bag?"). **Explain** that they should avoid the yes/no question which often provides no real information. The "**What's in the bag?**" activity encourages students to really practice problem solving and analytical thinking by asking, "What is it made out of?", "How big is it?", "What color is it?", etc.

    In my experience, students figure out that it is Mr. Potato Head about fifty percent of the time.

4. **Visual aid:** Continue their comprehension of the thinking skills with a picture, video, or illustration of a flame or fire and **Activity 3-1**.

5. **Oral review:** Call out the verbs on the left and challenge the students to respond with the thinking skill that matches it (answers provided):

List = Recall	Choose = Evaluation
Compare = Analysis	Identify = Recall
Invent = Synthesis	Predict = Creativity
Edit = Analysis	Judge = Evaluation
Contrast = Analysis	Label = Recall
Design = Synthesis	Organize = Analysis
Imagine = Creativity	Speculate = Synthesis

    [Keep in mind that students typically struggle with understanding synthesis and creativity, the more complex thinking skills.]

Homework options:

A. The assignment is termed the **Unrelated Items Essay (Activity 3-2)**. Here, students' skills of organization, grammar, and creativity are truly challenged. This is an excellent tool for doing a diagnostic assessment of their writing skills.

B. Students write a one page essay where they explain how they have used these specific thinking skills in any previous year of schooling, especially elementary school.

C. Students write a one page essay explaining the differences between an analytical writer and a creative writer.

D. Students write a one page essay describing a person they know who is very creative.

Name _____

Thinking Skills

Part I

1. Use *Recall* and describe a flame:

2. Use *Analysis* and explain what could make any flame burn more brightly:

3. Use *Evaluation* and list in order of effectiveness the various methods of putting out large flames (fires):

4. Use *Synthesis* and design a new method for teaching a toddler to avoid touching a flame:

5. Use *Creativity* to describe a loved one using the word flame:

Part II

1. *Recall*—List the qualities of an "A" student:

2. *Analysis*—Why are grades important? Why should students strive for them?

3. *Evaluation*—Compare students who get high grades with students who get low grades:

4. *Synthesis*—Design a method of evaluation that does not use the traditional grades of A-F:

5. *Creativity*—What *new* technology could help students get higher grades?

Name _____

Unrelated Items Assignment

Examine each of the fifteen items below. There seems to be no connection or relationship between them; they are, in short, quite unrelated.

Use creativity and your best writing skills to develop a detailed and organized composition where you relate these fifteen items. You can use ink or type this, writing on only one side of the paper.

Also, before writing your composition, make notes and/or do free-writing on this page to help organize yourself.

SPACE FLIGHT

TELEPHONE POLES

TEACHERS

TRAINS

TEXTBOOKS

GOING TO COLLEGE

CHRISTMAS

BOXING MATCHES

CHICAGO BULLS

TELEVISION

ROCK CONCERTS

BIG MACS

PICNICS IN THE PARK ON SUNDAY IN THE SUMMER

NUCLEAR ENERGY

SPOONS

Lesson 4   WRITING PORTFOLIO

Objective: Introduce the writing portfolio

Activities: [This lesson could take 1-2 class sessions.]

1. **Survey question**: "How do you usually react to a teacher's markings and comments on your writing?"

   [Answers vary. Some students prefer no marks because they become discouraged, while others want to see the teacher's analysis to make revisions. Consider these responses when marking their essays in the future.]

2. **Lecture:** Describe the purpose of the **Markings for Purpose of Revision** (**Form 4-1**).

3. Students then receive their essays on the unrelated items which have been evaluated and marked. Students examine the **Markings for Purpose of Revision Form 4-1** to clarify the markings and ask for help if there is anything they cannot read or understand. Always include at least one positive comment and one comment indicating an area in need of improvement on each paper.

   Along with the essay, they receive a **writing portfolio**.

Most students are unfamiliar with portfolios, so a good way to start is to refer to artists or advertising executives who often use portfolios to display their work to clients. Writers can do the same. Students can place in their portfolios all kinds of writing samples—freewriting, drafts, and poems. Teachers can use the portfolio to evaluate the student over an entire semester.

---

4. **Distribute:** the **Writing Chart (and Terms)—Form 4-2A** and **4-2B—** which is used to document students' strengths as writers. Students can check the appropriate boxes based on the markings. This can facilitate assessment and intervention.

Carol Avery, an author and classroom teacher, recommends teachers place great emphasis on the student's first experience with feedback about their writing. "It's important," she says, "to establish procedures, and, perhaps even more important, the workshop tone. A trusting environment is one that promotes risk taking, an essential behavior for the developing writer. A writer who feels inhibited by too much praise, overwhelming or unclear expectations, or lack of feedback will probably not feel comfortable with the process of writing."

---

5. **Oral reading:** Students who wrote excellent essays then read theirs and explain their strategies for completing the assignment. Or you may choose to read these aloud yourself before returning the essays to the class.

6. **Explain:** Organization of the Portfolio.

   • The Portfolio contains students' work in progress (prewriting) and their completed work (reports, essays, etc.). It will document their growth as writers—their revising and writing styles.

   • It will be organized by chronology or subject area—continually reviewed and updated.

   • The portfolio is part of the overall evaluation each nine weeks.

   • It leads to personalized instruction—one-on-one way of teacher communicating to student.

   • It must stay in the classroom (to prevent it from being lost); it will be used 2-3 times each week; it can be reviewed anytime by teacher, student, or parent.

   • Students can personalize the portfolio—drawings on the cover, devising a theme, etc.

   • Portfolios can be shared with classmates.

7. **Revising:** Students take several minutes to revise their original draft based on the markings. Move around the room to assist students **(Conferences)**.

   [This form of conferencing, which is simply a brief meeting between you and an individual student, requires you to discuss the writing. Having some parts read out loud and ask effective questions to help the student clarify his/her points. (What doesn't sound right? What do you like best?) All revisions go into the portfolio.]

Eventually, the portfolio and writing chart encourage self-evaluation by students. When they discover their strengths and weaknesses, you also allow them to control aspects of their own learning, and that kind of empowerment leads to more enthusiastic writing. Give students repeated opportunities to evaluate their work and monitor their own progress. You could, for example, have students compare two pieces of writing from different semesters to determine their growth as writers. Ask, "How has your writing changed?" or "What would you now change in the first piece?"

---

8. **Summary:** Review the strong connection between thinking skills and writing skills:

   • *Recall* for listing, defining, and summarizing in an essay (as in the prewriting stage of writing).

- *Analysis* for classifying, organizing, and explaining in an essay (as in the outlining stage of writing).

- *Evaluation* for persuading, recommending, and assessing in an essay (as in selecting the details and words when writing a first draft).

- *Synthesis* for developing, combining, and composing in an essay (as in arranging paragraphs in the body of an essay).

- *Creativity* for being unique, using figurative language, and showing fresh insights in an essay (as in developing a personal writing style).

Homework:

Students locate and write in their notebooks the definitions for the following writing terms: *Anecdote, Composition, Diction, Editing, Exposition, Grammar, Prewriting, Proofreading, Prose,* and *Revising*. Make reference to these terms during future writing assignments.

Students select any previous piece of writing or create a new one to include as the first document in their portfolio.

Students bring a copy of a favorite poem, letter, or essay to include in their portfolio.

Students dialogue with parents about the portfolio—its purpose, contents, writing chart—and return with a letter signed by the parents signifying that they understand. Use **Form 4-3**.

English—Markings for Purpose of Revising

Example Markings	*Explanation*
<u>It</u> was <u>kind of hot.</u>	Word choice or phrasing problem. I'm uncertain about your meaning here. Be more specific.
? The <u>environment</u> needs help.	Difficult to follow your reasoning. This is vague, unclear.
Flame colored leaves drifted around and crunched beneath me.	Good writing here. I like how you phrased this. Well done!
I live in the city of Richmond Hts.	Wordiness. Be more economical with your word choice.
She was a tired, old woman.	You have a punctuation error.
Her name was gerta.	Use a capital letter here.
Her Name was Gerta.	A capital letter is not needed.
I recieved ten dollers.	Spelling errors.
I like high school. But not homework.] **SF**	Sentence structure problem—Sentence Fragment.
[ ] **SR**	This is the abbreviation if you have a Sentence Run-on.
Expand	Explore this subject or point in greater detail. Be more explanatory.
¶	Begin a new paragraph here.
Students skills to study.	A word(s) is missing. This is a usage problem. Add the correct word.
Your not leaving.	Another typical usage problem. Replace the crossed out word.
VT	Verb tense shift. (Ex) You changed from present tense to past tense.
Intro?	The composition lacks an introductory paragraph.
Con?	The composition lacks a concluding paragraph.
Please sep*a*rate the parts.	Erase the misstroke and use the correct letter.
I'll get a long with out you.	Close up horizontal space.

Name _____

Writing Chart Criteria

Assignments	Risk	Topic	Prewriting	Introduction	Paragraphing	Transitions	Organization	Sentences	Spelling	Punctuation	Capitalization	Diction	Usage	Economy	Conclusion	Legibility	Style	Editing

Form 4-2B

Writing Chart Terms

Risk: The student takes risks, attempting new writing styles or vocabulary in his/her writing. There is a creative approach to the topic.

Topic: The student has narrowed the topic effectively for a composition.

Prewriting: The student has completed a freewriting, webbing, clustering, or mapping activity in preparation for the writing of a composition.

Introduction: The introduction successfully announces the topic and captures the reader's interest.

Paragraph: The paragraphs are unified, coherent, and thorough.

Transition: The student has used transitional words and devices in the composition.

Organization: The composition is well-organized and thorough. There is a logical arrangement of the main points.

Sentence: There are no sentence fragments or run-ons.

Spelling: There are one or no spelling errors.

Punctuation: There are one or no punctuation errors.

Capitalization: There are one or no capitalization errors.

Diction: The student has used specific, detailed wording that can appeal to a specific audience/reader. Clarity is important here especially.

Usage: There are one or fewer usage (verb tense, pronoun) errors.

Economy: The student has avoided wordiness and has been economical with words.

Conclusion: The conclusion successfully restates the thesis and summarizes the composition.

Legibility: The composition is legible and neat.

Style: The student demonstrates a personal and unique writing style.

Editing: The student effectively edited a first draft before submitting a final copy.

Parent Letter

Date ——————————————————

Dear Parent(s):

I would like to familiarize you with your student's Writing Portfolio.

This is a folder kept in our classroom so it is accessible to both the student and the teacher each day. Students place both their work in progress (prewriting, first drafts) and their completed work (essays, poems, reports) in this folder. The Writing Portfolio can be used several times each week and is reviewed by me at the end of each evaluation period.

The Writing Portfolio helps students recognize both their weaknesses and strengths as writers. To accomplish this, we will use the Writing Chart (enclosed) and various forms, which are distributed with a completed work. Another important aspect regarding the evaluation of the Portfolio is its thoroughness—that is, it contains all the writing assignments.

An important step for students is to share their work with you, especially their special pieces, through all stages of any writing project. In the same way I conference with students about their work, you can do the same. If you see any problems, especially while proofreading, please comment on the written work or contact me. Most important, try to say as many positive things about their writing as you can.

We will be working in the Writing Portfolio throughout each nine weeks, and I am confident that the benefits (and improvements in writing) will be noticed by both you and your student. I also feel sure that as concerned and involved parents I can count on your support.

Sincerely,

Section 2 : DESCRIPTION

"An abstract style is always bad. Your sentences should be full of stones, metals, chairs, tables, animals, men, and women."
(Emile Chartier)

Objectives: Define and suggest methods for using the parts of speech and sensory language
Verify the importance of standard English
Show how to use a dictionary and thesaurus
Indicate how diction relates to audience and purpose
Guide students as they compose a descriptive essay

Length: Approximately fifteen lessons

Introduction:

Knowing there is a genuine audience for their writing leads to better and more productive work by students. When they realize there is a reader who has a sincere interest in their essays, their effort becomes more purposeful.

Too many students enter our English classes with a dramatic indifference toward their own and, in turn, their classmates' writing. These students see any writing assignment as a depressing chore forced on them by merciless teachers. They stumble, sweat, and strain over the task of writing. When they have to write, most kids become cowards. Teach them to be heroes. Be their cheerleader as they take on the descriptive essay, and be their editor as they proceed through the writing process.

Students need to recognize the immortality of writing, including their own, and how literature has endured through the centuries. They need to make distinct comparisons between the literary classics and the linguistic sludge that appears on television, especially the soap operas. Tom Brokaw from NBC News says, "The written word is the most efficient, the clearest, and the most lasting expression of our thought processes. There will always be a need for writers and a job for them."

Lesson 5   STANDARD VS. NONSTANDARD ENGLISH

Objective: Eliminate students' reluctance to write

Make clear distinctions between standard and nonstandard English

Activities:

1. **Freewriting:** When did you first get the urge to write? Describe the first time it was important to you to be a writer.

   Some examples:

   "I think I began writing when I was in the first grade. All the kids in my class wrote little poems and stories, so I wrote a story about my cousin, a baby. I remember writing about his head. How his hair was real soft like a little chick."

   "It was probably when I was in the second grade and the teacher told us to write about our summer."

   "I was sitting in homeroom about two years ago filling out out an application. I noticed it said, 'Please Print.' Everything today says 'Please Print.' Then the bell rang and I thought how everyone everywhere was running their lives by a mechanical object that sits on their wrist. These things really bugged me and I wrote them down and handed them in for a paper in English."

James Britton in "Talking and Writing" (*Explorations in Children's Writing*) advises, "Every time a child succeeds in writing about something that has happened to him or something he has been thinking, two things are likely to have happened. First, he has improved his chances of doing so the next time he tries; his piece of writing has given him practice. And secondly, he has interpreted, shaped, coped with some bit of experience."

---

2. **Oral reading:** Several students read their responses.

3. **Discussion**: Why are we often compelled to write? How can working at writing benefit us?

   [Answers will vary.]

4. **Freewriting:** Students write notes to each other. Hand out half sheets of paper and designate 1-2 students to be message carriers. You might even choose to participate. Here is a typical example:

Kim,

Yo! Lighten up! Them scrags are playing it stupid in the big leagues and certain somebody is scrapping the bottom of the cess pool for friends. The whole thing is really a laugh. But I know how you feel. Too bad we don't have all of our classes together. Ooo la la! I noticed an exchange of a NOTE between you and Mr. Suave Beaucoup. You'll have to fill me in.

Karen

This brief activity quickly lessens any reluctance about writing that students might have, and they gain a clear understanding that writing almost always has a reader, either a classmate, or, in the future, a magazine editor. Their fear of any criticism of their writing is negated.

---

5. **Brainstorming:** Make clear distinctions between standard and nonstandard English. **List on the board** criteria students think should be used to evaluate good writing. (Show how at least parts of this criteria appear on their Writing Charts.) After a dozen items have been listed, point out expectations for standard English usage.

6. **Define:** Give definition of standard English or refer to the one in their textbooks: It is the accepted language of educated and literate people who follow traditional rules of grammar and usage.

7. **Discuss:** Determine their attitude toward this definition. Ask: Is it acceptable that there is one specific standard to follow? Why/Why not?

   [Answers will vary.]

8. **Song lyrics:** Play a tape of rap or rock 'n' roll music or, if it's available, distribute the song lyrics and ask how well the lyrics meet the criteria. Undoubtedly, they won't.

9. **Discuss:** Ask them to guess the slang words used during your high school days.

   • Ask the female students: Are you a *girl* or a *young lady*?

   • Ask the male students: Are you *macho* or *masculine*?

   • Ask: What makes some expressions like "spring fever," "sloppy joes," and "runny nose" awkward?

   Why is it often unacceptable to write the same way we speak?

10. **Explain:** Nonstandard usage persists in a variety of ways and the continuing challenge is to determine what is acceptable.

11. **Show:** Present examples of nonstandard usage found in newspaper headlines, in magazine advertisements, or even on T-shirts. **Discuss** the causes on incorrect usage.

Ask: Why does it happen if, in fact, we are educated every year to avoid it?

12. **Revising:** Students re-examine the notes they wrote earlier in the class and correct the nonstandard English. See if these revisions alter the meaning or intent of the note.

Homework options:

A. Read the list of nonstandard terms—**Activity 5-1**—which students are to correct.

B. Students explore our language in even greater depth by **listing** ten words they consider to be most ugly and ten words they consider to be most beautiful. They must explain their choices.

C. Students play with standard and nonstandard terms to describe themselves as if they were a recipe. For example: I am half cup of politeness, twenty-nine pounds of muscle, ten tons of courage, lightening quick, etc. This activity prompts them to carefully select terms—either standard or nonstandard—to describe themselves.

D. Students could write an opinion paper (editorial) on the controversy that persists with enforcing standard English on the American population.

The Ugly, the Bad, and the Good

Directions: Change the nonstandard (left) words to standard English terms.

1. aint _____

2. wanna _____

3. gonna _____

4. hafta _____

5. lemme _____

6. bursted _____

7. brung _____

8. oughta _____

9. sorta _____

10. theirselves _____

11. nowheres _____

12. hisself _____

13. kinda _____

14. wierdo _____

15. pooped _____

16. wimp _____

17. fatso _____

18. alot _____

19. must of _____

20. macho _____

21. brang _____

22. setted _____

23. chill out _____

Lesson 6 CONCRETE VS. ABSTRACT NOUNS

Objective: To make distinctions between concrete nouns and abstract nouns

Activities:

1. **Survey #1:** Use quotes (dialogue) said by Huck or Jim in "The Adventures of Huckleberry Finn," or Bigger Thomas in "Native Son," or another literary character. Is this standard English? Poll the students.

   Survey #2: Is it fair that the majority determines what is and is not standard English?

   Survey #3: What are the strategies for avoiding non-standard usage?

2. **Dictionary:** Students use the dictionary and their own text to locate and write definitions in their notebooks for the following: *Diction, Denotation, Connotation, Synonym,* and *Lexicon.*

   [Make sure every student is clear about the function and usefulness of both a dictionary and thesaurus.]

3. **Explain:** In order to compose the Descriptive Essay, students need to recognize the linguistic boundaries of our language. They should become skilled using the parts of speech which are a major part of standard English.

4. **Brainstorming:** Students work with **partners** on identifying and listing concrete nouns.

   A. **A-Z Activity**—One student in each pair lists down the left margin of a sheet of paper each letter of the alphabet. For each letter they are to write a noun that is associated with school—(ex) a—algebra, b—books, c—chalk, etc.

   B. **Paper Clip**—Students brainstorm other concrete nouns—(ex) bookmark, lock pick, fingernail cleaner, chain necklace, etc.

   Discuss the results and have students cite how nouns can refer to a person, place, thing, or idea. Pick several of the nouns they wrote and place them in two columns **on the board—Concrete** and **Abstract.** Point out how concrete nouns provide more specific information for description.

5. **Writing options:**

   A. Students with a background in a foreign language list concrete terms used in that language that refer to people, places, or things, and then for each, provide its English translation. What situation is each term associated with?

28

B. Students use dictionaries to locate concrete and abstract nouns. The students then copy their selections, writing for each why they chose it as an interesting or concrete noun.

You could suggest words like truth, courage, freedom, or love.

C. Students add in each of the blanks a more concrete noun to replace the abstract *sound* or *loudness*.

1. The _____ of her heels
2. The _____ of a door
3. The _____ of voices
4. The _____ of the brakes
5. The _____ of a truck engine

D. Students rank the following from most abstract to most specific: male, American citizen, Bill Clinton, Democrat, human, U.S. President, politician.

6. **Reading:** Students locate in their own textbook or available magazines examples of concrete and abstract nouns. Magazine advertisements are great sources of this.

7. **Discuss:** Students interpret "thingamajig" and "whatchamacallit." Also: Why is the word *thing* used so often in writing? How concrete is it?

["Thing" is obviously a vague term used too often to indicate an object or event. Review that a concrete noun is very specific—(ex) cactus, not plant; Monday, not just today.]

8. **Activity 6-1.** Distribute this descriptive essay that suffers from an overuse of abstract nouns. Have students replace the abstract nouns with concrete ones. Collect and evaluate their responses (extend this to homework if time runs out).

Discuss the results if time permits.

Homework options:

A. Students write one page essays where they use concrete nouns to describe any family member. Caution them not to use just adjectives. They should also read about nouns in their text.

B. Students edit the monthly menu from the school cafeteria or a local restaurant by replacing abstract nouns with concrete ones—(ex) vegetable—lima beans.

C. Students read all pages about nouns in their textbook.

Descriptive Essay

Directions: Read the following essay carefully and replace the abstract nouns with concrete (more specific) ones. Rewrite the entire paragraph below.

Going fishing on *opening day* of the *season* can be a challenge. *Early in the morning*, after I wake up, put on my *clothes*, and eat *breakfast*, I leave for *the lake*. Sometimes, it's raining, and that's not *fun*. Neither is waiting a *long time* to catch *a fish*. When a *fish* does nibble at my *bait*, it can be really difficult to keep the *boat* steady and pull it in. If *it* escapes I know then I have to narrate a fake story to *people* about catching *a lot* of *fish* on my trip.

Lesson 7   ANALYZING ADJECTIVES

Objective: To determine the best descriptive modifiers

Activities:

1. **Freewriting:** Students make two columns on their paper—titled BED-ROOM and CLASSROOM. Beneath each, students list words (probably adjectives) that describe these rooms.

   Discuss the results. Where are they similar? Where are they different?

2. **Explain:** Show how adjectives influence description, especially in relation to our understanding of a noun (like *road*). For example:

   A dusty road   A narrow road   A forgotten road

   A lonely road   A gravel road   A steep road

   Point out the importance of precision: *feverish* instead of *real hot* or *impressive* instead of *great*.

   Also deal with the comparative forms of adjectives. For example:

   hot—hotter—hottest / lucky—luckier—luckiest

3. **Visual aid:** Use a transparency, a painting, or a videotape ("Fantasia" is an excellent video to use) for students to describe with adjectives.

   Discuss the results, pointing out the most effective adjectives.

4. **Identification:** Use of Adjectives.

   A. Students refer to sentences in their textbooks or in any magazine ads where adjectives are used effectively or poorly.

   B. Students skim a dictionary to locate interesting and unusual adjectives. Prompt them by asking: What is the most unusual adjective? How would you use the adjective you've found in a sentence?

   C. Use a nonsense word like *dracky* and challenge the students to use it as an adjective.

5. **Discuss:** Evaluate the word *nice*. How descriptive is this word? How exact is it? How does it compare, for instance, to *cheerful* or *courteous*?

   What about *ugly, bad, beautiful,* and *good*?

   [Help students see that they are too general and are not effective modifiers.]

31

6. **Debate:** What would be the appropriate term?

   • Do male students want to be called *macho* or *masculine*?

   • Do female students want to be called *petite* or *small*?

   • To all students, *skinny* or *slender*? *Cool* or *chilly* ?

7. **Writing: Activity 7-1**

   Three examples are listed for each noun to assist students in getting started. Some other effective examples for the word *kitchen* would be *sizzling bacon* and *burnt toast*.

8. **Review:** Locate how adjectives are explained in their textbook (possibly use an exercise).

   Or: Describe their bare feet (let them take their shoes and socks off).

Homework options:

A. Students attach a picture of themselves to a piece of paper and then describe themselves using descriptive adjectives and concrete nouns.

B. Students evaluate and analyze the effectiveness of the modifiers they find in magazine or newspaper ads.

C. Students write 1-2 paragraphs that describe the interior of their body when they are scared, and then research the terms a doctor would use. (They should use a dictionary or medical journal.)

D. Students write a 200-word essay using effective modifiers to describe a *penny*.

Creative Adjective/Noun Combinations

Directions: Create interesting and descriptive "adjective-noun" combinations that relate to each of the following:

1. Kitchen: (ex) red linoleum, melting butter

2. Bodybuilder: (ex) slick bodies, thick necks

3. Cafeteria: (ex) greasy fries, smooth tables

4. Hospital: (ex) sterile tables, injured patients

5. Basement: (ex) musty couch, gray cobwebs

6. Theater: (ex) salty popcorn, red carpet

Lesson 8   SIGHT LANGUAGE

Objective: Explore sensory language and descriptive adjectives associated with SIGHT

Activities:

1. **Discussion:** How effective are the modifiers *black* and *white* ?

    [Lead students to identify how the connotations of some adjectives can influence an intended meaning of a noun. Black can connote blackmail, black magic, in the black, black mark, while white also suggests white flag, white hat (cowboy), whitey. Also, black is known to represent evil, while white represents good.]

2. **Contest:** Partners stare into each other's eyes. Who can stare the longest? Who is better at *observing* (vs. just *looking*)?

3. **Writing**: Have a colleague walk into the room, talk to you briefly, and then quickly exit. Challenge the students to describe him/her in great detail.

4. **Lecture:** Lead into the importance of making exact OBSERVATIONS. Writers need to observe carefully when describing, especially regarding modifiers related to SIGHT.

    Adjectives: chalky, foggy, glossy, muddy, grimy, tan
    Nouns: glitter, haze, glare, sleet, spark, cactus

5. **Writing:** Students do **Activity 8-1—"What do you see?"**—then **discuss** the results.

Homework options:

A. Students watch a television program like National Geographic, Biography, or even the news and write what they observe, writing a full page of effective modifiers.

B. Students describe their own facial features after staring into a mirror, listing even the most minor details (for example, "a half-inch scratch beneath my ear") until an entire page is completed.

C. Students read a story, poem, or essay in their literature text that has a lot of SIGHT words. Have them list those words on a paper. They also summarize the overall impact of those words and/or phrases that contribute to their understanding of the story, poem, or essay.

Name_____

"What Do You See?"

Part I

Directions: Write more exact statements using descriptive sight words for the following:

1. The school gym is big.

2. Many people have been hit on that street.

3. It is a gorgeous day.

Part II

4. Pick any object (for example, an oak tree outside the window, your desk, a map on the wall) and describe it:

5. List what you have seen that is heavy, solid, and white:

6. Examine a paper clip and describe it as if the reader has never seen it before. Devise a list of ways it could be used other than to hold papers—(ex) lock pick, chain necklace, navel/fingernail cleaner.

Lesson 9   TOUCH LANGUAGE

Objective: Identify sensory language and adverbs associated with TOUCH

Activities:

1. **Freewriting:** Students walk around the classroom (6-8 minutes), touch as many surfaces as they can, and list the sensations from what they touch.

    Discuss the results. Ask them to explain the differences in the feeling between their desk top and another smooth surface, like the ledge by the window or the blackboard.

2. **Lecture:** Describe the key factors that relate to the sense of touch. They are:

    *   Texture—what the surface feels like
    *   Temperature—Identify, if possible, the degrees.
    *   Solidity—What is it made of?
    *   Weight—in ounces, pounds, tons
    *   Dimensions—in inches or feet, its height, width, and length

    Some useful modifiers here are *slick, slippery, coarse, wrinkled, gritty, slimy, moist, damp, lukewarm, chilly, frigid, clammy, sharp, scratchy.*

3. **Freewriting:** Students must use single words to list (a) how you can touch someone—(ex) cautiously; and (b) how you can eat a plate of food—(ex) quickly, sloppily.

    Discuss the responses.

4. **Explain:** Terms like these are ADVERBS—modifiers which add description to sentences about when, where, how often, how long, or how little something is done.

    [Adverbs can be used anywhere in sentences, usually near the verb. Show them some more examples from their text.]

5. **Charades:** Students practice using adverbs in sentences they create based on a **charade** you (or volunteer students) perform of various physical gestures—(ex) crying, stomping around the room, waving arms.

    Examples: He waved his arms *wildly* in front of us.
                    He was *really* crying.

6. **Visual aid**: Show a video of any battle scene (such as one from "Red Badge of Courage"). Students list *how* a soldier might react to the charge of enemy soldiers in a battle—(ex) nervously, angrily.

7. **Research:** Adverbs—**Activity 9-1.**

   Discuss the results.

8. **Review:** Students close their eyes and touch the object you place in their open hands. Use acorns, stones, small toys, or whatever is available and allow students several minutes of tactile exploration.

   Then remove the object and challenge the students to write what it felt like. See how accurate and descriptive they are.

Homework options:

A. Students read all the pages in their text that deal with adverbs and complete 1-2 exercises related to adverb usage.

B. Students write a one-page analysis of various cultures' attitudes towards touching. The Italians, for example, are known for much hugging, while Asian people simply bow from a safe distance.

C. Students locate an object in their home that has the most unusual feel to it. They must caress it with their fingertips, grip it with their hands, weigh it on a scale (if possible), even rub it against their cheeks before writing 1-2 paragraphs about what it felt like.

D. Students make three columns in their notebooks—HOW, WHEN, WHERE—and list at least ten different adverbs in each and follow this with five sentences where they use at least ten of the thirty adverbs in these lists.

Adverbs and the Sense of Touch

Directions: Answer each of the following in detail.

1. How could each below be used as an adverb?

   quickly   urgently   quietly   soon
   tomorrow   yesterday   nearby   happily

2. What is a typical adverb suffix?

3. What is the purpose of an adverb?

4. How are adjectives and adverbs related modifiers?

5. What is meant by "out of touch?"

6. What is meant by a "touching experience?"

7. If someone says he/she is "touched," what does this mean?

8. If you had to hold hands with someone for an entire class period, how would you react? Why?

Lesson 10   SMELL LANGUAGE

Objective: Explore sensory language associated with SMELL

Activities:

1. **Freewriting: Activity 10-1.**

   Discuss the results.

2. **Mini-field trip:** Take students to the cafeteria, the school lawn, or the boiler room. (Get permission beforehand to do this.) Have students list the various smells.

   Discuss the results.

3. **Discuss**: How would you describe the smell of your favorite perfume or cologne?

   [This usually leads to students **comparing** one smell to another—(ex) my perfume smells like rose petals. Comparison is a common descriptive technique that students should employ.]

4. **Explain:** List some modifiers that are useful for describing scents: greasy, fetid, moldy, musty, putrid.

5. **Read:** Have students locate a story or poem in their literature text where smell modifiers are prominent, or find perfume/cologne advertisements in magazines.

Homework: Students write 1-2 paragraphs—**Activity 10-2.**

"What Smells?"

Part 1

Directions: Describe on the smell of:

1. August

2. November

3. January

4. April

5. Today

Part 2

Directions: Rank (Evaluate) the following list from the worst smelling place to the best smelling place (although they all have some foul smells):

1. school lavatory

2. locker room after a practice or a game

3. bottom of a cafeteria trash barrel after lunch

4. morgue when a new corpse is brought in

Part 3

Directions: Use the dictionary to define and compare the meanings of *stink* and *malodorousness*.

Name_____

Smells, Smells, Smells

Directions: Select any two of the following assignments and write 1-2 detailed paragraphs.

1. Describe the smells of any room in your house—(ex) the garage, basement, attic.

2. Explain the circumstances of any past event you might associate with a specific smell—(ex) spaghetti sauce reminds me of Sunday dinners at Grandma's house.

3. Describe the smells you could encounter at a store—(ex) a delicatessen, hair salon, drugstore.

4. Explain other descriptive modifiers that relate effectively to the sense of smell. (Use a dictionary and/or thesaurus.)

5. Identify and explain the *location* with the *worst* smell.

Lesson 11   TASTE LANGUAGE

Objective: Explore sensory language associated with TASTE

Activities:

1. **Taste test:** Pass out little candy treats like "Smarties," gum drops, or mints, and challenge students to describe the taste.

   Then pass out Tootsie Rolls and ask them to describe the taste beyond the obvious—"It tastes like chocolate," or "It's sweet." The more insightful student might write "It's like caramel," or "It has a waxy taste."

2. **Explain:** Some of the more descriptive modifiers to portray taste are *sweet, minty, spicy, sour, bitter,* and *refreshing.*

   Other modifiers students might have no familiarity with are *bland, sapid, gustable, palatable, and soporific.* This could be an opportunity to use the dictionary to define, compare, and rate these terms.

3. **Discuss:** Describe the differences between the following:

   A. crushed ice vs. cubed ice

   B. sweat vs. rain

   C. ham vs. turkey

   D. Big Mac vs. Whopper

   E. ocean water vs. lake water

4. **Freewriting:** "What does it taste like?"—**Activity 11-1.**

   Discuss the results.

5. **Visual aid:** Show a video of any scene from a movie that portrays people eating and prompt students to describe the taste of the meal.

Homework options:

A. Their evening dinner is the focus of this night's homework. Students are to describe the smells, sights, feel, and tastes of that meal (approximately one page).

B. Students research the physiology of our taste buds and how we acquire a sense of taste.

Name _____

"What Does It Taste Like?"

Directions: Complete each of the following in detail.

1. Describe the taste of any single item on our cafeteria menu:

2. Describe the taste of your favorite meal (other than by stating that it's *wonderful* or *good*):

3. List six pairs of wildly contrasting tastes:
    (ex) pickles and strawberries

4. Describe the taste of a non-food item:
    (ex) toothpaste or paper

5. Describe a meal you've seen movie or television characters eat:

6. Explain the recipe of a meal or dessert you especially enjoy:

7. Be creative. Describe what you think your desk, or the floor, or a tree, or whatever you choose tastes like:

Lesson 12   SOUND LANGUAGE

Objective: Study sensory language associated with SOUND

Activities:

1. **Freewriting:** Students remain completely silent for 3-4 minutes and simply listen and **list** the sounds they hear (lockers being slammed, coughing, papers shuffling).

   Discuss the results and praise effective listening.

2. **Discussion**: [Answers will vary.]

   A. What are the differences in sound between a church bell, a school bell, and a doorbell?

   B. Why can't we write the same way we speak?

   C. What is interesting about how the following words are *spelled* vs. the way they are *pronounced*?

   knife   choir   hiccough   night

3. **Role playing:** Be theatrical and dramatize the following sounds, prompting students to identify their spelling and meaning (which is in parentheses):

   - hmmm (a thoughtful pause)
   - shh (to urge silence)
   - uh-huh (yes)
   - uh-oh (oh no, there's a problem)
   - uh-uh (no)
   - yeh (a cheer)
   - arghh (an expression of pain or agony)
   - mmmm (a sign of pondering something)
   - gasp (a quick breath that shows surprise)
   - yeah (yes)

4. **Writing: "What does it sound like?"—Activity 12-1.**

   Discuss the results.

5. **Music:** Play cassette tapes of various musical sounds and ask, if possible, the musicians in class to describe the melodies in terms of musical terminology (notes, etc.).

   Have all students describe the sounds they hear.

6. **Explain:** List the modifiers that are useful to describing sound: *chime, clang, clatter, crackle, rattle, gurgle, murmur, hiss, whisper, monotone, whine, squeal, pitch, bass*

7. **Freewriting:** Students stay silent and listen to the sounds from the hallway, other classrooms, and outside. They must write on their paper those exact sounds.

Homework options:

A. Students describe the sounds they hear in their own homes in exact detail.

B. If they have a background in mechanics, students can describe the sounds of the loudest to the least noisy engines.

C. Students research the devices used by deaf or near-deaf people to hear and/or communicate. Other research topics include Helen Keller, "signing," and the physiology of the human ear.

Name _____

"What Does It Sound Like?"

Directions: Answer each of the following questions in detail.

1. Describe the most unique sound you've ever heard.

2. Describe the sound of the animal you think has the most unique sound—(ex) the howl of a coyote.

3. Describe the voice of your favorite singer/performer.

4. List the sounds you associate with the morning, the afternoon, and the night.

5. What sounds are associated with your kitchen at home?

Lesson 13   STRONG VERBS

Objective: To recognize the value of using strong verbs in descriptive writing

Activities:

1. **Explain:** Students are being evaluated as a group based on their **productivity in responses** and as individuals based on the **quality of verb usage** they show at the end of class. [Be sure desks are arranged ahead of time for group work.]

2. **Group work:** Explain or describe the differences between a strong and weak:

   A. person   B. building   C. song

3. **Explain:** The same differences can be found in action verbs. For example:

   Squirrels *scurried* across the lawn. (strong) vs. Squirrels *ran* across the lawn. (weak)

   A tree *crashed* to the ground. (strong) vs. A tree *fell* to the ground. (weak)

   He *smiled* at me. (weak) vs. He *smirked* at me. (strong)

4. **Contest #1:** Make students aware that strong verbs carry more meaning and better description than weak ones: Which group can list the most and the strongest verbs for a specific action?

   [Allow the groups 4-6 minutes to brainstorm their lists and then call on each group, in turn, to provide a strong action verb. The group that can still announce a verb after the other groups have exhausted their lists is the winner.]

   Round #1: Run
   Round #2: Talk
   Round #3: Throw

   Contest #2: Each group writes a strong verb, passes it to another group who must add a similar verb that is a synonym—(ex) *exclaim—announce.* Who can write the strongest verb? You can also make the second group write a verb that begins with the last letter of the first verb—(ex) exclai*m*—*m*ention.

5. **Writing:** Groups have to come up with strong action verbs—**Activity 13-1.**

   Discuss the results.

6. **Discuss:** Play a record or cassette tape of instrumental music and have students listen and announce the *action* they recognize—(ex) strumming.

Homework options:

A. Students read in their text everything about verbs and then practice using strong action verbs in a single paragraph about an assigned topic.

B. Students study their own hobby or extra-curricular activity and write a paragraph explaining any terms (concrete nouns) and actions (strong verbs) associated with it.

C. Students write a one page essay comparing and contrasting the actions (verbs) used by persons in any hobby (fishing, for example) or profession (doctor, for instance) a hundred years ago compared to the present.

D. In their textbook students examine sentences from any exercise for the verbs. How effective are they?

Name _____

The Strongest Verbs

© 1999 by The Center for Applied Research in Education

Part 1

Directions: For each of the activities below, list the strong action verbs associated with it.

(ex) Football: punt, sprint

1. Baseball:

2. Cooking:

3. Band:

4. Vacations:

Part 2

Directions: Skim the dictionary, locate, and then list the strongest and most interesting action verbs:

Part 3

Directions: Circle the verb that is the strongest in each pair:

5. build/construct   drink/gulp   eat/chew
    smirk/smile   freeze/chill   say/whisper
    ask/inquire   notice/note   clutch/grab

Lesson 14   VERB USAGE

Objective: To master usage of verbs and verb tenses

Activities:

1. **Tell a story:** Relay any story (about a trip you took or a concert, etc.). Afterwards, ask the students to explain *when* the event took place. Some might even guess the correct year, but almost all will identify that it was in the past.

2. **Discussion:**
    A. How do you know it happened before?
    B. How does the *when* or *time* of a story influence our understanding of it?

3. **Freewriting:** Students **write** two paragraphs, each about an important event in their life, the first paragraph in the present tense and the second paragraph in the past tense.

    Discuss the results. Encourage some volunteers to read their paragraphs and ask the others which paragraph they prefer and why.

4. **Lecture:** Teach students how to choose the appropriate verb tense for a writing assignment.

    *   The *present tense* is best for essays, editorials, and how-to articles since these writers' concerns are about their present feelings or suggestions.

        The present tense provokes a sense of urgency. The readers are encouraged to respond to the concerns immediately.

    *   The *past tense* is often used for stories, narratives, or news reports because most are about events that have happened before.

        The past tense suggests a reporter's viewpoint, and the readers readily recognize they are being informed after-the-fact.

    *   The *future tense* is useful in articles where the writer makes a prediction or a plea for action. It is most noticeable in interviews or editorials.

5. **Show sentences:** Select examples from the students' writing where verbs have been used incorrectly and have students revise them. This could also be the appropriate time to present avoiding the double negative with verbs.

6. **Discuss:** Go over active vs. passive verb constructions.

   Ask students which of the following sentences offers a better use of the verb.

   Someone banged the door shut. (active) vs.

   The door was banged shut by someone. (passive)

   The account must be updated every three weeks. (passive) vs.

   You must update the account every three weeks. (active)

7. **Explain:** Experienced writers use active rather than passive verb constructions. Active verb constructions are more forceful, they're less wordy, they're more clear.

8. **Quiz:** On verb usage—**Activity 14-1**.

Homework options:

A. Students examine a set of sentences found in the verb section of their grammar text and revise them, replacing incorrect or weak verbs with strong verbs.

B. Students write a persuasive speech about any school issue, using strong verbs of all types and tenses selectively.

C. (For more creative students) Students use the following nonsense words—*dreel, foop, jigger, gode, stip*—as verbs in sentences of a narrative paragraph.

D. Students create their own (8-10) questions about verbs and then pass them to a classmate to answer by the next day.

Name_____

Verb Usage Quiz

1. Write an action verb: _____

2. Write one helping verb: _____

3. Write one linking verb: _____

Verbs can be one, two, three, or four word phrases (ex) *eat, is eating, etc.*

4. Write a two word verb phrase: _____

5. Write a three word verb phrase: _____

6. Write a four word verb phrase: _____

Verbs can change form (ex) *play* can become *played,* or *take* can become *took.* Change the form of the following verbs:

7. sell _____

8. throw _____

9. sting _____

In the sentence, "*A lizard moved in front of me,*" the verb is *moved.* It is a weak verb. List below six stronger verbs for this sentence:

10. _____

11. _____

12. _____

13. _____

14. _____

15. _____

16. In a paragraph, explain and define "helping verbs," and "linking verbs." How are they used? What is their purpose?

Lesson 15   PREPOSITIONAL PHRASES

Objective: To introduce the importance of using effective prepositional phrases in descriptive writing

Activities:

1. **Freewriting:** Students locate a spot or object in the classroom they think no other student will select. They must **write** *phrases* that will guide their fellow classmates to that specific location or object without actually identifying it.

    For example: *It's near the door, next to the gray cabinet, beneath the flag, and on the floor* (ans.—the trash can)

    Discuss: Students read their lists of phrases and invite the rest of the class to determine the location of the object. Use this discussion as a teaching point about the relationship of *prepositional phrases* to *description*.

2. **Show:** List on the board some examples of prepositional phrases.

    We jogged *across the field*.

    The house *by the school* is vacant.

    The teacher strolled *into the classroom after lunch*.

3. **Review:** Adjectives and adverbs as modifiers. **Explain** how prepositional phrases function, at times, like single modifiers (adjectives and adverbs), showing, for example:

    WHERE (*across the field*)

    WHEN (*after lunch*)

    WHICH ONE (*by the school*)

    Prepositional phrases can appear anywhere in a sentence.

4. **Identification:** Students find where prepositions are listed in their **textbooks** and review the list of common prepositions. Also locate prepositional phrases in sentences, pointing out again how they contribute to description.

53

5. **Visual aid:** Put an illustration of a *tent* and a *tree* (on board). We camped _____.

6. **Modeling:** Show students how professional writers like John Steinbeck, Margaret Atwood, and John Grisham use prepositional phrases. Read from their literature. Use **Activity 15-1**.

7. **Writing:** Students do sentence combining using—**Activity 15-2**.

   Check or **discuss** the results.

Homework:

Students select a favorite writer and copy passages into their notebook where the writer has used prepositional phrases extensively and effectively.

Prepositions and the Professionals

Directions: Examine each of the following sentences by famous writers and locate (underline) the prepositional phrases. Beneath each sentence, explain how the writers use the prepositional phrases to add description and to highlight the sentence.

1. "At the heels trotted a dog, a big native husky." (from Jack London)

2. "The air at that height, about 6,200 feet, is like wine." (from Ernest Hemingway)

3. "I drew the blankets over my head and tried to think of Christmas." (from James Joyce)

4. "When the cake was done he set it on the window sill to cool, heated some condensed milk diluted with water, and beat eggs into an omelet." (from Albert Camus)

5. "That night they camped in a grove of oaks." (from Lucy Johnston)

Name_____

Sentence Combining
with Prepositional Phrases

Directions: Revise each of the following groups of sentences by combining the key prepositional phrases into one well-structured sentence.

1.   Sue drew a picture.
      She was in art class.
      The art class was at Riverview High School.
      The picture was of a winter scene.

2.   The Senator answered many questions.
      The Senator was from Ohio.
      The questions were about health care reform.

3.   The guests will be given a tour.
      The guests were in the lobby.
      The tour will be of the museum.
      The museum is downtown.

4.   Marty found a coin.
      Marty was at the park.
      The coin was from the 1920's.
      The coin was in the mud.

5.   Ann called her boyfriend.
      Ann called him on the telephone.
      Her boyfriend was from Iowa.
      She called him during school.

Lesson 16 THE DESCRIPTIVE ESSAY

Objective: To introduce the descriptive essay project and writing process

The previous weeks have established the foundation and fundamentals of effective description. They are the training sessions. Now, the direction and objectives for the actual descriptive essay you want them to write should be based on (1) the amount of time you wish to spend, (2) how difficult the subject is to describe, (3) why you have chosen to describe that subject, (4) how much they are willing to write, and (5) the intended reader.

Students should consider the writing of the essay as a goal, a competitive challenge which often prompts a better work ethic. This is particularly important for younger students who need frequent challenges to make the activities interesting and enjoyable.

Activities:

1. **Organize:** Here are some possibilities for the Descriptive Essay Project.

    (A) A field trip to the zoo, a museum, an open air market, a farm, a park, or even the school campus. If you live near a major metropolitan area, you could explore the downtown area—its streets, alleys, or offices.

    If you decide to take a field trip be sure to gain parental approval beforehand with a letter and the appropriate form. You can also announce this trip at parent-teacher conferences.

    If a field trip cannot be arranged, then take a trip through the school hallways, cafeteria (before or after the lunch period), and, if allowed, the boiler room. Make plans weeks in advance and contact the appropriate officials and school administrator.

    (B) Individualized Essay—**Form 16-1**.

2. **Lecture:** Outline the writing process. (They have just discussed Steps A and B above.)

    • Topic selection/select topic and audience (reader)
    • Prewriting (brainstorming, webbing, or clustering)
    • First Draft
    • Editing and Revising
    • Final Copy

3. **Discuss:** To help students understand the connection between the writer and an appropriate reader, put the following terms on the board:

1. Powder Room
2. Bathroom
3. John
4. Ladies Room
5. Washroom
6. Water Closet
7. Outhouse
8. Restroom
9. Lavatory
10. Port-a-Potty

For each, have them select an appropriate "audience"—for example, a farmer for Outhouse or construction worker for Port-a-Potty.

4. **Explain:** The writer must consider his or her audience in the same way regarding the essay's word choice.

5. **Contest:** Prompt students to practice prewriting using a contest. Who can list the most? (boys vs. girls, group vs. group) Do a brainstorming and/or clustering exercise about any topic (a wedding, for example). Other potential topics are accidents, sports, medicine.

   Send students in a **tag team** format to the **blackboard** to do their writing.

   Congratulate students for their thoroughness after the contest is over and have them study the results of their total effort. Make sure they realize they should follow this same process (either brainstorming, webbing, and/or clustering) when they begin their own descriptive essay.

Homework:

Students begin the prewriting based on the topic/field trip you have selected. They should write all that they know already on that topic and what they learn about it from others (parents, friends, relatives) or other resources. Suggest they try to fill an entire page. Distribute any permission forms as well if you plan to take a field trip.

Direct students to study any descriptive writing that appears either in their grammar or literature text. If possible, have them locate descriptive writing from any source found in the library (ex) travel section of the newspaper or the geography section of any country in an encyclopedia.

Descriptive Essay Possibilities

Topic to Describe	*Potential Reader*
restaurant, bowling alley, movie theater, store	the owner or manager of that business
your neighborhood	mayor or city council
billboards	Department of Transportation
any musical instrument or music video	band director of the school
the beach or local park	mayor or recreation department director
tools, computer, car, boat, machine, or model	a manufacturer
church	clergyman or church council
the attic, basement, or garage	parents
any animal or pet	directors of a zoo or owners of a pet store
flowers or other form of vegetation	landscaper, owner of a nursery, neighbor, gardener
cafeteria, bus, classroom, study hall, locker room, or stadium	superintendent or principal
doll, muppet, model	art teacher or manufacturer

Lesson 17   CONJUNCTIONS

Objective: To gain skill at writing a first draft
To master the use of conjunctions

Activities:

1. **Debate**: Which is the better sentence?

    *   *Hank is a friend to Larry.*

    *   *Hank and Larry are friends.*

    [If students mention the second sentence is more effective because it declares its meaning with less words, they have discovered one benefit of using conjunctions.]

2. **Explain:** Coordinating conjunctions (and, but, or, nor, for, yet, so) are useful for joining words, phrases, or clauses.

3. **Write:** Students analyze use of conjunctions—**Activity 17-1.**

    Check the results.

4. **Read:** In the text about conjunctions, especially note the list of coordinating and correlative conjunctions.

5. **Lecture:** Examine the benefits of using conjunctions:

    *   The writer can use less words (combine sentences).

    *   They help combine descriptive examples and main points.

    *   They prompt variety in sentence structure.

    *   They lead to coherence in writing.

    *   For other types of conjunction usage—Use **Form 17-2.**

6. **Discuss:** Choose any exercise in the text where conjunctions are used. First, have the students locate the conjunctions and the items being joined.

    Then select any of these sentences and ask, "How would these sentences be written if the conjunction was not present?"

Homework:

Students complete their first drafts (usually 400-600 words).

Using Conjunctions

1. Revise this sentence. Eliminate excessive conjunctions.

   This school has a lot of options for students and they should take advantage of them and these include sports and clubs and drama but if students lack the time they should try to budget their time or consider changing some non-school activities so they can participate in more school sports or clubs or drama.

2. Combine sentences using conjunctions.

   A. We love school. We hate homework.

   B. Helen Gurley Brown founded *Cosmopolitan* magazine. She also publishes it.

3. Locate sentences from your textbook or magazine articles that show effective use of conjunctions. Copy them.

4. Why should writers avoid beginning sentences with a conjunction?

5. Two conjunctions that are rarely used are *yet* and *so*.
   In separate sentences, use both effectively:

Crazy Conjunction Usage

1. *Asyndeton:*

   The omission of a conjunction where it would normally appear

   (ex) "I came, I saw, I conquered." (Julius Caesar)

   (ex) "That government of the people, by the people, for the people, shall not perish from the earth." (Abraham Lincoln in his Gettysburg Address)

   (ex) ". . . out of the heart of men, proceed evil thoughts, adulteries, fornications, murders, thefts, covetousness, wickedness, deceit, lasciviousness, an evil eye, blasphemy, pride, foolishness." (Mark 7:21)

2. *Polysyndeton:*

   The extended use of conjunctions, where only a single conjunction is necessary

   (ex) "When men drink, then they are rich and successful and win lawsuits and are happy and help their friends." (Aristophenes)

3. *Paradiastole:*

   The extended use of *nor* or *or*.

   (ex) "Not snow, nor rain, nor heat, nor night keeps them from accomplishing their appointed courses with all speed." (Herodotus)

   (ex) "He who greatly excels in beauty, strength, birth, or wealth, and he who is very poor, or very weak, or very disgraced, find it difficult to follow rational laws." (author unknown)

Question: How do these unconventional uses of conjunctions add to the intent or meaning of the statements?

Lesson 18   PEER EDITING

Objective: To work at peer editing

[For a more detailed overview on peer editing skills, see Section 13]

1. **Discussion:** In order to improve editing skills and establish the format of the peer editing task, **ask** students:

   A. What is a more specific word for the following?

       1. nice
       2. stuff
       3. person
       4. big
       5. wind
       6. loud

   [Be sure dictionaries and/or thesauruses are available for students.]

   B. How would you revise the following statements?

       1. James liked to read about farming, although he never lived on one.

       [Although he had never lived on a farm, James liked to read about farming.]

       2. It says in the book that jails are overcrowded.

       [The book says jails are overcrowded.]

2. **Explain:** One part of editing is replacing, as needed, words that lack clarity or strength with more descriptive and specific words (ex) replacing wind with *breeze*; cold rain with *chilly, December rain*; sound of the horn with *horn's shrill blast*.

3. **Partners:** Examine a paragraph of descriptive writing—**Activity 18-1.** Give each pair of students a specific task as indicated on the form.(If more pairs exist, then double up.)

   Discuss the results.

4. **Explain:** The intent of peer editing is, in short, one or more classmates assisting each other with their drafts by offering specific compliments or suggestions for improvement.

   [If you have any papers left over from your college or high school classes that your teachers have marked, show them now to prove that even accomplished writers must edit.]

5. **Exchange:** Students give each other first drafts. They examine them especially for word choice. **Monitor** their progress.

6. **Reminder:** Students must also engage in proofreading to complete the revising step.

Homework:

Students continue editing and revising their descrptive essays.

Peer Editing for Description

Directions: Examine the following paragraph for one of the following elements of descriptive writing. If you finish early, go on to edit the paragraph for another element. Has the writer used . . .

1. concrete nouns? Underline vague nouns and then replace them with concrete nouns.

2. strong verbs? Underline the weak verbs and then replace them with strong verbs.

3. colorful adjectives? Underline those words that lack precision and replace them with adjectives that are descriptive and precise.

4. adverbs appropriately? Indicate where any adverbs could be placed.

5. sensory language? Suggest spots where sensory language (words associated with sight, sound, smell, taste, and touch) can be used.

6. prepositional phrases effectively? Suggest where prepositional phrases can be placed for strong effect.

7. conjunctions to combine words, phrases, or sentences for more concise writing? Show where this could be accomplished.

8. phrases or sentences that are off the topic and do not add to the description? Cross out these phrases or sentences.

I remember going sledding during many bitter winters. Winter is really a beautiful time. Many animals leave their tracks in the snow. When we go sledding on our plastic sleds our boots fill up with snow after every footstep through the drifts. The wind also punishes our skin. After several trips down the hill the sledding track would get hard. We would go fast down the hill to see who could sled the farthest. Later, we would go home exhausted, pulling our sleds behind us.

Lesson 19 PRONOUNS

Objective: To recognize the importance of careful use of pronouns in descriptive writing

Activities:

[This lesson could take 1-2 class periods.]

1. **Read:** Distribute the "Leadership" paragraph (**Form 19-1**) for students to determine the humor in its content.

    Discuss: How do the pronouns here influence the intended humor? Why is it funny because of the pronouns?

    [The correct analysis is that the indefinite pronouns, which offer no specific reference to any person, tend to confuse any understanding of who is in charge.]

2. **Explain:** Pronouns can be useful to description as long as they are used effectively and judiciously. Be sure students are clear that pronouns take the place of nouns to prevent repetition and that these nouns are called *antecedents*.

3. **Review:** List the personal, indefinite, demonstrative, and interrogative pronouns. (Use students' grammar text.)

4. **Partners:** Students have a conversation without using pronouns, especially personal pronouns, as they speak. The topic—"Family and friends." **Monitor** their work, pointing out when they have used pronouns.

5. **Identification:** Use any exercise in the grammar text where students can identify the pronouns being used.

6. **Oral review**: Call out some nouns and ask students to identify a pronoun that could replace that antecedent (ex) *Billy*—him, he, his; *class*—they, us, everyone; *desk*—that, it, this.

7. **Visual aide:** Using a magazine photo, painting, or a transparency, students examine the picture and identify antecedents they can replace with pronouns. For example, a picture of a frontier scene could prompt the following: cowboy—him; horses—those; cowboys—everybody; cactus—it.

8. **Analysis:** Distribute **Pronouns and the Cafeteria—Activity 19-2**. [Students should eventually conclude too many or too few pronouns can hurt descriptive writing. Neither paragraph on this worksheet is truly

effective description.]

9. **Explain:** It is important to be selective about the use of pronouns. Students should not jeopardize clarity, nor risk awkward repetitions of nouns. Also, explore the use of "YOU." Use **Activity 19-3**.

   [Using "YOU" can show emphasis; make a direct link to the reader; and creates informality.

   Using "YOU" can also ruin economy in writing; makes the writing too conversational; and lessens emphasis if overused.]

10. **Discuss:** How pronouns are used in contractions—(ex) *that's* for *that is*; *it's* for *it is*; etc.

Homework:

Students read about pronouns in the grammar text, possibly memorizing the list of indefinite, personal, demonstrative, and interrogative pronouns.

Students also complete the revising and editing process of their descriptive essay.

If desired, students can review all the parts of speech and aspects associated with descriptive writing in preparation for a test. They should, of course, use any information in their textbooks to assist them with this review.

A Paragraph on Leadership

Once upon a time there were four persons named **Everybody**, **Somebody**, **Nobody**, and **Anybody**. When there was an important job to be done, **Everybody** was sure **Somebody** would do it. **Anybody** could have done it, but **Nobody** did it.

When **Nobody** did it, **Everybody** became angry because it was **Everybody's** job. **Everybody** thought that **Somebody** would do it, but **Nobody** realized that **Nobody** would do it.

Eventually, **Everybody** blamed **Somebody** when **Nobody** did what **Anybody** could have done in the first place.

Name _____

Pronouns and the Cafeteria

Directions: Read and examine each of these paragraphs and then decide which of the two is more effective and more descriptive. Be prepared to explain your selection.

Every day at lunch everyone rushes into line to buy their favorite food. I like to sit with my friends. We usually talk about someone or something that happened that day until everybody has had a chance to say this or that. After we eat nobody enjoys cleaning up, but we all have to do it. That is because another group comes in and they need their area clean.

Every day at lunch the 9th graders rush into line to buy the 9th graders' favorite food. I like to sit with Jonah, Sam, and Herbie. Jonah, Sam, Herbie, and I usually talk about Tricia or Tricia's problems that happened that day until Jonah, Sam, Herbie, and I finish talking about Tricia's problems or Tricia's family. After Jonah, Sam, Herbie, and I eat, Jonah, Sam, Herbie, and I do not enjoy cleaning up, but Jonah, Sam, Herbie, and I have to do the cleaning up. The cleaning up is necessary because another group comes in and the other group needs the other group's area clean.

The Pronoun You

Directions: Read and examine each of the sentences below and revise the sentence to eliminate the use of YOU to be more descriptive. Be prepared to explain your selection.

(ex)   If you find yourself not trusting your boyfriend, you can have a lot of problems.

(Rev.)   Not trusting a boyfriend can result in a lot of problems.

1.   You have to be able to respect other people.

   _____

2.   Being open with your friend is really important.

   _____

3.   In any relationship, you have to show them affection and support.

   _____

   _____

4.   To understand someone's feelings, you must first listen.

   _____

   _____

5.   In a relationship you must first meet your partner's needs.

   _____

   _____

6.   If you want your relationship to work you must really trust the other person.

   _____

   _____

7.   It can be really rewarding when you fall in love.

   _____

Section 3 : CHARACTER SKETCH

"Advice to young writers who want to get ahead without any annoying delays: don't write about Man, write about *a* man."
(E. B. White)

Objectives: Improve students' skills at descriptive writing
Teach effective paragraphing
Guide students as they compose a creative character sketch

Length: Five lessons

Introduction:

State the obvious. People surround us every day. Indeed, students have a tremendous variety of prompts and possibilities in this unit. Whether they choose to write about a real or imaginary person, students need only to observe family, friends, classmates, celebrities, and literary characters for subjects. Studying the people around us is the primary rationale behind this unit.

The description often seen in successful character sketches emerges from students who make precise observations, who provide detailed backgrounds, and who create unusual individuals. The main challenge here is to prompt students to be creative as they first select and then describe a person.

The character sketch helps students explore other people in an in-depth way—their behaviors, attitudes, appearances. This can lead, in turn, to students examining their own emotions and personalities. Ideally, when they deal intensely with both the outward appearance and the inner feelings of the person who is the subject of their character sketch, they usually reach self-awareness as well. This can lead to some new realizations for the student.

As always, be very clear about your expectations of students, and focus and build on quality work. Use remedial and individualized instruction whenever necessary—(ex) giving suggestions about figurative language. Finally, if desired, you can provide a list of persons you would prefer students not select as potential subjects.

Lesson 20 WHAT IS A CHARACTER SKETCH?

Objective: To introduce the character sketch

Activities:

1. **Freewriting:** Fictional person Jorge Gonzales—**Activity 20-1**, and Fictional Scenarios—**Activity 20-2**.

   Discuss the results.

2. **Explain:** The opening assignment is a typical way to begin formulating a character sketch. What is a character sketch?

   [It is a composition that profiles and describes a real or imaginary person's appearance, background, and behavior /attitude.]

3. **Brainstorming:** Write on the board the descriptive and concrete details that students announce about:

   A. An actual person all the students know well—other than school personnel (to avoid details that could make you uncomfortable).

   B. An imaginary person (much like Jorge Gonzales).

   Ask: What are his/her
   - physical features?
   - height and weight?
   - gestures?
   - behaviors?
   - job or avocation?
   - leisure activities?
   - family life?
   - attitudes?

4. **Visual aid:** Show pictures of unusual persons who appear in magazines, or in students' own text, or on posters in the room. Students cite these persons' characteristics using concrete nouns and descriptive adjectives.

   You can also use slides, wear a costume, or refer to a stage play the students might have seen.

5. **Brainstorming:** [Answers will vary.]
   - What are some unusual *names*—real or made up?
   - *Where* do these people live—real or made up?
   - What are some unusual ways of walking?

- What are some unusual types of clothing or jewelry? Tattoos?
- What about hair—braided, spiked, sideburns?

Homework (and options):

Students select the actual or imaginary person they plan to use for their character sketch—either someone they know personally (a parent, relative, or friend); someone they have seen or read about (a professional athlete, performer, actor); or someone they make up (like Jorge Gonzales). They brainstorm/prewrite a list of details about that person.

A. Students should also read any sample character sketches in their textbook(s).

B. Students write **Activity 20-3.**

C. Students closely observe family members and friends for one day, taking notes on the mannerisms and gestures as their subjects speak and move. For each gesture that is repeated, students explain how it reflects that person's personality.

D. Students expand their vocabulary related to the writing of a character sketch. Have them define CHARLATAN, CYNIC, INGRATE, NEOPHYTE, RENEGADE, URCHIN, IDEALIST, ZEALOT, PATRIARCH, and MATRIARCH.

Name _____

Jorge Gonzales

Directions: Answer each of the questions in detail.

1. Jorge Gonzales has a unique scar on his face. What does it look like? What other unique features does he have?

2. Jorge Gonzales hates where he lives. Why? Describe this place.

3. Jorge Gonzales leaves for work every day at midnight. What does he do for a living?

4. Jorge Gonzales doesn't have any friends. Why not?

5. Jorge Gonzales has some pretty bad habits. What are they?

6. Jorge Gonzales is dying. Why?

Scenarios for Character Sketches

Directions: A scenario is an outline of any real or imagined event. Read each of the
brief scenarios below and then answer the question in detail.

1. The police catch a poor, unemployed father stealing bread from a local grocery
   store. Who is this father and why is he stealing bread?

2. On a Christmas Eve news broadcast the anchorperson suddenly breaks down crying. What does this anchorperson look like and why is he/she crying?

3. The owner of a chocolate factory gathers all his employees together one Friday so
   they can hear his speech. What does this owner look like and what does he tell
   them?

4. John and Mary had planned to marry. However, John was kidnapped and held
   hostage for two years. Finally, he was released only to discover Mary married
   someone else. How does John react when he discovers this news, and what does
   he do next?

5. A marvelously talented wide receiver on a professional football team scores the
   winning touchdown in a playoff game and then collapses in the end zone. How did
   he behave in the end zone before collapsing, and what caused him to collapse?

Character Sketch—Extended Activities

Directions: Select any two of the following activities. All assignments should be 2-3 paragraphs.

1. Examine newspaper articles or obituaries for people who could be interesting subjects for a character sketch. Explain why you have selected them.

2. Observe closely family members and friends for one day, taking notes on their mannerisms and gestures as they speak and move. For each gesture that is repeated, explain how it reflects that person's personality.

3. Research any famous historical figure—(ex) Benjamin Franklin—and write an essay that portrays this person's most interesting qualities.

4. Make a chart of the heights, weights (possibly add any weight loss), shoe size, hat size, and shirt (jacket) size of all family members and friends.

5. Compare ancient man and modern man. Research *Homo Erectus* vs. *Homo Neanderthal* vs. *Homo Sapiens Sapiens*. Write an essay that clarifies and describes their major similarities and differences.

6. What are the major *diseases* affecting humanity? Select any three major diseases and explain in a detailed essay how they affect the human body.

7. Research "Australopithecus afarensis," the first known human. What was this human like—appearance, behavior, and social activities?

8. Look up a dozen names or terms related to professions and careers—(ex) technocrat. Define each and explain its origin.

9. Chart the ethnic and cultural background of people in your neighborhood.

10. Create a documentary about the lifestyle of a specific group of people—(ex) Eskimos. What are their general habits? Family life? Leisure activities? Etc.

Lesson 21   DESCRIPTION, CHARACTERIZATION, AND CARICATURES

Objective: To work at writing the details required in effective character sketches

Activities:

1. **Modeling**—Distribute **Form 21-1**—a sample character sketch—for students to read.

2. **Discussion:** What descriptive details do you notice about Modaki Czeressaborn? Why is it easy to make up details like this?

    [Be sure to point out the background (family, work, hobbies) of Modaki Czeressaborn.]

3. **Music:** Play a song about a person—(ex) "Barbara Ann" by the Beach Boys or "Billy Jean" by Michael Jackson. Ask: What is revealed about the person in the song?

4. **Explain:** Character sketches are more than just the description of a person's appearance. Sometimes the physical details can be exaggerated as in a *caricature*.

    Caricatures are illustrations (or at times written) that accentuate any person's most striking features (ex) Bob Hope's nose, Don King's hair, Jay Leno's chin.

    Most often, the caricature is associated with politics.

5. **Visual aid:** Show any caricatures from newspapers, their own textbook, or magazines. Look again at photographs of famous people. Possibly have some students draw one as a caricature.

6. **Write:** Students work on **Activity 21-2**—Caricatures.

    Discuss their responses.

7. **Discussion:** Lead into how to recognize writing that *shows* characterization, rather than *tells* it.

    A.   What is the difference between these two statements?

    Johnny becomes jealous easily.

    Johnny follows his girlfriend everywhere she goes except the bathroom.

    B.   An advertisement appeared in the classified section of the newspaper that read:

    "Gretchen, please come home. All is forgiven."

    Ask: What had happened here?

    Where is Gretchen?

C.   A baby was sitting alone in the grassy front yard of a house down the street crying.

       Ask: Why was the baby crying?
              Where were the parents?

D.   Plastic surgery is getting to be very common these days.

       Ask: Why are more and more healthy people getting plastic surgery?
              What are the benefits and/or risks of this type of surgery?

8.   **Write:** Students complete **Activity 21-3**—Showing vs. Telling. **Check** their responses individually.

9.   **Freewriting:**

Appearance—"Pretend you can travel in a time machine—into the past or future. Describe the appearance of the first person you see when you exit the machine."

Background—"What sports, clubs, or activities did your English teacher do when he/she was in high school?"

Behavior—"How did Snow White's eighth dwarf behave? Be sure you give him a name."

Check the results and remark on the most unusual or interesting features the students write.

Homework:

Students expand and complete the prewriting on the subject of their character sketch—brainstorming and clustering the following: What city is the place of his/her origin? Study an atlas; why did he/she appear in the newspaper one day? Study news articles; what is the unusual pet he/she has? Study a reference book on exotic animals; who is his/her enemy? Study any literary work to select an antagonist; what is a credo or saying that he/she lives by? Study a book of famous quotations and select one.

Sample Character Sketch— Modaki Czeressaborn

Modaki Czeressaborn is thirty-two years old and has lived in Belarus all his life. He has never traveled beyond his city of Rolenski and spends most of his time on his farm with his mother Lyuda and sister Sasha.

Although Modaki is very fit and athletic he rarely exercises, preferring instead to watch television when he is done with his farm chores. He has deep brown eyes and reddish-brown hair atop his six foot, 193 pound frame.

He enjoys television as his main leisure activity, especially the game shows, and collecting cardboard paper towel tubes. His girlfriend, or fiancee, Medka, spends time with him also, but her time is mostly spent with her studies. She wants to be a biologist. They've agreed to set a wedding date after she has graduated.

Modaki Czeressaborn rarely complains and is quite a passive person. He works on the farm during the day, watches his favorite television shows in the evening, and takes Medka to a local restaurant every weekend. This makes him satisfied and comfortable.

Caricatures

Directions: Examine the following example of a caricature from Washington Irving and then create your own.

"He was tall, but exceedingly lank, with narrow shoulders, long arms and legs, hands that dangled a mile out of his sleeves, feet that might have served for shovels, and his whole frame most loosely hung together. His head was small, and flat at top, with huge ears, large green glassy eyes, and a long snip nose, so that it looked like a weathercock perched upon his spindle neck, to tell which way the wind blew."

(From Irving describing Ichabod Crane, the schoolmaster, in "The Legend of Sleepy Hollow")

Your example:

Name _____

Showing vs. Telling

Part I Directions: For each of the following descriptions create a better one that **shows** characterization, rather than **tells** it.

(Ex) Telling: *Keith is funny.*

       Showing: *Keith is the Jerry Seinfeld of our class.*

1.   Telling: *Keith's hair is dark.*

     Showing:

2.   Telling: *Today has been a lousy day.*

     Showing:

3.   Telling: *It is really cold outside.*

     Showing:

4.   Telling: *He really worked hard on that school project.*

     Showing:

5.   Telling: *His family was very poor.*

     Showing:

Part II Directions: Answer the following questions in detail being sure to **show** the traits, and not **tell** them.

6.   What are the positive traits of your best friend?

7.   What are the negative traits of your best friend?

8.   What are the dimensions of the largest person you know personally?

9.   What are the characteristics of the wealthiest person you know?

Lesson 22   FIGURATIVE LANGUAGE AND APPOSITIVES

Objective: To explore figurative language and appositives

Activities:

[This lesson could take 1-2 class periods.]

1. **Review:** What are the differences between *showing* the reader and *telling* the reader?

   Does the following example show or tell the reader about the grandmother? [It shows.]

   Whenever it snows, my grandmother wears her thick red woolen socks, brown corduroy pants, royal blue sweater, and down jacket trimmed with white fur.

   What about these examples which are related to being frightened?

   "I was drowning. It was really bad, and I was really scared."

   "Any strength I had left me. The ocean water was like a giant rock pushing me down. My legs shook violently as I fell deeper and deeper, the water getting colder and colder, my arms trembling and quivering."

   [The second example shows the fear of a person drowning.]

2. **Pantomime:** Act out several moods and attitudes—puzzled, angry, frustrated, scared, in pain, excited by walking across the room—for students to identify and describe (showing).

   Student volunteers make their hands appear evil, angry, helpless, and guilty; their feet appear restless, angry, impatient; their faces angry, bored, embarrassed.

3. **Lecture:** Examine the use of allusions and similes for the character sketch. Figurative language helps writers *show* and not just *tell* about a person. Use **Activity 22-1**.

   Discuss the results.

4. **Analysis:** Use **Activity 22-2**.

   Discuss the results.

5. **Debate:** Which of the following is the best-phrased sentence? [Answers will vary.]

   My employer is Mrs. Filderbush. She loves chocolate.

   My employer, Mrs. Filderbush, loves chocolate.

   My employer, whose name is Mrs. Filderbush, loves chocolate.

6. **Lecture:** Go over the usefulness of appositives, especially when profiling a person and his/her traits.

7. **Read:** Locate in the grammar text more examples of appositives.

8. **Pair work:** Students exchange prewriting and offer suggestions for adding details and figurative language.

9. **Reminder:** Students should include unique gestures or habits (tapping a foot), character traits (coward or liar, for example), figurative language, and a comparison of their person to someone else—(ex) a celebrity. In this comparison, they should not, however, over-dramatize details about this person—(ex) an astronaut and an academy award winner.

Homework options:

Students expand their prewriting with figurative language.

A. Advanced students could expand their knowledge of characterizing a person by researching the background of prominent people in their city—a council member, the mayor, a police officer, or a local judge, the owner or employee of a local store, the director of the recreational department, or the director of the city service department.

B. Students could also research interesting names either from their literature text or the book couples may use to find a name for their child (or any other source). Have them investigate the meaning behind some names (or nicknames). They could even explore for unusual nicknames. What name do they find most appealing? Why? What names do they admire? Why?

C. Working in a thesaurus is also the focus of the homework. Students examine a series of words that could be used to describe people like *happy, funny, old, thin,* and *fast* and find more descriptive words.

D. Students consider television shows like "Seinfeld," songs like "Lucy" by Hansen, and movies, like "Rocky," which are based on people. What are their values? Beliefs? Personalities?

[Students need training in how the popular media (television, radio, films) portrays social skills and personal values. This type of examination can encourage critical thinking, especially about drug/alcohol references common in so many popular shows, the violent habits of movie heroes, and the exploitive depiction of females by musical performers, especially rappers.]

Allusions, Metaphors, and Similes

Allusions: References to historical or mythological persons or events

    (ex) You are a Benedict Arnold.
          He runs like a Sherman tank.

Similes: A comparison that uses *like* or *as* to connect the two items

    (ex) He ran like a marathoner on his last mile.
          Her brooding eyes were dark as night.

Metaphors: an *implied* comparison

    (ex) A storm raged in my mind.
          His rubbery legs gave out on the last lap.

- They enhance your writing style.

- They help clarify some descriptions by comparing something that it unfamiliar to that which is familiar.

- They can highlight description, especially of human beings.

Directions: Complete the following sentences with a simile, metaphor, or allusion.

1. His eyeballs bulged like _____

2. He twisted like a _____

3. His forehead was marked with _____

4. Hair hung over her forehead _____

5. Blood oozed like _____

6. _____ is the _____ of our class.
   (ex) John is the Hercules of our class.

Name _____

Figurative Language from the Professionals

Directions: Study these authors' figurative language and then create your own.

1. Thomas Pynchon wrote, "He had eyes which were the color of freezing rain."—What kind of figurative language is used here and how does it portray this person?

   How would you describe the eyes of a person who was happy?

2. Kurt Vonnegut wrote, "He didn't look like a soldier at all. He looked like a filthy flamingo."—What kind of figurative language is used here and how does it portray this person?

   How would you describe a soldier in battle?

3. Richard Wright wrote, "The sagging flesh of her face quivered; her eyes, large, dark, and deep-set, glared at me. Her lips narrowed to a line. Her high forehead was wrinkled. When she was angry, her eyelids drooped halfway down over her pupils, giving her a baleful aspect."—How would you describe the mood of this woman?

   How would you describe her face during a moment of delight?

Lesson 23

PREWRITING INTO PARAGRAPHS

Objective: To develop paragraphing skills

Activities:

1. **Explain:** Students' desks are arranged for group work. Be sure they are clear. They will be evaluated based on the *thoroughness* of their group work and the *creativity* and *cooperation* they demonstrate individually regarding proper paragraphing. Distribute **Form 23-1**—Character Sketch Evaluation.

2. **Group work:** Paragraphing

   A. **Knowledge check:** Ask: How does a writer know when he/she has an effective paragraph?

   [It has a topic sentence; 4-6 sentences; all sentences relate to one topic; coherent sentences]

   B. **Writing:** Groups write a paragraph comparing a team player to a super star.

   C. For the given body parts written on index cards, each student creates a supporting sentence. The group as a whole creates a topic sentence.

   D. **Analysis:** What is the difference between a topic sentence and a thesis statement?

   [The topic sentence expresses the main topic of a paragraph while the thesis expresses the main topic of an entire essay.]

3. **Discuss:** Paragraphing [Refer to group work.]

   A. How can a writer develop a topic sentence?

   [By using supporting sentences that are examples, reasons, or description about the topic sentence.]

   B. How can a writer achieve paragraph coherence?

   {By using transitional words—second, third, finally, also, etc.—and varying sentence length.]

   C. How can a writer improve a faulty paragraph?

   [Check for unity, remove grammar errors, count for 4-6 sentences, evaluate the topic sentence, etc.]

4. **Analysis #1:** Students examine and compare paragraphs they find in fiction (literature text), newspaper articles, and essays. How are they similar? Different?

Analysis #2: Students compare any stanza from any poem from their literature text with any well-structured paragraph from their grammar text. Why have both writers grouped those lines/sentences together?

5. **Summary:** Every paragraph should stand on its own and deal with one specific topic. Any sentences unrelated to the topic should be deleted—this is unity. Transitions should be used to create coherence. Finally, you can find differences in paragraph length between fiction and essays, however, typically there are 4-6 sentences.

Homework options:

A. Students read selected pages in their grammar text about specific paragraphing skills (and possibly do an exercise in the text).

B. Students write the first draft of the character sketch, transforming their preliminary prewriting into a sequence of paragraphs with an introduction, body, and conclusion.

C. Students select any abstract term associated with human behavior—love, loyalty, kindness, etc.—and write a paragraph that defines that term.

Name _____

Character Sketch Evaluation

Low . . . Needs some work . . . Adequate . . . High
1 . . . . .2 . . . . .3 . . . . .4 5

Points   *Criteria*

1. _____ The character sketch has an interesting introduction that leads effectively into the thesis.

2 _____ The sketch is effectively organized—logical and coherent arrangement of paragraphs. The order is correct, clear, and easy to follow.

3. _____ Paragraphs are well-structured and unified.

4. _____ The person is described thoroughly.

5. _____ The individual is presented in an interesting and creative way (uniqueness).

6. _____ Various types of figurative language (allusions, similes, metaphors) are used effectively/creatively.

7. _____ Concrete, descriptive words are evident throughout the character sketch. Dull language is avoided.

8. _____ Spelling and capitalization have been checked.

9. _____ Punctuation and sentence structure are correct.

10. _____ Uniqueness, insight, and editing are evident.

_____ Total Points

Lesson 24 — PEER EDITING—CHARACTER SKETCH

Objective: To work at character sketch organization and coherence

Activities:

1. **Review:** Proper paragraph structure.

   [An effective paragraph should have: 4-6 sentences; a topic sentence as its first or final sentence; unity—all the supporting sentences relate directly to the topic sentence; coherence—transitional words or devices are used.]

2. **Warm up:** Use **Activity 24-1** to introduce the peer editing of the character sketch.

2. **Peer Editing**—First drafts are exchanged and edited. Refer, if necessary to **Activity 23-1**.

   What would you take out?

   What would you add?

   What about figurative language?

   What descriptions remain unclear?

   What descriptions are precise and interesting?

3. **Writing:** Students work at revising and editing while **conferencing** (formal or informal) with the teacher (or a classmate).

Homework:

Students complete (type) the final copy of their character sketches.

Editing—The Character Sketch

Directions: Examine the following character sketch and do the following:

1. Delete unnecessary details.
2. Check words or phrases that are especially precise and descriptive.
3. Mark sentences or paragraphs that lack description.
4. Offer suggestions for figurative language.
5. Comment on the introduction and conclusion.

    My character sketch is about Jackie Jones. She is five eight inches tall. She has golden brown hair. Her eyes are a leafy green color. My character has a B average in school. She is well mannered and has a lot of friends.

    She dresses in stylish clothes. She loves to shop at the mall. She loves to talk on the phone with her friends. She never misses an episode of "General Hospital."

    The character I have just described has lived in this town since the 6th grade. My character is Jackie Jones.

Section 4 : SENTENCE STRUCTURE

"It has taken me years of struggle, hard work and research to learn to make one simple gesture, and I know enough about the art of writing to realize that it would take as many years of concentrated effort to write one simple, beautiful sentence."

(*Isadora Duncan*)

Objectives: Identify the sentence core
Teach methods for expanding the sentence core
Explain the importance of using a variety of sentence types (simple, compound, and complex)
Show how to avoid sentence fragments and run-ons

Length: Ten lessons approximately

Introduction:

By the time they reach 7th grade all students should be competent enough to write complete, coherent, and cogent sentences. Unfortunately, too many essays still have run-ons and fragments, wordiness and strings, punctuation errors and misplaced modifiers. Even the students who turn in papers that are free of such grammatical mistakes may still show little variety and complexity in their sentences, preferring, it seems, to stick with the basic subject-verb pattern. In short, students at the secondary level still fall into the same traps that can lead to errors in sentence structure and they take too little risk in attempting any form of diversity with their sentences.

We need to intensify their knowledge of how sentences work and then to open their eyes to the dynamics of manipulating sentences to demonstrate *meaning* clearly, coherently, and creatively. To accomplish this, first identify the specific, technical rules all writers must follow when writing sentences. Then, like an engineer, demonstrate the various ways of building a sentence with modifiers, phrases, and clauses. Finally, be prepared to answer questions dealing with syntax, semantics, and patterns in sentence structure.

To encourage students to engage themselves in this unit with intensity and diligence, it is best to follow a sequence of steps that can take the student from his or her present skill level to a more advanced level. Students need to see that improving their skill at writing sentences is helpful, and that this adds a more mature element to their writing style. Writing a comprehensive sentence can be a challenge for some students.

Work with them, therefore, to set individual goals regarding improving their skill with sentences and provide less comprehensive techniques for expanding sentences.

Lesson 25 WHAT IS A GOOD SENTENCE?

Objective: To introduce the importance of writing strong sentences

Activities:

1. **Discuss:**

   What are the characteristics of an effective sentence?

   How do sentences differ between *speech* and *writing*?

   How would you *define* a sentence?

   Consider—*The lazy carpet ate a false shovel*? Is this a sentence? Why/Why not?

2. **Review:** Find out the students' knowledge of sentences. Some students have probably identified the necessity for a subject and predicate (verb), and the relationship of punctuation (end marks) to sentence writing.

3. **Discuss:** Distribute **Form 25-1.** Show how grammarians have defined the sentence through history. Students select the definition they find most appropriate. Ask them to explain why the others are not useful.

4. **Analysis:** Determine what are complete and incomplete sentences. Use any of the following:

   A. *Song lyrics* from a contemporary and popular song copied onto paper. Ask: What is missing?

   B. *Exercises* in the textbook about sentence errors (e.g., missing subject or verb).

   C. *Script from a play* (possibly from their own literature text or a work by Shakespeare)—Students identify complete and incomplete sentences spoken by the characters.

   D. *Videotape* of a movie. Students identify those actors' dialogues that are fragments and complete sentences.

   E. *Role playing*—Two students have a conversation about their favorite after-school activity. Ask the rest of class to point out any incomplete sentences in the conversation.

5. **Lecture:** Examine the sentence core. Review the basic subject-verb relationship that forms any sentence and makes a sentence make sense.

6. **Freewriting:** Students practice *expanding* the sentence core, which is like the core of an apple (it contains the seeds, the basics, the subject and verb). Use **Activity 25-2.**

7. **Oral reading:** Students read their sentences out loud. Comment on their use of adjectives, prepositional phrases, and adverbs.

8. **Identification:** Show students detailed sentences found in their literature text, grammar textbook, or other supplemental source for them to see how other writers use expanded sentences.

9. **Reading:** Locate in the grammar text the opening sections on sentence structure and parts of sentences. You might also spend some time **discussing** any exercise that deals with the sentence core.

Homework options:

A. Students research and define in their notebooks—sentence subject and sentence predicate (the core).

B. Students practice more sentence expansion by expanding sentences that appear in their grammar text, or by using sentences copied from a children's book.

C. Advanced students can research famous sentences from Thomas Jefferson, Abraham Lincoln, John F. Kennedy, Martin Luther King, and Richard Nixon.

Name _____

Definitions of Sentences

Date *Definition*

1762 "A sentence is an assemblage of words, expressed in proper form, ranged in proper order, and concurring to make complete sense." (by Robert Lowth)

1856 "A sentence is a portion of a composition or utterance as extends from one full stop to another." (from an English grammar text)

1924 "A sentence is a complete and independent utterance—the completeness and independence being shown by . . . its capability of standing alone." (by Otto Jespersen)

1933 "Each sentence is an independent linguistic form, not included by virtue of any grammatical construction in any larger linguistic form." (by Leonard Bloomfield)

1941 "It is a collection of words by means of which a meaningful idea is expressed about a being, place, or thing. It is a thought expressed in words so arranged and constructed as to have a subject—that about which something is said—and a predicate—that which expresses action or state or condition about the subject." (from Harper's *English Grammar*)

1963 "Sentences in English develop about patterns . . . in which a subject introduces a topic, and a verb, and usually a complement comment on it." (from the *Modern English Handbook*)

1963 " . . . a group of words containing a subject and predicate." (from the *Standard College Dictionary*)

1965 "A set of words complete in itself, having either expressed or understood in it a subject and a predicate and conveying a statement or question or command or exclamation." (by H. W. Fowler)

1966 "A sentence is not just a linear string of words; it is a sequence grouped in a particular way." (by N. R. Cattall)

Sentence Expansion

Directions: Expand each sentence below with modifiers, phrases, and clauses.

(ex) The campers roasted marshmallows.

The twenty starving campers from Boy Scout troop #46 eagerly roasted marshmallows over a roaring fire at Camp Winnetonka last weekend.

1. A visitor arrived.

2. A stranger entered.

3. His face looked mean.

4. No one spoke.

5. The man walked around.

6. The crowd stared.

7. A bell rang.

8. The stranger left.

Lesson 26 EXPANDING THE SENTENCE CORE

Objective: To review expanding the sentence core

Activities:

[This lesson could take 1-2 class periods.]

1. **Review:** Ask any student to read his/her expanded sentences from the Lesson 25 homework assignment. Ask: What parts make up a complete sentence? What is the sentence core?

2. **Freewriting:** Students work on sentence expansion.

    A. Expand the following: *"This class is interesting."*

        1. by adding adjective(s)

           (ex) This *English* class is interesting.

        2. by adding prepositional phrase(s)

           (ex) This English class is interesting *on Fridays.*

        3. by adding a compound part

           (ex) This English class is interesting *and enjoyable on* Fridays.

        4. by adding a subordinate clause

           (ex) This English class is interesting and enjoyable on Fridays *when we go on field trips.*

    B. Use a sentence like *"Today I expect . . ."* on the board and then direct students to complete and expand it with the following words:

    HOMEWORK   LUNCH   TALKATIVE   FUN   FRIENDS   TEST

    Review their results.

3. **Explain:** With the direction to add a compound part or a subordinate clause, many students might become confused. They might also end up with the run-on effect. Therefore, they need to be careful when expanding.

    Using conjunctions—and, but, or—at times can help the writer use less words. They are also for convenience.

    Point out these typical problems (possibly by sending some students to the **blackboard** to write their sentences).

4. **Locate:** The list of subordinate conjunctions in their text and examine how they are used in sentences.

97

5. **Discuss:** Which is the best subordinate conjunction to place in the blank? Choose from:

Although, If, Since, When, Because

_____ *you have no teeth, you have to eat pizza from a blender.*

[Correct answers are either *If* or *Because*. *Although* is grammatically incorrect; *Since* and *When* imply a reference to time. *If* means "supposing that," and *Because* refers to a cause/effect relationship.]

Which is the most effectively written sentence?

> *The students left <u>because</u> the teacher never showed up.*
>
> *The students left <u>since</u> the teacher never showed up.*

[Be sure that at least five students have dictionaries to look up each conjunction. Once these definitions are announced, students can more readily make the best choice, which should be *because* which again suggests a cause/effect relationship.]

6. **Identification:** Show students examples of complex sentences (from their grammar text).

7. **Explain:** Differences between a compound sentence and a complex sentence.

[A compound sentence has two independent clauses joined by a coordinating conjunction (and, but, or), while a complex sentence has an independent clause and a dependent clause joined by a subordinating conjunction (because, as, while, which, etc.)]

8. **Charting:** Using a newspaper or magazine, students chart how writers often use complex and simple sentences.

9. **Writing:** Students do **Activity 26-1**.

   Check the results.

10. **Reading:** Students locate the section in their text about complex sentences, and possibly discuss 1-2 exercises.

Homework options: Students continue to explore complex sentences.

A. Students study a book that appeals to them and make copies of five different pages. Using a highlighter, they identify the complex sentences.

B. Since complex sentences are often found in more advanced forms of writing, it could be suggested that the less skilled reader can be easily discouraged from reading this type of literature. Students write a brief, persuasive essay on the advantages or disadvantages of complex sentences.

C. More advanced students can research and define the *noun clause*, the *adjective clause*, and the *adverb clause* and write several example sentences of each.

D. Students research interesting sentences from a published author that demonstrate sentence expansion.

Writing Complex Sentences

Directions: Complete the sentence starters below, developing them into complex sentences. Use the subordinate conjunction in parentheses.

1. (after) My dog jumped out the window

2. (before) A frog landed in my lap

3. (when) It wasn't funny

4. (which) I finished my homework

5. (because) I never expected

6. (although) I wanted to win

7. (as) The coach applauded

8. [Create your own complex sentences]

Lesson 27   VARIETY IN SENTENCES

Objective: To work at showing variety in sentence writing

Activities:

1. **Introduce:** Discuss the importance of variety in sentence writing. Give examples from a favorite author, a selection in their literature text, or a magazine article. Especially useful are sentences from William Shakespeare, Ernest Hemingway (short sentences), James Fenimore Cooper (lengthy sentences), Irwin Shaw, Saul Bellow, and Raymond Carver, among others.

2. **Write: Activity 27-1**—Students combine simple sentences to make more comprehensive sentences and restructure complex sentences (deconstruction or working backwards) into short, simple ones.

   Discussion: Which types do you prefer? Why?

3. **Analysis:** Students work in **pairs** or **individually** on **Activity 27-2** and **Activity 27-3**.

   Discuss their responses.

4. **Review** how to *build/expand* sentences by compounding. *Show* how to construct compound subjects, verbs, objects, and sentences. Compare the following:

   (ex)   The dog growled. He snarled. He attacked.

         The dog growled, snarled, and attacked. (Compound verb)

5. **Summary:** Varying sentence lengths and types can make writing smoother and less dull.

Homework options:

A. Students locate writing that demonstrates true variety in sentences. They bring that article or story to class along with an article or story they've written themselves imitating the professional piece (the same subject matter).

B. They write a paragraph or a page where they describe a dream they've had either using short, tense sentences or lengthy, complex sentences to create the mood or tone of that dream (possibly a nightmare).

C. They locate a piece of writing (not poetry) and analyze it for its sentence structure.

101

Constructing and Deconstructing Sentences

I **Combine** (Construct) the following groups of sentences into one comprehensive sentence each in the space to the right.

   1. A new student entered the classroom.
       He was blond.
       He was lanky.
       He smiled at us.
       He seemed shy.

   2. The third baseman reached his mitt into the air.
       He snagged the ball.
       He threw it to first base.
       He was a veteran player.

   3. The girl grasped the handlebars of her bike.
       She grasped them tightly.
       She was nervous.
       She was about seven years old.
       The bike was her first two wheeler.

   4. Barb's parents watched her on the diving board.
       They were smiling.
       She stood at the end of the diving board.
       She was nervous.

   5. The school bell rang.
       It was finally three o'clock.
       We stepped quickly to our buses.
       It would be a fifteen minute bus ride.

II **Split** (deconstruct) each of the following sentences into 2-3 sentences.

   6. The dog perked up its ears, barked, and raced to the door when the car's tires crunched onto the gravel of the driveway, knowing its owner had returned with dinner, which was a can of expensive dog food, for the evening.

   7. The Red Devils, who hadn't won a game all year, gloated after winning the football game against the Eagles, their arch rivals, who had been undefeated and ranked first in the state before losing this one 24-14 on a cloudy day.

   8. I always leave the cigar box I use for my spare coins, which I eventually use to buy birthday presents, hidden behind my books on the top shelf in my bedroom.

Name _____

"At the Foul Line"

Read each of the paragraphs below and then answer the questions that follow.

Paragraph #1

He stood at the foul line. He was alone. All the other players were at the sidelines. The pep band was silent. No fan cheered. Everyone watched breathlessly. He gripped the ball tightly. He bounced it once. He bounced it twice. He shot the ball. It went in.

Paragraph #2

He stood at the foul line alone because the rest of the players had been instructed to go to the sidelines. The pep band was silent, and even the fans didn't cheer. Everyone, in fact, watched breathlessly as he gripped the basketball tightly. He bounced it twice before shooting and making his shot.

Questions

1. How do these paragraphs differ in terms of their sentence structure?

2. What mood or "tone" is established in the first paragraph?

3. Why does the second paragraph seem to have better sense of coherence?

4. Which paragraph offers more details?

Sentence Tension

Part I

Directions: Short sentences tend to create a feeling of tension or suspense, while longer sentences are generally more useful for description. Read the following paragraph, answer the questions, and then create your own series of short sentences.

The guards finally finished and left. The Row was now locked down. Every inmate in his cell. All doors secured. All windows closed. Sam had begun shaking with the closing of the windows. His head dropped even lower. Adam placed an arm around his frail shoulders. (from John Grisham's "The Chamber")

1.   How does Grisham convey a sense of fear?

2.   Why do you think Sam is shaking?

3.   What is the *image* you get from these sentences?

4.   Write your own sentences that convey a sense of fear or tension:

Part II

Directions: Continue to practice writing short, tense sentences about driving a car, riding a bike, or any other activity.

Lesson 28 — SIMPLE, COMPOUND, AND COMPLEX

Objective: To review simple, compound, and complex sentences

Activities:

1. **Writing: Activity 28-1. Check** results individually or **discuss** as a class.

2. **Identification:** Use the literature text or a novel for students to locate compound and complex sentences.

   Ask: How do these sentences add to the interest we take in the narrative? What are the differences between an independent clause and a dependent clause?

3. **Read: Form 28-2**—Each type of sentence—simple, compound, complex—has a distinct purpose for a writer. **Discuss** reactions to the contents.

   Ask: What distinctions can you make between each paragraph?

   What audience/reader seems appropriate for each?

   What tone or mood is established by each paragraph?

4. **Discuss:** What is the best placement of a clause? In which sentence is the subordinate clause placed best?

   A. When the judge entered the courtroom everyone stood.

   B. Everyone stood when the judge entered the courtroom.

   C. Everyone, when the judge entered the courtroom, stood.

5. **Review:** Remind the class how sentences can grow from simple sentences to compound sentences to complex sentences. Simple sentence—add coordinating conjunction and another main clause to make a compound sentence—add a subordinate clause and a subordinating conjunction to make a complex sentence.

Homework options:

A. Give students 5-10 different subordinating conjunctions and have them create a 1-3 paragraph narrative using them in complex sentences.

B. Use the exercise in their textbook to analyze for subordinate clauses.

C. Students do **Activity 28-3**.

Name _____

Sentence Challenges

Challenge #1: Transform the following into 1-2 sentences:

The boy has a dog. The boy has a cat. The dog has black hair. The cat has red hair. The dog is cute. The dog is friendly. The dog is a beagle. His name is Sancho. The cat's name is Buttons.

Challenge #2: Who can write the longest sentence without making a grammatical mistake?

Challenge #3: Locate more examples of complex sentences in the literature text and copy them.

Challenge #4: Make complete and coherent sentences from the dependent clauses below.

(1) how to publish a short story

(2) while studying for an important test in English

(3) before she realized it

Examples for Simple, Compound and Complex

Simple Sentences

Two Austrian dead lay in the rubble in the shade of the house. Up the street were other dead. Things were getting forward in the town. It was going well. Stretcher bearers would be along any time now.

(By Ernest Hemingway from one of his short stories)

Compound Sentences

The skids dug in, and all the weight of the aircraft struck hard, and above the wind they heard the wood splinter and crack. The aircraft bounced once . . . and settled back to the sands, the forward elevator braces askew, broken so that the surfaces hung at an angle . . . It had happened; he had flown for fifty-nine seconds. No one ever recorded what Wilbur's words were at that moment, and no amount of research has been able to unearth them. It is unfortunate, but they are lost forever.

(By Harry Combs in his narrative about the Wright brothers' first flight at Kitty Hawk, North Carolina)

Complex Sentences

The occupants of the few cars which came toward him saw a man in a ball-cap with his head held down against the glare and his hands stuffed into his pockets. The shadow of the cap's visor would defeat all but the most insistent glances, and if they had looked more closely, they would have seen only the bandages. The cars which came from behind and passed him going north had nothing but his back to get a good look at, of course.

(by Stephen King from his novel "The Dark Half")

Create Complex Sentences

Directions: Complete each of the following to create complex sentences:

1. I felt foolish because

2. If a chipmunk spoke to me I would

3. I worry most when

4. I can get really angry after I

5. It is important to win because

6. I have a goal in school which is

7. I remember when

8. I wonder how

9. I just learned why

10. One place I would like to visit

Lesson 29 EMPHASIS AND VARIETY

Objective: To explore emphasis and variety in sentences

Activities:

[This lesson could be completed in 1-2 class sessions.]

1. **Jumbled sentences: Activity 29-1**—Students rearrange the words. **Discuss** the results.

2. **Writing options:** Use any of the following:

   A. Select one of the following topics:

      An unforgettable person
      A big blunder
      A favorite movie
      A prized possession
      The strangest animal

   Students select one topic and begin a narrative with a *simple* sentence. Upon command they pass the paper to any classmate who adds a *compound* sentence. On the third pass that student writes a *complex* sentence. Continue until 5-6 different sentences have been written.

   B. Challenge students to compose coherent (and complex) sentences based on the following pattern:

   E_____ p_____ because c_____ d_____
   (ex) Everyone played because Carlotta did.
   E_____ p_____ if c_____ d_____
   E_____ p_____ when c_____ d_____
   E_____ p_____ since c_____ d_____

   C. Students create an interesting paragraph of five sentences on a self-selected topic based on the following formula: Simple Sentence—Compound Sentence—Complex Sentence—Simple Sentence—Complex Sentence. Emphasize the importance of *variety*.

   D. Students write a sequence of sentences where they never use the letters *i* or *d*.

   Discuss the results.

3. **Discuss:** Emphasis in sentences. Students examine the following sentence:

The best state for employment opportunities in the 1990s is (fill in your state name).

Ask: What part of the sentence is being emphasized?

[Correct answer = the state name.]

4. **Write:** Students rewrite it emphasizing next *employment opportunities* and then *the 1990s*.

   [In the 1990s (fill in your state name) is the best state for employment opportunities.]

   [For employment opportunities (fill in your state name) is the best state in the 1990s.]

5. **Writing: Activity 29-2. Check** their work individually as students create at least two additional versions for each sentence.

6. **Visual aid:** Show a scene from a popular PG movie. Preview the tape by naming the character you want them to study. After 3-4 minutes, stop the tape and have students write 3-5 sentences about that character. Check for emphasis and variety.

7. **Charting: Activity 29-3**—Students examine sentences in their own grammar or literature text.

8. **Discuss:** Explore how they can *begin* sentences. Work on the following examples:

   A.   The young man with intense blue eyes stared at the girl.

   B.   With intense blue eyes, the young man stared at the girl.

   C.   At the girl the young man stared with intense blue eyes.

9. **Debate:** Should writers begin sentences with And or But?

   [Only if it seems natural; this shouldn't be overdone; traditionally, this is grammatically incorrect and is more common in fiction, not essays etc.]

10. **Explain:** Discuss how the dash can aid the writer in showing a variety in sentence structure. Have students consider the following example:

    Money, fame, and power—these are the goals of many businessmen.

    This could be written:

    The goals of many businessmen are money, fame, and power.

11. **Summary:** Varying sentences helps make writing coherent and smooth. A skilled writer uses a variety of word orders. For example:

    • The boy was up all night. He was extremely tired.

    • The boy was up all night, so he was extremely tired.

    • The boy who was up all night was extremely tired.

- Because the boy was up all night he was tired.
- The boy was up all night; he was extremely tired.

Proper emphasis helps the reader better comprehend the key element of the sentence. Therefore, place the most important words at the end.

Homework options:

A. Students examine a play script for emphasis in dialogue. Also analyze the type of sentences that appear in the dialogue and explain the author's intent here.

B. Students study wording in magazine or newspaper ads to learn the kind of sentences that are being used and what is being emphasized, then write a paragraph that explains their analysis.

C. Students describe a family member or celebrity using a variety of sentences and proper emphasis.

Name _____

Jumbled Sentences

Directions: Reorder the words in each of the following to make simple, compound, or complex sentences. After writing the sentence, label its type.

1. Fog that January for dangerous dense comes hazard drivers the a in is

2. Fog driving make on hazardous this dense can road

3. Fog in in early often low morning areas the occurs

4. Fog low level water is particles ground a mass the near of

5. Fog fogbank dense that surface motionless the on remains mass a is of a

6. Fog foghorn ships gives to warning a during a

7. Fog sometimes a in someone confused who said is is be to

8. Fog sometimes with mixed be rain can

9. Fog but to fog-alarm fogbell on on land ship is is a during a a give warning used used a

Emphasis in Sentences

Directions: Rewrite each of the following sentences to emphasize another aspect in the statement.

1. For one hundred years, "Romeo and Juliet" was performed with the lovers still alive at the end.

2. Of all of Shakespeare's plays, "Romeo and Juliet" has been produced on film the most times.

3. In the 18th century (two hundred years after he wrote it), Shakespeare's "Romeo and Juliet" was performed over 400 times in London.

4. Shakespeare borrowed some of the plot of "Romeo and Juliet" from Chaucer and other earlier poets.

5. The play involves an ancient feud between two families in Verona, Italy named the Montagues and the Capulets.

Name _____

Sentence Chart

Directions: Take any twenty sentences, in order, from the page you have selected and identify the type of sentence it is (Simple, Compound, or Complex) and then what is being emphasized.

Be prepared to explain the author's intent.

Number	*Type of Sentence*	*What Is Being Emphasized*
1	_____	_____
2	_____	_____
3	_____	_____
4	_____	_____
5	_____	_____
6	_____	_____
7	_____	_____
8	_____	_____
9	_____	_____
10	_____	_____
11	_____	_____
12	_____	_____
13	_____	_____
14	_____	_____
15	_____	_____
16	_____	_____
17	_____	_____
18	_____	_____
19	_____	_____
20	_____	_____

Lesson 30 VERBALS AND VARIETY

Objective: To define, identify, and use verbals correctly (more variety in writing)

Activities:

1. **Brainstorming contest:** Who can list the most action verbs ending in -ing beginning with the letter P? [You may choose to have students focus on physical gestures and actions—(ex) pushing.]

   Then use the letter D (ex) dancing.

2. **Charades:** Either you or a student volunteer perform physical gestures—(ex) rotating a finger to represent *dialing* on the telephone or moving a cupped hand to the mouth to imitate *eating*. Students must list those action verbs with -ing endings—(ex) dialing.

3. **Freewriting:** Students select any five of these verbs to write sentences, using them as the action verbs.

   (ex) I was pointing my finger at my brother.

   (ex) I was eating my dinner.

4. **Review:** Go over the importance of *variety* in sentences. Students write sentences using the same action verb as the subject in a sample sentence.

   (ex) Pointing a finger at someone can be dangerous.

5. **Lecture:** Verbs used this way (as subjects of sentences) are termed **verbals**. They are used in a different way in a sentence. Verbals can add a dynamic quality to sentences and help the writer be more creative and flexible with sentences. Compare the following examples:

   She stamped her feet, feeling the damp creep through her shoes.

   She felt the damp creeping through her shoes.

   There are three kinds of verbals:

   • Gerunds   Verbs used as nouns

   • Participles   Verbs used as adjectives

   • Infinitives   The preposition *to* followed by an action verb
                      (ex) to run, to think

6. **Writing: Activity 30-1.**

   Check the results.

7. **Reading:** Students read about verbals in their text and study sentences that have verbals—Gerunds, Participles, and Infinitives.

8. **Closure options**:

A. **Discuss:** Consider an exercise from the **textbook** where students can identify verbals in sentences.

B. **Debate:** Examine the use of verbals in sentences—for example, which of the following is a better sentence?

- To play in an all-star game is any athlete's goal.

- An athlete accomplishes a goal when he plays in an all-star game.

- Playing in an all-star game is a typical goal for any athlete.

C. **Writing:** Select any ten action verbs and use each in two different sentences—as a main verb in one and as a verbal in the other.

D. **Lecture:** Discuss how verbals can add description to any writing and how they add a dynamic quality to sentences.

Homework options:

A. Students can work on an exercise from their grammar text along with reading any pages that deal with verbals.

B. Students create their own sentences for each type of verbal: gerunds, participles, and infinitives.

C. Research the gerund phrase, participial phrase, and infinitive phrase—how these can be used effectively in sentences.

Introducing Verbals

Part I

Directions: Use the following verbal phrases in several different ways in sentences (*not* as main verbs):

Sample phrase: celebrating the victory

> (ex) Celebrating the victory, the team dumped the Gatorade jug on Coach Smith.
>
> (ex) We plan on celebrating the victory at Coach Smith's house.

1. waiting anxiously

2. leaving them behind

3. resting by the lake

4. hoping for better luck

5. wrestling the bear

Part II

Directions: Brainstorm action verbs that begin with the letter *C* and then use these verbs as action verbs and as verbals.

Lesson 31 MASTERING VERBALS

Objective: To demonstrate a mastery of verbals

Activities:

1. **Review:** How do you define each verbal?

    What are some examples of verbals? [Send students to the board to write these]

    Where can verbals be placed in sentences? [Nearly anywhere]

    How can verbals be preferable to nouns? [This can prompt more economy in word choice—(ex) Utilization of the computer in payroll preparation will bring about a reduction in clerical costs.]

    Using the computer *to prepare* the payroll will reduce clerical costs.

2. **Lecture:** Discuss awkward and incorrect use of participial phrases— the dangling participle and the misplaced modifier.

    *   Dangling Participial Phrase

        (ex) Sitting in the grandstand, the horses ran a great race.

    In this example, *Sitting in the grandstand* incorrectly modifies horses. In fact, this phrase has no noun to modify. It's *dangling*. A correct version would be:

    > Sitting in the grandstand, the spectators watched the horses run a great race.

    *   Misplaced Modifier

        (ex) Running to catch the bus, a truck almost hit me.

    [The obvious error is that the participial phrase *Running to catch the bus* seems to be modifying the truck. It is misplaced. A correct version would be:

    Running to catch the bus, I was almost hit by a truck.]

3. **Freewriting:** List the following verbs on the board for students to use in sentences as *verbals*.

Canoeing	Skydiving	Skipping
Broken	Fired	Published
Cheated	Stolen	Dressing
Writing	Screaming	Written

    Discuss the results. {You may send students to the board].

4. **Identification:** Have students locate verbals in any story or narrative in their literature text or other source.

5. **Quiz**: Students select from the following:

   A. Explain in a detailed paragraph the differences between gerunds and participles.

   B. In a coherent paragraph, use the verbs *learning* and *believing* as gerunds, participles, and regular action verbs.

   C. Write a complete and coherent paragraph where you use gerunds, participles, and infinitives successfully.

Homework options:

A. Students skim magazine articles to examine the variety of sentence types from professional writers.

B. Students do **Activity 31-1.**

C. Students do an exercise from their grammar text on dangling participles and misplaced modifiers.

Understanding Participles

Participles are action verbs that occur in sentences used as adjectives. Using them enables any writer to be more expressive and creative in his/her writing.

             hv   av
(ex) The ship was sinking quickly.—A basic subject-verb sentence

           part.   av
(ex) The sinking ship capsized beneath the waves.—Expanded sentence with participle and prepositional phrase

Directions: In the following examples, combine simple sentences into one expanded sentence by moving participles near the nouns they describe.

1. The coach was trying to quiet the crowd.
    The coach was embarrassed.
    The crowd was booing.

2. The goose chased the boys.
    The goose was hissing.
    The boys were yelling.

3. The passengers evacuated the ship.
    The ship was sinking.
    The passengers were screaming.

4. The pilot brought the plane to safety.
    The pilot was trained.
    The plane was disabled.

5. We found a photograph in the attic.
    The photograph was faded.
    The attic was crumbling.

6. The Boy Scouts were gathered around the fire.
    The Scouts were singing.
    The fire was blazing.

Lesson 32 THE RUN-ON

Objectives: To expand sentences without creating run-ons
To recognize the importance of correct punctuation (semicolons and end marks)

Activities:

1. Be sure the desks are arranged ahead of time for group work. After students are arranged in their groups, announce that you are evaluating them both as a group based on their **productivity** and as individuals based on their **quality of skill** with **semicolons** and **end marks.**

2. **Group work:** Work on run-on sentences.

   Contest #1: Distribute **Activity 32-1**—the passage from Jack Kerouac's novel "The Town and the Country." Have students **revise** this passage, eliminating the run-on.

   Monitor their work—answer any questions as they proceed through the activity for 10-12 minutes.

   Contest #2: Which group can write the longest sentence without making a grammatical mistake?

3. **Discuss:** Proper sentences vs. Run-ons.

   A. What problems did you encounter with the Kerouac passage? [Run-ons, improper punctuation, etc.]

   B. What are the characteristics of run-ons? [They are lengthy, over-extended sentences with too many words and possibly too many conjunctions.]

   C. Why do they sometimes occur? [Answers will vary.]

   D. Why would a writer like Kerouac intentionally use a run-on? [For dramatic effect, to be different, etc.]

4. **Lecture:** Semicolons can prevent run-ons and comma faults. Explain the connection between semicolons and using conjunctions. Compare the following examples:

   Keith is a talented athlete, and he's also a great singer.

   Keith is a talented athlete; he's also a great singer.

   The conjunction in a compound sentence can be removed if the writer chooses to use a semicolon.

5. **Group work:** Practice avoiding the run-on.

    A. Have Students write a 26-word sentence with each word in succession being the next word in the alphabet without creating a run-on.

        (ex) **A**llen **b**uried **C**onnie's **d**ead **e**agle **F**riday, **g**rieving **h**eavily **i**nside.

    B. For the total numerals in all their street addresses (ex) 2113 (4) + 45567 (5) + 3688 (4) + 131 (3) = 16, have students create a sentence with that many words.

    C. To stimulate fluency with sentences (and creativity), have students create sentences that hide the following household items:

chair	tables	sink	plate
fork	lamp	shelf	bed

        (ex) My sister al**so fa**res well in science.

    D. Review strategies for avoiding the run-on and sentence fragments.

6. **Lecture:** Discuss the problem of overusing *so* and *then* in sentences. These create run-ons. Compare:

    (ex) Ralph made the tackle, then he stood and yelled at his teammates.

    After Ralph made the tackle, he stood and yelled at his teammates.

    *   Run-ons also occur when sentences are separated with a comma, instead of a period

    *   Sentence fragments result when writers think a dependent clause is itself a complete sentence. **Show** students several dependent clauses alone—(ex) While I was waiting for Dad. Explain how they violate the rules of proper sentence structure.

7. **Summary:** With careful proofreading, most sentence run-ons and fragments can be eliminated. Students must also review sentence structure and punctuation marks, especially the end marks and semicolon.

Homework options:

A. Students read any pages on run-ons and fragments in their textbook. You might even have them work on an exercise.

B. Students read about the end marks and semicolon in their text. They could write a paragraph or two explaining the proper distinctions between using the period or semicolon in a compound sentence, or work on 1-2 exercises.

Run-on Sentences?

Directions: Examine the following passage from Jack Kerouac's novel "The Town and the Country." Where necessary, insert punctuation, delete words, and re-structure the sentences.

Afternoons in Lowell long ago I'd wondered what the grimy men were doing with big boxcars and blocks of wood in their hands and when far above the ramps and rooftops of the great gray warehouse of eternity I'd see the immortal canal clouds of redbrick time, the drowse so heavy in the whole July city it would hang even in the dank gloom of my father's shop outside where they kept big rolltrucks with little wheels and flat silvery platforms and junk in corners and boards, the ink dyed into the oily wood as deep as a black river folded therein forever, contrasts for the whitepuff cream-clouds outdoors that you just can see standing in the dust moted hall door over the old 1830 Lowell Dickens redbrick floating like an old cartoon with little bird designs floating by too, all of a gray daguerreotype mystery in the whorly spermy waters of the canal.

Thus is the same way the afternoons in the S.P. redbrick alley, remembering my wonder at the slow grinding movement and squeal of gigantic boxcars and flats rolling by with that overpowering steel dust crenching closh and clack of steel on steel, the shudder of the whole steely proposition, a car going by with a brake. . . .

Lesson 33   ECONOMY IN SENTENCES

Objective: To avoid wordiness in sentences

Activities:

1. **Contest:** Students first **write** a sentence on a self-selected topic using 17-19 words. Then students must convey the same meaning they have in the first sentence in:

   - 12-13 words.

   - 6-7 words.

   - 5 or fewer words (if possible).

   Check or **Discuss** the results. [Possibly award extra points to any students who accomplish this.]

2. **Discuss:** Economy in writing.

   A. When someone is asked to be economical with money, what is he/she supposed to do?

   [Save the money; use money wisely; be frugal; etc.]

   B. How would you define the word *economy*?

   [Could refer to freedom from waste; proper management of items or resources; saving things; etc.]

   C. How could a writer be economical with words?

   [Using fewer words to convey the same meaning]

3. **Writing:** Students practice eliminating repetition, wordiness, and unrelated items from sentences. Use **Activity 33-1.**

   Discuss or **check** the results.

4. **Explain:** Effective writers should be economical with words—that is, they eliminate unnecessary words. They "cut to the bone" sometimes and are *concise*. This leads to more forceful writing. Compare:

   To describe my room, it is messy. = My room is messy.

5. **Discuss:** Consider an exercise in the text on wordiness.

6. **Analysis:** Examine magazine or newspaper advertisements and cross out unnecessary or repetitious words.

7. **Summary:** Almost any piece of writing can be improved by careful cutting of words. Writing should be concise and sharp, not long and blurred. Writers achieve this by deleting repetitious words—(ex) He

repeated *again* . . . and unnecessary details—(ex) The cucumber was green *in color*—from sentences.

Homework options:

A. Students write a one-page essay explaining how the state transportation department practices economy and conciseness in writing, offering a variety of examples.

B. Students read selected pages in their text on avoiding wordiness (possibly doing 1-2 exercises).

C. Students write an editorial that cites some public examples—in magazines, on billboards, on T-shirts—of excessive wordiness and how it should be corrected.

D. Advanced students could research some famous speeches that could be reduced if the speech-maker had eliminated any unnecessary words.

Economical Sentences

1. Write a new 4-6 word slogan for a T-shirt.

2. Cross out the words in the following sentences that are repetitious:

   A. If we cooperate together, we can win.

   B. His final conclusion was to resign immediately.

   C. In my opinion, I think everyone should graduate at the end of four years.

3. Cross out the words in the following sentences that are unnecessary:

   A. It was in 1960 that John F. Kennedy was elected President of the United States.

   B. There were ten students who failed the test.

4. Read the following passages by Henry David Thoreau and then answer the questions.

   #1 *And now I see the beauty and full meaning of that word sound. Nature always possesses a certain sonorousness, as in the hum of insects—the booming of ice—the crowing of cocks in the morning and the barking of dogs at night—which indicates her sound state.* (Journal entry 1841)

   #2 *All these sounds, the crowing of cocks, the baying of dogs, and the hum of insects at noon, are evidence of nature's health or* sound *state.* (published in "A Week on the Concord and Merrimack Rivers" in 1849)

   A. Why did he eliminate so many words in the second passage?

   B. Why did he eliminate "in the morning" after "the crowing of cocks"?

5. What are your personal feelings about lengthy sentences or writing (in general)?

Lesson 34 SENTENCE REVIEW

Objective: To master all aspects of sentence structure

Activities:

[This lesson could take 1-2 class periods.]

1. **Discuss:** True/False to the following:

   A. All sentences are clauses. [T]

   B. One word can be a clause. [F]

   C. Simple sentences are always short in length. [F]

   D. A compound sentence and a complex sentence are basically the same. [F]

   E. Every complete sentence must have at least one independent clause. [T]

   F. A phrase can be in a clause. [T]

   G. A clause and a phrase are the same thing. [F]

   H. A dependent clause and a subordinate clause are the same thing. [T]

   I. Semicolons can replace conjunctions. [F]

   J. Important details should be at the end of a sentence, not the beginning. [T]

2. **Freewriting:** Challenge students to expand the following sentence. Who can add the most modifiers, phrases, and clauses without making a grammatical error?

   The game was canceled.

   Discuss the results.

3. **Analysis:** With the following sentences **on the board**, ask students to determine the awkwardness in terms of word order and overall structure.

   A. Many students at this college balance a job, perhaps even a family, in addition to a full academic course load.

   [It's wordy—*in addition* should be deleted and it could be written, *Many college students . . .*; the word *balance* implies *two* things, not three.]

   B. When students have jobs, families, and try to study as well, they sometimes make high demands on themselves.

127

[Note the ill-phrased dependent clause that begins the sentence—it should be written, *When students have jobs, families, and studies, they . . .*]

4. **Debate:** Are contractions appropriate in effective sentences? [Responses will vary, yet a more formal tone to the sentence is established if no contractions are used.]

5. **Freewriting:** Students write sample test questions about sentence structure (ex) What is a dependent clause?

6. **Pair work:** On sentence structure.

    A. Students write a paragraph on a self-selected topic that follows the pattern of Simple Sentence, Compound Sentence, Complex Sentence, Simple Sentence, and Complex Sentence.

    B. Students revise: I couldn't sleep last night I'm very exhausted today.

       • By adding a single word

       • By adding a single punctuation mark

       • By adding one word and a punctuation mark

    C. Students write two more versions of the sentence to show different emphasis (and variety):

       He soon became exhausted and dropped out of the marathon.

    D. Students review the sample test questions.

7. **Discuss:** Go over any review exercises in the grammar text on sentence structure.

8. **Writing:** Students do **Activity 34-1.**

    Discuss the results.

9. **Review:** Any remaining questions from students.

Homework:

Students work on **Activity 34-2.**

Name _____

Analyzing Sentences

Directions: Read the memos from the principal below and then rewrite them changing the sentence structure.   Be ready to explain how the rewrite alters intent.

1. **Memo from the principal**

   It is obvious from the condition of the study hall that there is a lot of "Fooling Around" by the students. There were papers and cards all over; desks were out of order; the place was a mess by the close of school yesterday. I'm not sure when this happened; therefore I am sending this memo to all study hall teachers.

   Study hall is for quiet time and students should be working. I have heard comments that students do not finish homework assignments. Insist on students bringing homework to study hall!

2. **Memo from the principal**

   It has come to my attention that an increasing number of students are in the halls during the class periods. This can be both disruptive to the classes they pass by and the classes they are from. Please do not allow students out of your classes unless it is an emergency! Please do not leave students unattended in your classrooms. Thank you for your attention and help in this matter!

Mastery of Sentence Structure

Part I

1. Write one simple sentence with two prepositional phrases:

    _____

    _____

    Write two original compound sentences:

2. _____

    _____

3. _____

    _____

    Write three original complex sentences:

4. _____

    _____

5. _____

    _____

6. _____

    _____

    Write the definition of a sentence:

7. _____

    _____

    List examples of subordinating conjunctions:

8. _____

9. _____

10. _____

Part II Short Answer Essay

Answer each of the following questions in 2-3 sentences. Be detailed and insightful.

1. How does a writer achieve sentence expansion?

2. Why do we need to use a variety of sentence patterns?

3. What advantages are there to using compound and complex sentences in our writing?

4. What are the key differences between independent and dependent clauses?

5. Sentence fragments and run-ons should, of course, be avoided by writers of formal essays. Explain or suggest how these typical sentence errors can be avoided.

Bonus points: Write a paragraph where you describe your home. You must use expanded simple sentences, com-pound sentences, and at least two complex sentences.

Section 5 : PERSONAL NARRATIVE

"Writing from experience does not, of course, mean just transcribing experience. You have the responsibility to sift and shape your material until it makes sense as a unit and until that unit can be fitted into the context of the reader's life."

(Judith Applebaum)

Objectives: Review Prewriting, Drafting, and Revising
Expand students' skills at descriptive writing
Guide students as they compose a personal narrative

Length: Approximately five Lessons

Introduction:

Clearly, we shouldn't expect students to walk into our classrooms at the beginning of the school year with a positive attitude, eager to improve their writing skills and ready to work hard. Often, they bring their personal problems and accomplishments directly into the classroom. These potential distractions can, in fact, provide an excellent focus for the personal narrative assignment.

When you instruct students to write about experiences in their lives be sure not to violate their privacy. Inform them that all work will be confidential. Because students are describing some very personal experiences, they need to see your genuine level of concern—both for their personal lives and their skill as a writer. This can be accomplished through a personal conference or through comments on drafts. They also need the freedom to write about their experiences, without fear of detailed criticism.

As they work toward a final copy, students sometimes discover a way to deal with their psychological and emotional responses related to a past experience. The teacher could, therefore, function as a counselor. You don't have to be Sigmund Freud, but you should be ready to deal with all the emotions on the spectrum. Remind them that they are learning as much about themselves as they are improving their writing skills, and be careful and sincere with your evaluation and feedback. You should encourage them, in fact, to write about their positive accomplishments.

Consider the incentives you could provide that will motivate students to write truly detailed personal narratives. Their age, sex, maturity level, interests, and culture are important here. It is important to break down their reluctance to open up to you in an essay about a personal experience. In short, be more attentive to *teaching* than *judging* for this essay.

Lesson 35   WHAT IS A PERSONAL NARRATIVE?

Objective: To introduce the personal narrative

Activities:

1. **Introduce:** Recalling past events—**Activity 35-1.**

   Discuss the response:

   A. Why did you select the events you did?

   B. How did it feel to look back on those events?

   C. Why would any writer want to describe an event or experience in his or her past life?

2. **Lecture:** A personal narrative is simply a composition that describes a memorable experience in the life of the writer. It could also include a thematic purpose.

   The experience must be *important* and *memorable*.

3. **Writing:** Students describe in a single paragraph the events they've experienced that day.

   Check individually and praise descriptive and/or detailed writing. Be sure events appear in chronological order.

4. **Discussion:**

   A. How do we distinguish the important events in our lives?

   B. What makes some experiences more special than others?

   C. What could be turning points in our lives?

   D. Why could it be helpful to review and re-create an experience or event in our life?

   E. How is a personal narrative like an autobiography?

   F. What events might not merit the focus of a personal narrative?

Homework:

Students do **Activity 35-2.**

Name _____

Past Events

Directions: Recall a single memory in your life associated with any seven of the following:

1. Neighborhood bully

2. Getting hurt

3. The attic (or basement)

4. The dentist

5. An older friend

6. A nightmare

7. The first time you got dressed up

8. An important promise

9. A costume

10. Glasses or braces

11. A birth

12. Haunted house

13. Cemetery

14. Railroad tracks

15. Grocery store

Name _____

When and How and Why?

Directions: Answer each question in detail.

1. When and how did you learn the truth about Santa Claus?

2. When and how did you learn to climb a tree?

3. When and how did you stick up for a friend?

4. When and how did you perform in front of an audience?

5. When did you try something that flopped?

6. When and how did you play at a construction site?

7. When and how did you play at an abandoned house, a barn, or a tree fort?

8. When and why were you accused of something you didn't do?

9. When and how did you lose something that was very valuable to you or your family?

10. When and why did you stay up the latest you ever stayed awake?

11. When and why were you talked into something you later regretted?

12. When and how did you forget something that was really important?

13. When and why were you ever locked out (or in)?

14. When and how did you ever outsmart someone?

Lesson 36   EXPERIENCE AND EMOTION

Objective: To identify the specific emotions connected with past experiences

Activities:

1. **Freewriting:** Students describe their first experience at riding a two wheel bike—where it happened, how they felt, what happened, etc.

    Discuss the responses.

2. **Check** and **discuss** their responses on the **When and How** responses—**Activity 35-2**.

3. **Freewriting options**: Write about personal experiences.

    [Answers will vary.]

    A. What have been the most dramatic or interesting experiences you have ever had *on a bus*?

    B. What are some of the humorous side affects of falling in love? [Consider Valentine Day's messages.]

    C. Which month of the year can you associate with a specific emotion? Explain.

    Discuss the responses. Connect *emotion* to *events*.

4. **Lecture:** Clarify keys to effective personal narratives:

    •   They are about past events/experiences.

    •   These are significant events, both for the writer and the potential reader.

    •   Personal narratives focus on strong description and chronological organization.

    •   Personal narratives are told in the first person (the writer uses "I").

    •   The reader should also be able to learn from it (the thematic purpose).

    To clarify the thematic purpose, you should **explain** that it is the judgment derived from the experience; it refers to what was learned, why it was important. This is often expressed in the final paragraph.

5. **Explain:** Types of Personal Narratives. Distribute **Form 36-1**.

6. **Writing:** Students do **Activity 36-2**.

    Discuss the results.

Homework options:

A. Students read any examples of personal narrative that appear in any of their texts. Encourage students to be experience-oriented.

B. Students describe briefly any experience from their childhood and an event they anticipate in their future. Then compare the two.

C. Students write a one-page personal narrative associated with spending money.

D. Students write a one-page personal narrative associated with a sleep-over.

Types of Personal Narratives

1. A trip or journey that had a dramatic influence on you—(ex) a vacation to the Grand Canyon or visiting another country

2. A personal achievement or triumph—(ex) winning the baseball game with a home run

3. An experience with another person (perhaps a sibling) that caused a change in attitude for you—(ex) breaking up with a boyfriend/girlfriend

4. An ordeal or tragedy that affected you or your family—(ex) a death in the family

5. A family custom or tradition—(ex) a wedding

6. An emotional experience associated with a certain place—(ex) visiting Grandma's house one Sunday

7. A memorable experience you had at school

8. A baby-sitting experience or other experience requiring a challenging responsibility

9. A time you cheated in school and were caught

10. Finding a stray animal and bringing it home

11. A memorable experience you had shopping—(ex) getting new clothes

12. The difficulties you had learning to drive

13. A time you got lost in a strange town

14. An experience at work (possibly getting fired or quitting) or looking for a job

15. The first time you spent the night away from home

16. Running away from home when you were much younger

17. An experience you had riding in a limousine, helicopter, horse-drawn carriage, or other unusual vehicle

18. A traumatic experience you had at a fire, tornado, flood, hurricane, or other dangerous storm

19. The best concert you've attended

20. Saving someone from getting hurt

21. An account of the time you and/or your family had to move to another city

22. A game you used to play outside in the spring, summer, fall, or winter

23. When you became disillusioned with someone you admired or respected

24. A time when you stuck up for someone

25. A time when you tried to help a friend and made things worse

26. A time you had to prove yourself to someone older, like a parent, older brother or sister, or teacher

27. Working in the yard—(ex) mowing the grass, burning leaves, weeding the garden, avoiding frogs or snakes, etc.

Name _____

Events and Emotions

Directions: For each emotion listed below briefly describe an event in your life associated with it:

1. Triumph

2. Grief

3. Happiness

4. Disappointment

5. Jealousy

6. Anger

7. Relief

Lesson 37   DESCRIPTION AND MOOD

Objective: To focus on descriptive details that convey a specific mood (for personal narratives)

Activities:

1. **Survey #1:** Poll each student—What is your *mood* today?

   Survey #2: How would you describe the moods of the teenagers at a school dance?

   Survey #3: How would you explain the mood of the teen who said the following quote:

   "It doesn't matter what you wear. People are going to fight if they're in their underwear," says a California high school student who was suspended for wearing a bandanna to school.

   Discuss the results. Connect mood to events.

2. **Freewriting:** Students do **Activities 37-1** and **37-2.**

   Discuss the responses, focusing on effective description.

3. **Read: Form 37-3**—Present a sample personal narrative and deal with students' reactions to it—description, thematic purpose, emotion, mood, etc.

4. **Summary:** Students should be able to write their personal narrative from a variety of angles. They should be prepared to organize the details and create a first draft.

Homework:

Students select the experience/event that they want to use as the focus of their personal narrative and begin prewriting on it. They should also write the final paragraph—the thematic purpose. What are they going to write about? Why are they going to write about this experience? What would a reader learn from reading about this event in their life?

Events

Directions: For each of the following, connect one event or experience in your life to it. Explain briefly.

1. Traveling:

2. Injury:

3. Chocolate:

4. Doubts:

5. An argument:

6. Money:

7. Grandparents:

Name _____

How Description Creates Mood

Part I

Directions: Examine each group of phrases and list the mood you connect to that description to the right.

(ex) coffin of dark oak
    dim lights
    tearful praying
    sniffling
    plush red carpet
    yellow, pink, purple flowers

(ex) sorrow, remorse
anguish, faith

1. jagged rocks
    dark clouds
    crashing waves
    tossing the flimsy boat
    gulls screeching overhead
    frigid wind

2. faded Persian rug
    crutches lying on the floor
    quiet as a cemetery
    her 1912 World's Fair lamp
    dimly lit living room
    quiet smile

3. sunny June day
    warm breeze
    open windows
    children laughing in the front yard
    ice cubes clinking in the cups of lemonade
    the buzzing of insects

4. December 21
    raging blizzard
    shingles tearing loose from the roof
    windows rattling
    blankets pulled tight
    news reports on the radio

Part II

Directions: Describe a person at work on his/her last day before retirement.

Sample Personal Narrative

The Autograph

I had already waited outside the locker room for two hours. My eyes stared at the door. I felt faint. I was nervous. I could only hope that _____ would stop and give me his autograph.

My sister waited next to me, as did what seemed to be a hundred other fans, all of them pushing and straining to be near the barricades the security personnel had set up to keep us away. Then suddenly he was there, wearing a dark leather jacket with tan fur at the collar. He was listening to headphones and peering straight ahead. I waved my hands, my notebook, my pen, praying he would notice me and stop.

My stomach was churning.

He stopped and smiled and signed on the open page. At that moment, nothing else in the world mattered. He even winked at me.

I learned that even superstars knew what we felt as their fans, how much we adored them.

Lesson 38　　DRAFTING THE PERSONAL NARRATIVE

Objective:　　Guided writing on the personal narrative

Activities:

1. **Discuss:** a series of prompts to get students focused on developing details in their own personal narratives.

   A. What is the taste of paper? [description]

   B. What does a basketball smell like? [description]

   C. What are the feelings associated with competition? [emotions]

   D. Why would one person want to have more money than his/her best friend? [personality]

   E. Who would want to win the school cookie contest? [personality]

   F. Why would a student want to hurry up and get out of school? [emotions, attitudes]

   G. What if someone lost an eye in an accident? [emotion, appearance, attitudes]

2. **Writing:** Students write the first drafts—conferring with you when necessary—focusing on the more interesting and dramatic elements of the experience and sensory details—sight, sound, smells.

3. **Mapping:** Students draw or illustrate the locale of their personal narrative—where the event or experience occurred.

4. **Reminder:** Due date and format of final copy. Distribute and discuss **Form 38-1**.

Homework:

Students should read at least another sample personal narrative or any pages in their grammar text that deal with narrative writing.

They should complete the first draft.

Name _____

Evaluating the Personal Narrative

Points	*Criteria*

5 _____ **Significant Experience** (SE)—Was the event or experience a truly important one? Can it be seen as a turning point? Was it crucial?

5 _____ **Content** (CO)—Did the writer apply effective *insight* to his/her own experience? How much analysis can be seen?

10 _____ **Description** (DES)—How descriptive was the writer? Sensory details? How effectively did the writer re-create the experience?

10 _____ **Organization** (ORG)—Did the writer follow the guidelines associated with writing a personal narrative? Has the writer been thorough?

5 _____ **Structure** (STRU)—Is there proper paragraphing? Are events described in a well-arranged, chronological order?

5 _____ **Thematic Purpose** (TP)—How effectively did the writer express the theme of the narrative? What is the lesson associated with the experience?

10 _____ **Grammar Errors** (GRA)—Sentence structure, spelling, usage, capitalization, and punctuation will be evaluated here.

_____

50 _____ **Total Points** (TP)

Section 6 : PERSUASION

"What I admire in Columbus is not his having discovered a world, but his having gone in search of it on the faith of an opinion." *(from Jacques Cousteau)*

Objectives: Show how to support an argument with evidence
Make distinctions between facts and opinions
Develop a persuasive thesis
Help students gain skill in using precise diction
Show logical and coherent organization of an essay

Length: Nine Lessons

Introduction:

Often, the best persuaders are the best talkers and writers. Since discussions are the backbone of most classroom activities, their value and effectiveness depend on students being prepared and respecting each other's opinions. If students don't see any value in communicating with each other, then learning will suffer, and the objective of this essay will not be achieved.

Persuasive writing requires the same kind of preparation and respect. You can gauge students' listening skills during a discussion (either in a small group or an entire class) by having them evaluate a comment; ask a question of the commentator; interpret a comment; or advise the speaker. The teacher serves as a mediator who will not only challenge students with controversial topics but also mediate the arguments that surface afterwards.

Lesson 39   OPINIONS AND PERSUASIVE LANGUAGE

Objective: To introduce persuasive language

Activities:

1. **Prompts:** Encourage students to express opinions.

    A. **Writing:** Write one paragraph explaining why this is or is not a beneficial policy:

    Gold chains, bracelets, and "large or extravagant" earrings are not permitted in Baltimore schools.

    Discuss the results with the goal to challenge the students to **clarify** and then **defend** their opinions.

    B. **Visual Aid:** Show a videotape of a cartoon that displays a character—human or animal—being injured or harmed in some way (ex) "Inspector Gadget," "Tom and Jerry," "Bugs Bunny and Pals." Students **write** one paragraph explaining why cartoons like this (that show violence) should or should not be seen by children.

    Discuss the results with the goal to challenge the students to **clarify** and then **defend** their opinions.

    C. **Discuss:** Talk about the following statistics:

    According to the American Psychological Association, the typical American child spends 27 hours a week watching television. In a lifetime he/she will witness 100,000 acts of violence, including 8000 murders. Ask:

    What would you say to parents about this? Why?

    What would you say to our lawmakers about this? Why?

    How has television influenced you?

    What would you say to television executives about this? Why?

    D. **Role-playing:** Two students role-play an argument on a given topic—(ex) The school should abandon study halls, or teenagers today are too greedy. Before beginning, take one student out into the hall. Tell this student to disagree with his/her classmate no matter what is said.

    Discuss the results.

2. **Freewriting:** Explain Lord Palmerston's meaning when he said: *"Opinions are stronger than armies."*

    Discuss their responses. Hopefully, students will soon comment on the

During discussions an effective teacher listens carefully and praises frequently. Breakdowns occur when students ignore classmates or attack personalities, not views. Be prepared to deal with disruptive behaviors. How?

1. Discipline any belligerent behavior
2. Remind them to use evidence, not excuses, when arguing
3. Set a proper example when a student challenges your opinions
4. Watch for students dominating discussions and/or berating classmates
5. Seek apologies from students who show disrespect for you or their classmates
6. Remain calm, disarming, and patient no matter how heated any argument may get

Some nonconformity, rebelliousness, and rejection of others' ideas are to be expected, but confrontations between students have to be arbitrated.

---

power of words, how they can hurt or ruin a person or a group (like an army can destroy another army).

3. **Review**: the power of persuasive words by having students recall and discuss a list of advertising slogans from the television, radio, and magazines. What does this suggest about the power of a slogan?

4. **Discussion:** On Persuasion. [Answers will vary.]

   A. Why are some people unwilling to listen to the other side?

   B. Why do some people struggle to be persuasive?

   C. How is persuading a reader different from persuading a listener?

   D. What words are commonly associated with persuasion?

   E. What are some effective ways to persuade others verbally (without threats)?

   - be knowledgeable (do research)
   - be clear (easy to follow your main points)
   - be thorough (consider all the angles)
   - be friendly (a negative tone can turn them off)
   - be fair (show an understanding of the opposing viewpoint)

Homework options:

A. Students investigate the amount of violence on 2-4 selected television shows. How many violent acts are there per minute? They should obtain research from the National Coalition on Television Violence and write a brief summary of their findings in a persuasive essay that also explains their views on this situation.

B. Students locate and list persuasive language found in more newspaper and magazine advertisements. They then summarize the specific intent of each.

C. Students write persuasive sentences about each of the following topics, declaring their importance in society: Music, Teachers, Neighbors, Heroes, Movies.

D. Contact parents and ask them to write a persuasive letter to their children. These could be mailed to the teacher and kept sealed until the end of the unit. This letter could express appreciation of the importance of a shared event. This can truly make parents partners in learning.

Lesson 40   PERSUASION AND PRECISE LANGUAGE

Objective: To make distinctions between precise language and generalizations, jargon, and clichés

Activities:

[This lesson could take 1-2 class periods.]

1. **Analysis**: Choose any of the following prompts.
    A. **Writing:** Students do **Activity 40-1. Discuss** the results.
    B. **Role-play:** One student tries to persuade another student in school to cheat (or sell him/her drugs), with a third student wondering what he/she should do about it. **Discuss:** What are students' attitudes toward this scenario?
    C. **Debate:** Discuss the location for the best vacation (or fast food restaurant or musical group).
    D. **Pair work:** List the benefits of chores and homework in preparation of convincing classmates to do one but not the other.
    E. **Videotape:** Run tape of an Oprah Winfrey show or other talk show where guests are asked to express opinions, then **discuss** students' reactions.

    [In any of these activities, look for language that is truly precise. Also point out generalizations and clichés. Are students stating the obvious? Showing insight? Are they relating personal experience, textbook knowledge, or generalization?]

2. **Debate:** Have students exchange views on the following issues until their comments become repetitious or unclear, then point out the problems with both their wording (are there generalizations?), and opinions (are they supported by evidence?)

    • Children should adopt the same religious beliefs of their parents.
    • Spoiled children become selfish teenagers.
    • Parents should treat younger children better than older children.

3. **Lecture** on generalizations, jargon, and clichés
    • Generalizations: a general conclusion based usually on an isolated event.

    (ex) Teachers are boring.

- Jargon: speech or writing that is full of unfamiliar or technical terms which are incomprehensible to most persons and expected to impress more than inform.

  (ex) ameliorate (improve), peruse (read), epistaxis (nosebleed)

- Clichés: overused phrases or statements.

  (ex) light as a feather, crystal clear, flat as a pancake

4. **Debate:** Consider the use of language in arguments. [Responses will vary.]

   - Formal, complex language is more impressive.

   - Shorter sentences in an argument make it easier to convince another person.

   - Expressions like *Spring Fever*, *Sloppy Joes*, and *Going Coconuts* truly portray their intended meanings.

5. **Discuss:** Language and audience.

   A. What kind of language would a leader use with a subordinate? [authoritative, forceful, rude]

   B. What kind of language would a store clerk use with a customer? [polite, selling, flattery]

   C. What kind of language would a thief use with a police officer? [deceptive, rude, sly, etc.]

   D. What kind of language would a bully use with a small child? [taunting, abusive, obnoxious, etc.]

6. **Write:** Revise the following jargon so that young students can understand it.

   Management has become cognizant of the necessity for the diligent elimination of undesirable vegetation surrounding the periphery of our facility.

   [The owner wants the weeds around the building removed.]

7. **Identification:** Students locate clichés, jargon, and generalizations in magazine/newspaper articles and ads.

Homework options:

A. Students write a letter to Mom or Dad explaining their feelings about a family issue that upset them. They must avoid using any generalizations and clichés.

B. Students should also read any pages in their textbook relating to persuasive language, especially those that deal with generalizations, clichés, jargon, and/or loaded words.

C. Students write two paragraphs using language carefully: in the first, they pretend to be a groom writing a letter to his bride-to-be, and in the second, they pretend to be the bride writing to the groom.

D. Students write an editorial on the positive and negative aspects of dating in high school without using jargon.

E. Students write a narrative describing a "date from Hell" without using generalizations or clichés.

F. How important is profanity? Students explain in a one page essay the appropriate audience and use of profanity in an argument.

Name _____

The Language of Arguments

Directions: Answer each of the following in detail.

1. Describe the last argument you had with your parents and the words, other than profanity, that were said.

2. What could be the words of an argument used by a couple who are in a romantic relationship?

3. What is the language used by men versus women in tense moments?

4. Write a Sweetest Day or Valentine's Day message that would prompt someone to forget a past argument; (who can be the most compelling?).

5. What words and evidence can you use to persuade a reader that you have the best relative?

Lesson 41 SUPPORTING YOUR OPINION

Objective: To recognize the importance of supporting an opinion with effective sources

Activities:

1. **Survey:** On marriages.

   A. Fifty-two percent of marriages today end in divorce. How do we know that?

   [Court records, church records]

   B. Trust is the most important characteristic of a successful marriage other than love. How do we know that?

   [Talking to people who have been married a long time]

   C. Today, more men and women are waiting until they are thirty and forty to get married. How do we know that?

   [Census results, talking to people, etc.]

2. **Explain:** Statements need to be backed up with evidence—especially statistical evidence, if possible.

3. **Review:** Reexamine the importance of using evidence that supports an opinion by **asking** students to explain what sources they could use to deal with the following issues. The intent here is not to answer the questions but to cite the sources one would locate and use to defend an answer. [Answers will vary.]

   (ex) Is gun control constitutional? [National Rifle Association, U.S. Senator, Supreme Court]

   • How can famine be reduced?

   • Is Affirmative Action effective?

   • How does pornography promote violence?

   • How does rap music promote violence?

   • Should teenage violent offenders be treated like adult offenders in the courts?

   • Can regulation of tobacco marketing prevent teenage use of cigarettes? Should the government regulation of smoking be increased?

   • Should women serve in military combat?

   • Does legalized gambling benefit state and local economies?

- Do IQ tests truly measure intelligence?

- Does illegal immigration harm the United States?

- What are the causes of police brutality?

- How effective has recycling been to reducing waste in the United States?

- What rules or regulations in the student handbook should be eliminated? Which are rarely enforced?

4. **Read: Form 41-1**—This is a sample persuasive essay on drug use that has decent evidence and research to support the opinion, but weak insights on this broad issue. **Ask** students to cite the kind of language used, to explain the opinion, and to evaluate the evidence and insight.

5. **Debate:** Of the following, which is least likely to be supported by facts or statistics?

GOSSIP   COMPLAINT   OPINION

Homework options:

A. Students watch a **videotape** from "Nightline," "Crossfire," or other television news program that features a debate and ask students to cite the opinions and the evidence the speakers use to support them.

B. Students write an argument—possibly on the subject of the ideal date—where they use specific evidence to support a viewpoint.

C. Students research some of the great historical debates—Lincoln/Douglas, Kennedy/Nixon, etc.—and explain (1) who performed better and (2) why.

Sample Persuasive Essay

"Drugs"

Drugs are the most harmful element of schools today. If you take them, they will ruin not only your life but someone else's, most likely someone in your own family.

I say this because nearly 6 in 10 ten students say that drugs are sold at their schools. It is estimated that illegal drug sales reach $100 billion a year. Since 1981, the federal government has spent over $120 billion on the war on drugs. This information comes from a 1996 National Household Survey on Drug Abuse.

We really must do something about this major problem that is affecting kids and schools across the country.

Lesson 42   ARGUMENTS, OPINIONS, AND OUTCOMES

Objective: To explore the characteristics of an effective argument

Activities:

1. **Talk Show:** Use any of the following prompts for students to express an opinion orally and back it up with evidence. You can assign students roles for this activity—expert, parent, audience, celebrity, etc. Be sure to provide as many students as possible the opportunity to participate.

   A. Does everyone deserve good housing even if he/she can't afford it?

   B. Why is it important to make contributions to others (charity)?

   C. Celebrities—do they deserve our attention? Why/why not?

   D. Use a current event (ex) a political scandal.

   E. Should science alter a person's genetics, even if it meant eliminating a potential disease that has been passed down in a family?

   F. **Visual aid:** Show a videotape(s) of professional athletes and then **ask:** Who is the best professional athlete?

2. **Discuss:** Arguments, Language, and Feelings. [Answers will vary.]

   A. At home, when are you asked to voice your opinion, how does this make you feel?

   B. In school, when are you asked to voice your opinion, how does this make you feel?

   C. At work, when are you asked to voice your opinion, how does this make you feel?

3. **Summary:** The language used to persuade should be formal, dynamic, and concrete. Oprah Winfrey has become the first American female billionaire because she possesses superior skills at persuasion and communication. She knows how to persuade, collaborate, appreciate, philosophize, and show feelings. Arguments always have some type of outcome.

Homework options:

A. What is the *ideal* family? Students locate any news and magazine articles that deal with families to use as evidence. They must also study the language the writer uses.

B. Students locate a famous quotation about family life, write it down, and explain its intent. What point was the author trying to get across to the reader?

C. Students complete an exercise in the textbook on persuasive language.

Lesson 43   DANGEROUS LANGUAGE

Objective: To examine the harmful effects of persuasive language

Activities:

1. **Freewriting:** How could persuasive language harm someone?

2. **Discuss:** Talk about students' examples and then cite the following:

   A. In the 1930s, Adolf Hitler used propaganda to incite violence against Jewish people in Germany.

   B. In the 1950s, Senator Joe McCarthy claimed communists occupied positions inside the American government. His accusations soon ruined the careers of many persons.

   C. In the 1970s, their shouts of protest against the Vietnam War caused National Guardsmen to shoot at Kent State University students.

   D. In 1989, Washington journalists suggested in their articles that former House speaker Thomas Foley could be a homosexual although the information was false. These articles nearly ruined Foley's political career.

3. **Review:** Persuasive language. [Answers will vary.]

   How could persuasive language harm or affect a person in each of the following professions: medicine, rock 'n' roll, the government, an insurance agent, chef?

   What are some examples of the language that could harm or affect them?

4. **Lecture:** Selecting the appropriate language depends on who the audience/reader is for the essay. To help students select a topic for the persuasive essay, distribute **Form 43-1.** To help them further consider what makes for a meaningful topic, use the following triangle illustration to show that the writer must pick a topic that appeals to the reader and use words that are both understandable and appealing to the reader:

> **An effective writing prompt should be developmentally appropriate for your students. The prompt should contain no racial, sexual, religious, or social bias; it should permit the writer to respond in a variety of modes; it should be easy for the student to generate ideas; it should cause the student to think before writing; it should require the student to go beyond generalities; it must allow for an honest response; and it must have genuine reader appeal.**

Homework:

Students select their topic and reader for the persuasive essay and begin Prewriting (listing ideas, gathering evidence, and generating statements). Also, consider essay contests—**Form 43-2.**

Persuasive Essay Topics

1. Write an essay about the importance of safety in the home.

2. Compose a letter to the mayor about increasing or reducing the speed limit on a road near your home.

3. Write an editorial that relates your opinion on any issue related to the community or school for submission to the school newspaper.

4. Write a traditional essay about any school rule, policy, or area that should be changed. Submit this to the principal.

5. Write a journal entry where you agree or disagree with a famous quotation. Use personal experiences as one element of your research to support your argument.

6. Create an advertisement on videotape about an activity that the entire public should see or do. Present this to your classmates.

7. Cut out a newspaper or magazine editorial that interests you and write a reaction paper. Include both in your report.

8. Construct an outline detailing the reasons for changing any school board policy and then share it at a meeting.

9. Write a letter to the president of any television network giving an opinion on the content of current children's cartoons. Are they too violent? Realistic? Humorous? Cite specific examples.

10. Make a chart detailing the best way to spend $10,000 at a homeless shelter. Submit this to the city council where the shelter exists.

11. Create a speech against or for the -ism of your choice (i.e., communism, nationalism, racism, etc.). Deliver this speech to the school's government class.

12. Write a report for the mayor of your city detailing the improvements you recommend for the city parks. Include an overview on the benefits of these improvements.

13. Write a detailed essay persuading the reader to accept your definition of one of the following abstract terms: courage, love, friendship, equality, or happiness.

Form 43-1 (*continued*)

14. Make a chart that details and evaluates all of the types of music, books, or movies. Present this to your classmates.

15. Write an essay where you compare the attitudes people have towards smoking in public places. Submit this to a smoker.

16. Write a detailed essay where you present the problems with television cameras in courtrooms and offer solutions.

17. Make a chart of the school's graduation requirements, rating them from most to least important with a detailed explanation for your rating system. Present this to the superintendent.

18. Write a personal reflection on final (or semester exams). Present this to a committee of teachers and/or guidance department.

19. Write a response to any piece of literature declaring its merit or faults. Present this to the dean of the English Department.

20. Write a profile/character sketch of the person you think has made the most valuable contribution to the school or community. Present this to that individual.

21. Write recommendations and advice to the class behind you about the attitude and preparation they should have toward their academics and athletics. This could be distributed the next year by the teacher.

22. Write a letter to a parent or teacher describing your most memorable high school academic or athletic experience and explaining why every high school student should have a similar experience.

23. Prepare an oral presentation to classmates that explains in detail the meaning of graduation and the best career path (or future plan) a graduate should take.

24. Locate a poem or story whose theme reflects the importance of graduation or moving on in life. Write a persuasive essay that analyzes how effectively the writer presents that theme. Deliver this to the teacher, publisher, and, if possible, the writer.

25. Assess the course content and lesson plans. Write an essay that persuades the teacher and principal to maintain and/or improve any aspects of the course just completed.

Essay Contests

"Fountainhead" Essay Contest
or "Anthem" Essay Contest
The Ayn Rand Institute
P.O. Box 6004
Inglewood, CA 90312

Stein Roe Funds Essay Contest
1-800-586-KIDS

21st Century Magazine
P.O. Box 30
Newton, MA 02161
1-800-363-1986
Fax# 617-964-1940

Scholastic Art and Writing Awards
555 Broadway
New York, NY 10012
212-343-6931

Women Making History Essay Contest
c/o Susan McKinley
Women's Division
Ohio Bureau of Employment Services
145 South Front Street
P.O. Box 1618
Columbus, OH 43216-1618
614-466-4496

National Essay Contest
The Korea Society
950 Third Avenue
8th Floor
New York, NY 10022
1-888-355-7066

USA Today Essay Contest
The University of Rhode Island
2 Butterfield Road, Suite 2
Kingston, RI 02881-0104

World's AIDS Day Creative Crayons and Composition Competition
c/o American Association for World Health
1825 K Street
Suite 1208
Washington, D.C. 20006

Black History in Music Student Essay Contest
Rhino Records
Lifetime Learning Systems
203-705-3600

"Technology and Education" Contest
P.O. Box 3933
Milford, CT 06460-2088

Veterans of Foreign Wars Youth Essay Contest
c/o the local VFW Post or Ladies Auxiliary representative

Veterans of Foreign Wars Voice of Democracy Essay Contest
c/o the local VFW Post or Ladies Auxiliary representative

Lesson 44   DEVELOPING A THESIS, INTRODUCTION, AND CONCLUSION

Objective: To develop an effective and persuasive thesis

Activities:

[This lesson could take 1-2 class sessions.]

1. **Lecture:** Present principles of developing a thesis—a persuasive, direct, and narrowed statement about a topic, which often is controversial in nature.

   The reader expects to find the thesis in the introduction.

   (ex) Teenagers should not be exposed to video games like "Mortal Kombat" because they display too much violence.

2. **Writing:** Students practice creating thesis statements using **Activity 44-1. Check** or **discuss** their responses.

3. **Lecture:** Discuss introductions and conclusions.

   • The introduction needs to grab the readers' attention and lead them smoothly into the thesis.

   How? Study **Form 44-2.**

   • The concluding (final) paragraph should summarize, suggest solutions, or plead for action—**Form 44-3.**

4. **Reading:** Read any pages in their grammar text about thesis statements, introductions, and conclusions.

5. **Visual aid:** View a videotape of 2-3 movies that begin very dramatically and **discuss** the reasons the directors/writers did this.

6. **Identification:** Locate and identify thesis statements, introductions, and conclusions in magazine articles or newspaper editorials. Students label them as to the type and method.

   Deal with the *angle* writers take. How do they appeal to a reader?

Homework:

Students must write the introduction and thesis for their topic.

Name _____

Writing a Thesis Statement

Directions: Practice writing thesis statements for each of the following general topics. First, narrow the general subject and then write the statement.

1. Today's teenage fashions

2. The importance of exercise for teens

3. Weight loss treatments or programs

4. The dropout rate in urban high schools

5. High school cliques

6. Grandparents and their values

7. Divorce rate in the United States

8. Salaries of professional athletes

Types of Introductions

Provocative Statement

Too many professional basketball players in the National Basketball Association act like spoiled brats. The NBA has become a home for all those athletes who just never grew up. They seem to care only about their contracts, their cars, and their jewelry. Of little concern to them are the management, their teammates, or the fans who pay, of course, for those high salaries and, in turn, expensive cars and jewelry. *The executives of the NBA should establish stricter guidelines for the players' behavior and actions on and off the court.*

Challenging Question

How can any senior afford going to a prom these days? Of course, the prom is a traditional event every spring, but the costs of renting a tux, buying a dress, and renting a limousine have made paying for it very difficult. Too many seniors just don't have the necessary funds. This is a major concern for some kids, and a major headache for others. *However, with long range planning and careful shopping any senior's prom can be both affordable and enjoyable.*

Famous Quotation

"Winning isn't everything, it's the only thing," said Vince Lombardi, who coached the Green Bay Packers to three National Football League championships. Never has one statement been used by so many coaches to emphasize the importance of winning games. That is why so many of them put too much pressure on their athletes. *It is truly disturbing to see so many high school coaches emphasize winning above other values.*

Story

The young teenagers—Jamie was the oldest at 16—entered the principal's office, and declared their grievances. "We should have an open campus," said a junior. "Underclassmen should be allowed to go to the prom," added a sophomore. "We'd at least like to be asked," Jamie requested, "whenever the school board decides to make a new policy."

This type of scene is becoming familiar across the country as groups of students—often members of student councils or class officers—are participating in school management. *In fact, many high school administrations are enjoying positive results when they join with students in managing their schools.*

Types of Conclusions

Strong Summary

Thus, it is unfortunate that each year too many high school seniors find them-selves dealing with the difficult task of paying for their prom. Although raising the money does take effort, following the suggestions and guidelines mentioned in this essay can help make the job easier. Any senior who follows them can benefit and enjoy the prom.

Plea for Action

Our city must change the local zoning ordinance that permits fast food restau-rants to be built next to the high school. The temptation for students to use them before, during, or after the school day could cause some serious injuries as kids rush across the street or hang out in the parking lot. Our students' safety is at risk if the city council does not change the zoning ordinance.

Prediction

It is evident that marijuana use is truly harmful to teens, and if this trend isn't stopped, we could see a generation of young people grow into adults who are not ambitious, diligent, or healthy. Even more worrisome is the strain illegal sales of marijuana would place on law enforcement and municipal courts when these teenagers are apprehended. In short, entire communities will be affected if mari-juana use continues as a habit for young people.

Climactic Description

They ran into the locker room and cheered for their victory. Their football jerseys were damp with sweat, their pants caked with mud, and their muscles sore from the pounding, but none of that mattered now that the league championship was theirs. The season now over, they dumped their shoulder pads into a pile and returned to their celebration, clapping their hands and yelling into the shower steam. This was their first championship.

Lesson 45

COHERENCE IN THE PERSUASIVE ESSAY

Objective: To work at essay coherence

Activities:

1. **Survey:** On transitional words. Students respond **orally** or in **writing**:

   A. In what situation would you use the word *indeed* in a sentence?

   B. How would you define the word *moreover*?

   C. What transitional word would best complete the second sentence?

   Running keeps me in shape. _____ , it keeps my weight down.

   D. Which of the following is not a transitional word or phrase?

   next, to be sure, because

   E. In what situation would you use the transitional word *therefore*?

   Discuss the results.

2. **Read**: Study any information about transitional words or methods in their text.

3. **Discussion:** Go over an exercise, if available in the text, to pick out transitional words in the sentences.

4. **Lecture:** Speak on the importance of using transitional words and devices which lead to **coherence**:

   • They help link main points or ideas from sentence to sentence, paragraph to paragraph.

   • They usually appear at the beginnings of sentences.

   • They are often set off by commas.

   • They are also adverbs in other situations.

   • They can reflect: time   (ex) finally

a contrast   (ex) however

additional   (ex) also

emphasis   (ex) in fact

a summary   (ex) thus

5. **Reading:** Examine the persuasive essays in **Form 45-1** for coherence, language, and content (evidence). Be sure to cite the type of organization: order of importance or chronological order, etc.

6. **Visual aid:** Examine the following diagrams. How do they model the concept of a transition?

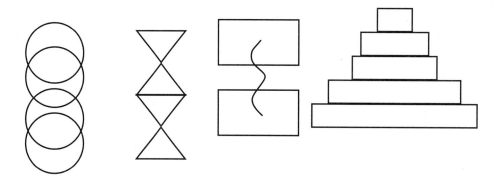

7. **Writing: Activity 45-2**—Monitor students' progress and point out effective use of transitional words, any persuasive words, and the proper use of the data. If students finish early, you may choose to have some of the paragraphs read out loud.

Homework:

Students should complete the prewriting on the topic of their persuasive essay and also write the first draft (in preparation for peer editing).

Students read selected pages on essay coherence in their text.

Sample Persuasive Essay

New Year's Resolutions

Each new year almost everyone seeks improvement. Most of us swear, in fact, that we're going to take positive action and eliminate nasty habits. We promise to lose weight, stop smoking, begin exercising, save money, or make new friends. During those first weeks of January we remain excited about our pledges, but by the middle of February our new year's resolutions are too often abandoned.

Making the resolutions is not the problem. Making the *right* resolution is the challenge. Unfortunately, most people set themselves up for failure because they don't, for example, enjoy exercising or really don't need any more friends. If, however, your health depends on exercising more, then select an activity you truly enjoy, like bowling, golf or dancing. You could, moreover, join a group in a volleyball league, or just bike or walk in the park during the spring and summer.

Some recent studies say that over fifty-five percent of the American population is overweight. If your new year's resolution is to lose weight, you are not alone. Instead of just beginning another dreaded diet, increase your level of exercise during the week. Furthermore, eat only when you feel hungry and stop when you feel full. Eat healthier by reducing the fat in your diet and the portions at each meal.

In conclusion, resolutions are a wonderful way to begin the new year. Sticking to them can surely improve your mental (self-esteem) and physical health. Making them work depends on making them enjoyable. Making them work also prevents you from having to make the same resolution again.

Sample Persuasive Essay

Motivation

What is motivation? How does it influence an athlete's performance? Today, a common lament of many coaches is that their athletes are unmotivated, that they don't work hard enough, that they're not willing to sacrifice to achieve success. Furthermore, since the athletes are giving up time after school to participate, too many coaches take for granted that they're already motivated. Coaches need to understand (1) what motivates athletes to participate in any sport; (2) how athletes stay motivated; and (3) how motivation influences athletic performance.

"To coaches, motivation means finding ways to get players to do things they might not want to do on their own . . . To players, motivation means having reasons for acting or failing to act," says sports psychologist William Warren. Motivation refers to techniques used on athletes to encourage them to maximize their efforts in practice and games; maintain persistence toward a specified goal; handle obstacles, failures, and criticism without quitting the team; display a positive attitude; express an enjoyment for practicing and competing; and work cooperatively with teammates and the coaching staff.

Motivation is designed, in short, to get athletes *addicted* to the sport, and the means to achieve that end certainly vary from athlete to athlete. In fact, motivation should be individualized for best results. Warren calls this "salesmanship, communication, and psychological conditioning."

In summary, a coach needs to set up the circumstances and conditions that make athletes receptive to being motivated. Moreover, motivation is closely linked to emotion. Truly, the coach is a salesman: selling a love for the sport, dialoging about its benefits, inviting athletes to participate, and offering them rewards for that participation. Coaching is motivating.

Coherence?

Directions: Examine the data on recycling below and then use some of it in a persuasive paragraph where you use transitional words and devices effectively.

Audience: Classmates and, for a newspaper or magazine of your choice, in the form of a letter to the editor

Data:

1. Recycling aluminum cans saves 95% of the energy used to make them from scratch, which means you can make 20 cans out of recycled material with the same energy it takes to make one can out of new material.
2. Americans throw away enough aluminum every three months to rebuild our entire commercial air fleet.
3. Aluminum is used for window frames, screen doors, lawn furniture, cans, etc.
4. We get 27.8 pounds of air pollution for every ton of new glass produced. Recycling glass reduces that pollution by 21%.
5. Recycling glass saves 35% of the energy used to make new glass.
6. One ton of glass is formed from 1330 pounds of sand, 433 pounds of soda ash, 433 pounds of limestone, and 151 pounds of feldspar.
7. One ton of glass produced from raw materials creates 384 pounds of mining waste.
8. Less than 40% of American communities have curb side recycling.

Lesson 46 WRITING WITH STYLE

Objective: To identify distinctions in writing styles

Activities:

1. **Brainstorm:** Students make lists.
   A. Styles of clothing
   B. Classmates who have *style*
   C. Professional athletes with the most style
   D. Authors who they think have unique writing styles
   Discuss the results.

2. **Discuss:** Word choice related to writing style.
   A. What are the differences between being *psyched* and *motivated* ?
   B. What are the differences in the following statements?
      Sue loves Sam.
      Hey, Suzi digs Sammy's bod.
      At her school, in her home, at her place of employment—Susanne continually reviews her affection for Samuel.

3. **Lecture:** Speak on writing style. Distribute **Form 46-1**.

4. **Discuss:** What would be the appropriate writing style for
   A. an audience in tuxedos?
   B. an audience in heavy metal T-shirts?
   C. a rapper?
   D. an elementary school student?

5. **Analysis:** Determine the writing style of the following:
   A. Dude has a phat car, crazy beeper, and mad money.
   B. Judith fastened her deep blue eyes on the open, frank countenance of her companion, as if she would read his soul.
   C. I'm having conceptual difficulty with these mandates.

6. **Freewriting:** Students change the writing style of the above statements—the first, from slang to formal diction; the second, from formal to slang; the third, from jargon to informal.
   Discuss the results.

7. **Discuss:** Developing a writing style.

   A. What is flowery language?

      [It contains too many adjectives and adverbs.]

   B. How can you develop your own writing style?

      [Be sincere, show personality, compare your writing with any professional, keep a journal, etc.]

   C. How does using clichés affect a person's writing style?

      [Clichés are to be avoided; they reflect a lack of originality; generally, they are not useful; etc.]

8. **Review:** Students examine selected works from their text(s) and select those they think have unique writing styles. Ask for the reasons behind their selections.

Homework:

Students read any pages in their text about writing style.

Students do **Activity 46-2** and analyze various writing styles.

Students revise the first drafts of their persuasive essays to try for a unique writing style.

Guidelines for Developing a Personal Writing Style

- Writing style is determined by the writer's word choice, sentence structure, and *tone*.

- Better writing styles show unique use of figurative language and descriptive phrases.

- Accomplished writers always try for creativity and variety in their expressions.

- Examples:

  Ernest Hemingway had a simple, journalistic writing style (1-2 syllable words, short sentences).

  Jack Kerouac was known for complex sentences, much figurative language, and wild descriptions.

- The writing style is often determined by the intended reader.

- Here is a partial list of types of writing styles—academic, journalistic, literary, loose (unstructured).

- No matter the writing style you have, you should always try for *clarity*.

- Avoid repetitious sentences and and cute words or phrases that do not strengthen sentences.

- Use strong verbs—(ex) *swaggered*, not *walked*.

- Study the writing style of famous writers.

- Look to establish a rhythm to the writing—(ex) *My brother's room is full of smelly sweatshirts, wrinkled shorts, and dirty socks*. [Note the even balance of adjectives to nouns in the list.]

- Repetition can be effective at times—(ex) *"We shall fight on the beaches, we shall fight on the landing grounds, we shall fight in the fields and in the streets, we shall fight in the hills; we shall never surrender."* (from Winston Churchill)

- *"Writing style can be the make-or-break skill in a business career."* (from Lewis Spence, writing teacher and consultant)

What Is the Writing Style?

Directions: Read each passage below that is a response to the book "The Adventures of Huckleberry Finn" by Mark Twain and then answer the questions.

1.   Anyway you look at it, "Huck Finn" is a cool book. The way Huck sees things makes the book funny. This Twain may be an old writer, but he sure digs what it's like to be young. You won't find many guys who can scratch it out like he can. He's got this way of making you wonder what's next, like I kept wondering if Huck and Jim would make it. Even kids who don't dig reading could go for "Huck Finn."

2.   "The Adventures of Huckleberry Finn," by Mark Twain, is a literary triumph that is terrific in its combination of folk lore and the Southern experience.

   The author's background as a river boat pilot obviously helped him select with great clarity the details related to Huck and Jim's adventures on the Mississippi River, and the characters they encounter. The reader is introduced to the human drama of Huck and Jim's journey to freedom down the Mississippi River.

   This novel is truly a wonderful and educational read for any student who is interested in both an exciting adventure and excellent descriptions of the Mississippi River.

3.   Viewed educationally and literarily, Mark Twain's "The Adventures of Huckleberry Finn" is a major triumph. Poetic in its perception, lucid in its phrasing, and dramatically original in its scope, this novel both delights and educates the reader. This outstanding narrative deserves to be ranked among the exceptional literary works of the 20th century. Possibly the most noteworthy evidence of Twain's talent lies in his capacity to describe the Mississippi River as both commonplace and exotic, to elicit the reader's compassion for the runaways Huck and Jim, and to create a breathless tale of suspense and adventure. All young persons should peruse and study this classic narrative.

Questions

1. How would you characterize the writing style of each passage?

2. Which passage appeals to you? Why?

Lesson 47   PEER EDITING— PERSUASIVE ESSAY

Objective: To complete effective peer editing

Activities:

1. **Lecture:** Discuss the key points of editing persuasive essays:

   • React positively when classmates offer reasonable suggestions for change.

   • Avoid being judgmental; show tolerance for any inadequacies in the persuasive essay.

   • Don't overemphasize the areas needing improvement, especially as a means to change their point of view.

   • Avoid power struggles or hostilities.

   • See the value in receiving direct feedback from a helpful reader.

2. **Review: Form 47-1**—Persuasive Essay Evaluation Form. Consider having students use this during peer editing.

3. **Peer Editing:** Study the persuasive essays.

   A. Each writer first explains orally his/her intent in the persuasive essay—i.e., a brief introduction to the argument—and the *specific* audience (reader) for the essay (not *anyone*).

   B. Essays are exchanged.

   C. Editors look especially for vague wording, effectiveness of introductions and conclusions, and thoroughness (and supporting evidence) in content.

   Editors make marks on the manuscripts.

   D. Each essay is discussed by the group (using a time limit) as members make suggestions to each other

Homework:

Students finish the editing and revising of their persuasive essays.

Form 47-1

Persuasive Essay Evaluation Form

RATING SCALE—1 Weak . . . . 3 Average . . . 5 Strong

CONTENT & CRITERIA   *POINTS*

1. The writer's opinion is clearly stated in an effective introduction. There is a good lead into the thesis statement.   _____

2. The thesis or central idea of the composition is clear and effectively expressed.   _____

3. The writer develops the thesis with appropriate details. There are no generalizations.   _____

4. There are no lapses in logic. The argument is clear and strong throughout the essay.   _____

5. There is a well-arranged sequence of paragraphs. Their order is correct, clear, and easy to follow. There is essay unity. Demonstrates coherence and a clear sense of organization.   _____

6. Appropriate transitional words and phrases between sentences and paragraphs are used.   _____

7. The writer includes sentences with a variety of lengths and structures. They are complete and well-phrased.   _____

8. Uses vivid, precise language that is appropriate to the audience. The writer has specific, concrete diction.   _____

9. The author includes a conclusion that sums up reasons or prompts a plea for action. It is an effective summary.   _____

10. Grammar, usage, and mechanics: spelling, sentence structure, and punctuation are correct.   _____

Total Points   _____

Section 7 : RESEARCH

"Perhaps the most valuable result of all education is the ability to make yourself do the thing you have to do when it has to be done, whether you like it or not."

(Aldous Huxley)

Objectives: Identify the origins of stereotypes and prejudice
                      Help students take pride in their own ethnicity
                      Encourage students' appreciation of others' race, culture and ethnicity
                      Show students how to locate and use research
                      Guide students as they write a research essay

Length: Approximately ten Lessons

Introduction

It's rare to have students who love gathering research. Experience teaches that it is even less likely you will have students who can analyze, organize, and utilize that research effectively. Nevertheless, the importance of research cannot be underrated by the effective teacher. Gathering and using research, in fact, is the foundation of academia.

Our job then is to help students recognize first how research can be important to them and, second, how a writer goes about obtaining and using it in a composition. They need to know that research can be found in sources other than encyclopedias, that it isn't just a collection of useless data, and that through research, they can discover more about their community, their family, and themselves than they had ever realized.

Like most other essays, the research essay is a carefully planned work, but it differs with respect to the diversity of information presented to the reader from a variety of sources. Teachers need to recognize that the goals of student researchers often differ and shouldn't expect, therefore, that student essays will possess comprehensive research and dramatic insights. The main objective is for students, especially younger ones, to master the format and process of the research essay and to learn something new about history, an issue, or their world.

The keys are to help them enjoy the challenge of researching an interesting (though possibly complex) topic, to encourage them to be diligent and thorough and to assist them in mastering a task that remains a part of all academic programs at all levels.

Lesson 48   PERCEPTION VS. REALITY

Objective: Evaluate our perceptions of other cultures, races, and nationalities

Activities:

1. **Prompts:** Introduce the unit with the following:

   A. **Survey: Activity 48-1** or **48-2**—These will help reveal the depth of students' awareness of other cultures and nationalities.

   [**Answers** to **Activity 48-2:** (1) Japan; (2) Vietnam; (3) Indonesia; (4) Muslim; (5) Jewish; (6) Iran; (7) Greece; (8) Italy; (9) Korea; (10) England; (11) China; (12) Bulgaria; (13) India; (14) Cuba; (15) Mexico]

   B. **Word Association Game:** Most students have played these since elementary school. For example, if you say "day," they would probably say "night." If you said "teacher," they'd probably say "students."

   You can do this activity **orally** or **in writing** to identify the perceptions students have of other nationalities and cultures. Students must say or write their first response to the following words:

   1. Mexican
   2. German
   3. Japanese
   4. Egyptian
   5. Italian
   6. Jewish
   7. Greek
   8. Russian
   9. Korean
   10. French

   [Responses related to food (like Taco Bell, pizza, spaghetti), buildings (the pyramids, Eiffel Tower, temples), and clothes (togas, kimonos, veils) are quite common.]

   [The exercise clearly illustrates that much of what we know about other nationalities and cultures is based on perceptions rather than true awareness. Other typical responses include Mafia for Italians, vodka for the Russians, and Nazis for Germans.]

C. **Read:** Find a brief narrative or poem from their literature text that relates an image or experience related to another nationality, race, or culture.

D. **Magazine advertisements**—See how different racial and ethnic groups are portrayed—(ex) ethnic women for recipes or food products.

E. **Music:** Find recordings associated with various nationalities or cultures (see your school music director or shop at a local music store for tapes or CDs) and challenge students either **orally** or **in writing** to identify the various selections.

2. **Discussion**: Explain the word *perception* first, then ask:

   A. How do we acquire these perceptions?

   [From family members, friends, books, television, newspapers and movies, etc.]

   B. Why do we lack more detailed and accurate information?

   [Not interested, don't follow the news, don't spend time around others who have different backgrounds, might be prejudiced, etc.]

   C. Is it important to learn about other cultures, races, or nationalities? Why?

   [Answers will vary]

3. **Discovery:** Demonstrate the diversity in your classroom. Distribute blank index cards to all students. They are to write their name (optional), the main nationality (ies) in their background, their religion, and the languages they can speak. When finished, students pass the cards around the classroom until everyone has read at least 10-15 cards.

4. **Discussion** on traveling and immigration:

   A. Who has traveled in another country? Any personal experiences?

   B. What do you think it would be like to travel to ___?

   C. What do you think it's like for foreign travelers in the United States?

   D. What do you think it would be like to live in another country?

   E. Why was America once known as the "Melting Pot"?

   F. What is our government's policy on immigration now?

   G. How can we improve our awareness of other cultures and nationalities?

   H. What are some television or radio programs that help us learn about other cultures or nationalities?

Homework options:

A. Students **write a description** of a typical school day of a teenager in an Asian or European nation of their own selection. To locate this information direct them to the Education subheading in the encyclopedia article for the country they select.

B. For a topic, like Chinese communism or Native American dances, students **list 5-10 facts** about it and the sources they used to locate the research on that topic—(ex) encyclopedia, textbook.

C. **Writing:** Students investigate their own culture or family heritage. They describe in 2 paragraphs some customs or traditions associated with it—(ex) marriages, holidays. Students with mixed backgrounds should choose the most dominant origin. They should practice researching by interviewing parents and grandparents and examining relevant encyclopedia articles.

D. **Identification:** Students locate and explain any pictures or films that present an unfair or biased image of another nationality or culture—(ex) how Native Americans are portrayed in movie westerns from the 1940s and 1950s.

E. **Discovery:** Students **clip 5-8** newspaper and/or magazine articles that deal directly or indirectly with their personal ethnic or cultural heritages.

Cultural Awareness Survey #1

1. List those nationalities where bowing is an expected part of their greeting:

2. List three nationalities where hugging and/or kissing are an expected part of their greeting:

3. What are some of the countries located in the Middle East?

4. The term *Native American* has replaced *Indian*. Why?

5. What are some of the traditional foods and religions associated with Greeks?

6. What are some of the marriage customs associated with the Jewish faith?

7. From whom are the Mexican people descended?

8. How would you make friends with a teenager who didn't know any English?

Name _____

Cultural Awareness Survey #2

Directions: Match the following countries or cultures to the descriptions. Each country or culture is used only once.

MEXICO	VIETNAM	JEWISH	ENGLAND	JAPANESE
INDIA	CUBA	CHINA	INDONESIA	IRAN
KOREA	BULGARIA	GREECE	ITALY	MUSLIM

1. _____ These students have a school year of 240 days.

2. _____ Students here go to school six days a week for 4 hours a day for nearly the entire year.

3. _____ These people never touch any part of another person's face or scalp because it's bad luck.

4. _____ These children never attend school on Friday.

5. _____ In this religion a couple is married under a *huppah*, a canopy held by four poles.

6. _____ This country is said to have begun the wearing of veils by women.

7. _____ These people began sporting events now known as the Olympics.

8. _____ Children here express a promise by tracing an invisible cross on their chests.

9. _____ To beckon someone here people hold a hand palm down and wiggle their fingers.

10. _____ To say good-bye here children often use the word "cheerio."

11. _____ The people here celebrate their New Year with a Lion Dance.

12. _____ Here, shaking the head means "yes."

13. _____ In some households in this country, it's considered a bad omen to say "good-bye." Instead, they say "Go and come back."

14. _____ On this island near Florida all the children must learn to speak Russian starting in the seventh grade.

15. _____ This country's culture is a mixture of Aztecs, Mayans, and Spanish peoples.

Lesson 49

LABELS, NAMES, AND GROUPS

Objective: Gain an appreciation of other nationalities, races, or cultures and practice narrowing a research topic

Activities:

[Desks should already be arranged for group work.]

1. **Explain:** Present your expectations for groups—Evaluation will be based on individual contributions and the thoroughness of the group effort.

2. **Group work:** On recognizing diversity.

   A. **Share and Compare:** Students compare backgrounds (Lesson 48 homework) by reading or exchanging papers.

   [Give the groups time as well for each member to share why he/she is *proud* of his/her ethnic heritage and/or some of the *problems* they might have experienced, (an example could be grandparents who can't speak English) because of their ethnic or cultural background.]

   B. **Discovery:** Students wander the classroom to locate and list 12-15 different *labels* they find. You might offer a few hints: "What's written on your shoes?" or "Check out the bulletin board." Some labels they could discover are Nike, English Grammar, JC Penny, your school name, etc.

   This could be a contest to see which group can list the most labels. After they return to their groups they total the number of labels. Possibly award the winning group with extra points.

3. **Discuss:** various labels—Cadillac, Oscar, Grammy, Disney, Friday, Cheerios, Air Jordans, etc. What do these labels suggest? (ex) Cadillac suggests wealth; Disney suggests family entertainment.

4. **Explain:** Students have just engaged in obtaining Primary Research, that is, research they generate on their own. Another example would be hiking in a forest and taking notes on the plant life.

5. **Visual aid:** Continue their exploration of labels and primary research. **Show pictures or a videotape** of people of various nationalities or cultures. Groups must **identify** and **list** the characteristics of those people—(ex) Greeks—usually dark complexions, hardy people.

6. **Discussion:** Do we need labels on people (*races*)? Why/Why not? Give time for deliberation and then poll each group.

7. **Summary options:**

   A. **Collage**: Make a collage that represents the group. Students cut out pictures and headlines from magazines or draw illustrations on paper. Add a creative title—(ex) "Unity in Diversity."

   B. **Writing:** Students cite a **label** they've heard used in school to profile students (ex) nerds. They explain how that label came into being and how it could be eliminated.

   C. **Lecture: Discuss** the connection between stereotyping and labeling. First, explain the foundation of the word stereotyping (stereo + type), then some examples such as, *blondes are ditzy* or *teachers are boring*, and then the reasons stereotypes are common and often cruel.

   D. **Analysis:** Students choose any two of the following groups and **explain** the labels or stereotypes the public has of this group and how this perception could be altered.

Hockey players	Rock 'n' Roll stars
Grandmothers	Grandfathers
Bankers	Professional athletes

Homework options: [These lead students into doing Secondary Research, that is, research they gain from someone else's primary research]:

   A. Students could do some research on how labeling and stereotyping have caused conflicts between nations (ex) Greece and Turkey, Iran and Iraq, England and Ireland.

   B. Why do we label one section of the planet the "Third World"? How did this label come about?

   C. America was once considered the "Melting Pot"—What does that mean? Is it the same now? Why/Why not?

   D. Students research the labels car manufacturers use for their vehicles (ex) why Mustang, not Stallion.

   E. The atomic bomb dropped on Hiroshima was called "Little Boy." Students research why they used that label.

Lesson 50   WHAT IS RESEARCH?

Objective: To identify what *is* and *isn't* research

Activities:

1. **Survey: Activity 50-1.**

   [Desks are arranged for cooperative learning. Give each group 6-8 index cards. **Reminder:** Their evaluation will be based on all group members participating and the group doing thorough work.]

2. **Group work:** Explore aspects of Research.

   A. **Share and Compare:** What is research?—**Activity 50-1.**

   B. **Writing:** Write a topic on one index card that could be developed by adding research (ex) AIDS, WW II weapons.

   C. **Exchange:** Groups exchange cards and list on that card the resources a person could use to research that topic. [Answers will vary.]

   D. **Writing:** What is common knowledge? Each group writes a topic on another index card that could be developed by anyone *without* research (ex) January is a cold winter month.

   E. **Exchange:** Groups exchange cards and add details about that topic to determine if it is truly common knowledge. [Answers will vary.]

   F. **Listing:** Who can list the most resources a person could use to research the origin of paper money or spray deodorant, or the subject of electric guitars? Write these on an index card.

   [Paper money: encyclopedia, interview with banker, pamphlets from U.S. Mint, books, history texts, biographies, historical magazines, etc.]

   [Deodorant: interview with chemist, brochures and advertisements from companies, personal observations, reference books, magazine articles, etc.]

   [Electric guitars: encyclopedia, brochures from companies, interview with musician, reference book, college text, interview with music teacher, possible advertisements, etc.]

   G. **Brainstorming:** What are curds and whey? Groups combine common knowledge (what they know already) and research (dictionary, books, etc. in the classroom)

   Put two headings on the blackboard—Research and Common Knowledge.

[Research = information previously unknown obtained from other sources; Common knowledge = information the general public already knows.]

(ex) *Research*   *Common Knowledge*
        AIDS   January is a cold month.
        WW II weapons   White House is in Washington, D.C.

Which group can produce the most topics for each category in four minutes?

H. **Listing:** On each of the remaining index cards, each group writes the name of a nationality or culture the group collectively finds interesting.

Collect all cards and **discuss** the results, and ask:

"How can we learn more about other nationalities and cultures ?"

[Talk to persons of different nationalities, travel, learn a foreign language, read books, newspapers and magazines, *do research,* etc.]

3. Once students have grasped the idea of research, **review** the definitions of Primary and Secondary Research.

4. **Summarize:** Primary Research is obtained most frequently from personal observation. Secondary Research is obtained from investigating other sources which can either be print or oral sources.

Gathering research is important because:

A. It helps students practice effective organizational skills.

B. A student's knowledge base is increased.

C. It can demonstrate a student's capabilities.

D. It serves as a means for individualized instruction:

E. The research essay can become part of a permanent reference section for future students to use as a resource.

5. **Assessment**: On Research.

A. What will make research easier for you?

B. What difficulties have you had in the past?

C. How much time should be spent on actual research?

D. How does one go about finding research in a book? In a magazine?

E. Skim your grammar textbook—what *isn't* research?

6. **Preview:** Give homework assignment on research. [And inform the librarian(s) of the students' obligations and deadlines in completing the assignment.]

Homework:

Generally, students research *research*—a fact-finding mission on how to use computers, card catalogs, and the reference area found in almost all libraries. They should also find out how magazines, newspapers, recordings (records and tapes), and videos are organized. They then prepare a report—an easy-to-follow list of guidelines locating research materials, including pamphlets the library makes available to patrons. The more comprehensive this report, the better their evaluation.

As a preview activity, students can do **Activity 50-2—Facts and Sources** which introduces them to locating facts and specific sources.

Name _____

What Is Research?

Directions: Answer each question in detail

1. How do you define *research*?

2. Where can a writer find research?

3. What are some topics that you would have to research in order to understand them better?

4. What is the best way to locate information in a book?

5. What is the best way to locate information in a magazine?

6. What other sources are available to us as research?

7. What *isn't* research?

8. What research have you done in the past?

Name _____

Facts and Sources

Directions: For each topic below list one fact and the source used to locate that fact.

Topic	One Fact	Source
(ex) Bull fighting	began 6 thousand years ago	Encyclopedia Americana
1. Wetlands in Venezuela		
2. German Nobel prize winners		
3. Aztec jewelry		
4. Egyptian pyramids		
5. Russian prisons		
6. Weather in Ireland		
7. Divorce in the Catholic religion		
8. Australian rugby		
9. French art		
10. Turkish tobacco		
11. Japanese schools		
12. Native American dances		
13. London mass transit		

Lesson 51   TOPIC AND AUDIENCE

Objective: To prepare students to research a specific topic related to a nationality, race, or culture

Activities:

1. **Discussion:** Put the name of a specific nationality—(ex) China—on the board and have students announce what they already know (Primary Research and Common Knowledge) about it.

2. **Explain:** Clarify that they will be researching a nationality or culture, possibly one from their own background. The intent for them is to pick one they are truly interested in learning more about.

    First steps in the process:

    Step #1 Selecting an appealing topic and narrowing it

    Step #2 Listing primary research related to that topic (Prewriting)

3. **Discussion:** How will you go about selecting a topic?

    [Often the best topics are related to their personal family history, a certain place they know well, or a subject they have studied in the past.]

4. Create an interest in the project by **discussing** any of the following:

    A. Compare our president with the political leader of any African country.

    B. Who might be involved in a future WW III? Why these nations?

    C. The London police force doesn't carry any weapons. Why do you think they don't?

    D. What do you think the suburbs of Mexico City are like?

    E. What were some of the historical events leading to the building of the Berlin Wall?

    F. What are some martial arts by name, origin (country), and their definitions?

    G. What is the weather like in Central and South America?

5. **Freewriting:** Use **Activity 51-1** to continue generating interest in possible topic selections.

6. **Contest:** Decide teams (girls vs. boys, groups, rows)—on narrowing a topic (since it is the habit of too many students to attempt to research topics that are too general, like WW II or Drugs). Give points to the group who can best transform the following broad topics into one that is more specific.

(ex)   Weather—Rain—Monsoons in Burma

Round #1   Crime

Round #2   Art

Round #3   Armed Services

Bonus Round   Education

7. **Discuss:** Explore the various options for this assignment; also consider the expected audience/reader:

   A. Create a newsletter per month on a specific culture or nationality.

   B. Include art work from art classes to coincide with the research on a nationality or culture.

   C. Work with the Social Studies Department (history and/ or geography of a nationality or culture) and Science Department (geological and natural formations found in certain countries) as students start their formal research.

   D. For any nationality or culture, have students include the prominent literary figures and literature from that country or culture.

   E. Work with the Home Economics teacher to make the prominent foods and dishes associated with that nationality or culture.

   F. Include some guest speakers—parents, community members, or teachers from a local college—to make presentations about ethnic/traditional customs that are associated with any nationality or culture.

8. **Explain:**   **Activity 51-2**—the possible projects—and **Activity 51-3**—The Checklist.

   This assignment could be, if desired, an "*I*-Search" project, rather than a *R*esearch project. The I-Search essay begins with the writer's own natural curiosity about a topic and then focuses on a personal search (primary research) for information from visits, interviews, and observations. Printed sources are only used when they are recommended by someone during an interview.

Homework:

Students read in their grammar text any of the pages that apply to selecting a topic and audience.

Students complete Step #1 of the Checklist—**Activity 52-3**.

Students could also begin work on listing the sources they plan to use to complete their research. The most obvious is an encyclopedia, yet many other reference books are useful.

Name _____

Prompts for Selecting a Topic
for the Research Essay

Directions: Complete each of the following statements.

1. If I could talk to any person in history from another country, he or she would be
_____.

2. If I could travel to any country, it would be _____.

3. If I read about any current events they would be_____
_____
_____.

4. If I could watch any television program related to another nationality or culture, that nationality or culture would be _____.

5. If I could read a story about any nationality or culture, it would be about _____
_____
_____
_____.

Form 51-2   Name _____

Cultural Awareness Research Essay Project

I Objectives—Students must

1. show an appreciation and understanding of another culture or nationality
2. obtain specific research about that culture or nationality
3. compose a complete and coherent essay

II Projects—Select a single nationality (Italy, for example) or culture (Shawnee Native American tribe, for example) that interests you. Narrow down to a specific topic that relates to *one* of the following:

1. Describe the origin, use, and style of veils worn by women in the Middle East.
2. Describe the origin, rituals, and garments related to the wedding customs of any culture or religion.
3. Describe a historic area, district, or avenue associated with any culture or ethnic group (ex) the Vatican.
4. Describe a single geographic region (ex) the Black Forest in Germany.
5. Describe a monument (or historic structure) associated with any culture or nationality (ex) the Eiffel Tower.
6. Describe the origin, tradition, rhythm, lyrics, and theme of any nation's national anthem. Bring in a tape of the song.
7. Describe and chart the seasons or weather of any Asian, Middle Eastern, or South American country.
8. Describe the clothing or fashions of any nationality or culture that is particular to that culture or nationality. Be sure to deal with how it is made and any traditions related to the garments (ex) Hawaiian lei.
9. Describe the origin, tradition, and style of play of any sport associated with a nationality or culture (ex) hurling in Ireland. **Do not select a sport that many nations play** (ex) soccer.
10. Describe the origin, tradition, and creation of any food associated with a culture or nationality (ex) Italian pastries.
11. Describe the appearance, habitat, and uniqueness of any animal particular to any foreign nation (ex) the Australian kangaroo.
12. If another topic appeals to you that relates to researching another culture or nationality, discuss it with the teacher.

Key Points:

1. Investigate your topic systematically and thoroughly.
2. Organize your essay logically and coherently. Be sure you are thorough and accurate.

3. Follow the checklist (**Activity 47-3**).

4. Be sure to incorporate your own thoughts on the subject in the body of the essay.

5. Try not to say something old in a new way, but to say something new, using the most current and interesting research.

6. **Do not** select a *person* associated with a nationality or culture.

Name _____

Research Essay Checklist

Step #	*Points*	*Responsibility*
1	5 ____	Select a narrowed and accessible topic that can interest both you and the intended reader.
2	5 ____	Write a persuasive, focused thesis statement about that topic.
3	5 ____	Write an introductory paragraph that presents the topic in an interesting way.
4	5 ____	What do you know already about the topic? Freewrite a list of ideas, examples, main points, etc. about the topic. You may also choose to cluster or web these points (prewriting).
5		Gather research and take notes, choosing either to paraphrase or quote information from among the following:
	5 ____	books by an authority on that topic
	5 ____	a reference book related to that topic (encyclopedia, for example)
	5 ____	a magazine article about that topic
	5 ____	a newspaper article or another magazine article
	5 ____	an interview with an *authority* on that topic
	5 ____	any other acceptable source (pamphlet, video, recording, etc.)
6	10 ___	Type the bibliography page where you list your sources in alphabetical order arranged in block style. Use the appropriate abbreviations where necessary and follow proper punctuation rules. You must have at least **six** different sources. Do **not** number them on the page.
7	10 ___	Organize your research and prepare a detailed outline that consists of at least 4-6 major topics (I-VI) and two subtopics for each major topic.
8	20 ___	Write a first draft, converting each major topic of the outline into complete paragraphs which should be arranged in a logical order. Each major topic should become, in order, the topic sentence of a paragraph, and the subtopics should become the support sentences.

Form 51-3 (*continued*)

Each paragraph should have a combination of research and your personal insights. In this way you will avoid **"jammed"** research.

Use transitions effectively here and be sure to place quotation marks around all quoted words or passages.

Plagiarism is a problem if direct quotes or paraphrased material is not documented correctly. At least 40% of this paper should be the writer's personal insight.

9   5 ___ Write a concluding paragraph which reflects a forceful ending to your research essay. Do not include any research in this paragraph. It must be the writer's own insights.

10   25 ___ Revise and edit the first draft and prepare a typed (double-spaced) final copy of 750-1000 words. Be careful about proofreading.

11   5 ___ Type your title page. This will have (1) a creative title (middle, center); (2) your name beneath the title: (3) the course name and period; and (4) the date.

12   25 ___ (Optional) Prepare, rehearse, then deliver a 4-5 minute presentation to the class about your topic. This oral presentation must consist of the key points of your research and analysis. Also, reveal your attitude or opinions about the topic.

Include an audio/visual aid to clarify these main points.

Total Points ___

Lesson 52

TOPIC, THESIS, AND INTRODUCTION

Objective: To prepare students to research a specific topic related to a nationality, race, or culture and write a thesis statement and introduction

Activities:

1. **Lecture:** Discuss writing a Thesis Statement. It is:

   - a statement that expresses the essay's topic

   - not a question

   - a single sentence, never more than two

   - persuasive in some way (that is, it is capable of being developed into an essay)

     Key words in a thesis statement to indicate persuasion can be *classify, compare, contrast, prove, identify,* and *establish*

   - the final sentence of the introduction

2. **Writing:** Students examine thesis statements—their weaknesses or strengths—in **Activity 52-1**.

   Discuss the results.

   Example #1   Not a complete sentence

   Example #2   It can't be a question

   Example #3   Very specific but not persuasive

   Example #4   Specific and persuasive

   Example #5   Not very persuasive or stylistically mature writing

   Example #6   Shows specific intent and persuasiveness

   Example #7   Reflects a specific topic and intent

3. **Visual aid:** Show the opening scene of a dramatic movie or the first segment of a strip cartoon. Ask: How does the director or cartoonist get you interested?

4. **Review:** Refer to **Form 44-2—Types of introductions.**

5. **Analysis:** Use **Activity 52-2**—an introductory paragraph for students to analyze and evaluate.

   [The paragraph begins effectively—the question does get a reader interested—but then gets too technical with references to experimental animals, information more appropriate for later paragraphs. Also, the thesis needs improvement.]

201

6. **Identification:** Students examine introductions and thesis statements in magazine articles, chapter openings in their text, or in previous essays to determine the type of introduction and quality of thesis that was used.

7. **Writing:** Students work on writing their own introduction and thesis statement, and **confer** with teacher when work is completed.

Homework:

Students continue work associated with researching their topic and composing a thesis statement—Checklist steps #2-4.

Students should read any pages in their text that deal with the writing of a thesis statement (sometimes called a thematic statement, controlling purpose statement, or topic statement).

Students should be listing the sources they plan to use to complete their research. They need to evaluate what will be the most beneficial resource. This evaluation should be based on the following questions:

#1 How authoritative is the source?

#2 How up-to-date is the source?

#3 How detailed is the source?

Name _____

Thesis Statements

Directions: Examine each of the following potential thesis statements and then explain why it is or is not an effective one on the line below it.

Example #1   China's national sport

_____

Example #2   What is China's national sport?

_____

Example #3   China's national sport is table tennis (ping pong).

_____

_____

Example #4   China dominates the sport of table tennis (ping pong) internationally.

_____

_____

Example #5   My paper is about China's national sport which is table tennis (ping pong).

_____

_____

Example #6   My intent is to explain the main causes of the destruction of Brazil's rain forest.

_____

_____

Example #7   The Eiffel Tower in Paris can be considered as France's most important monument.

_____

_____

What Is an Effective Introduction?

Directions: Evaluate the following paragraph to determine if it is an effective introductory paragraph.

Why has the solution to the common cold so long eluded us? Perhaps the fact that it is not a dangerous disease has lessened the pressure to solve the problem. There are, however, more important reasons. Viral diseases are studied mainly by observing the effects produced in experimental animals and plants, for viruses cannot be grown in an artificial way. Unfortunately, there is no convenient experimental animal for studying the cold virus. Neither the mouse, guinea pig, nor other animal can be infected with colds. Therefore, the common cold still is a mystery.

Your evaluation:

Lesson 53   BIBLIOGRAPHY

Objective: To gather research and create an accurate bibliography (or list of resources)

Activities:

[This lesson could last 1-3 class periods, depending on the skills and experience of the students.]

1. **Explain**: Present the importance of using the following resources for gathering research. If possible, have an example of each in the classroom:

Computerized card catalogs	Interviews
Dictionaries	Reference books
Encyclopedias	Atlases
Periodicals	Almanacs
Videotapes	Musical recordings

2. **Group work:** Locate the bibliographic information in a source. Each group should have the following items (which could be borrowed from your school library):

   A. Encyclopedia

   B. Non-fiction book

   C. Magazine

   D. School newsletter

   E. Edited book (anthology)

   F. Teacher as interviewee

   Students determine the bibliographic information and **write** it on a sheet of paper or index card.

3. **Explain:** Cover if necessary, how to locate any source's bibliographic information. Consider it in terms of four W's:

   WHO: Who originated the information (author, interviewee, editor, organization)?

   WHAT: What is its title (article, magazine, book, encyclopedia, interviewee title, etc.)?

   WHERE: Where was it published (city, state)?

   WHEN: When was it published (copyright date)?

4. **Discussion:** On Sources

   A. Why should you use a variety of resources?

      [This provides credibility and thoroughness to the research. At times, information from one source could be biased.]

   B. What makes one source better than another?

      [Look for one which is more up-to-date or more detailed; check which is more authoritative; evaluate the diction for comprehension.]

   C. How do you determine the effectiveness of a source?

      [Preliminary reading = surveying a source first before taking notes. If the section looks helpful, you should read the first several paragraphs and decide then if it should be part of the bibliography.]

5. **Explain:** The Bibliography Page (also called List of Works Cited)— Distribute **Form 53-1**.

6. **Read:** Have students read pages in their text associated with gathering research and constructing a bibliography.

7. **Group work:** Challenge groups to write the bibliographic information for the following sources, using imaginary sources (correct format is in brackets).

   A. a computer web site [(ex) "Iowa Wrestling," University of Iowa web site, www.hawkeyes.com, May 15, 1997.]

   B. a pamphlet [(ex) "CPR," American Heart Association, New York, 1990.]

   C. someone else's research essay [(ex) Somrak, Danielle, "The Death of Leon Trotsky," Essay, Richmond Heights High School, 1992.]

   D. a CD [(ex) Guthrie, Woody, "Do-Re-Me," Dust Bowl Ballads, CD, Rounder Records, 1166-10040-2, 1988.]

   E. a television program [(ex) "Civil War," Dir. Andrew Harris, Prod. Ken Burns, PBS, New York, May 18, 1996.]

   Check the responses and then **show** the correct format.

8. **Summary:** A researcher first needs to select the best sources available. There need to be several different types of resources. The bibliographic information needs to be documented accurately.

Homework:

Students continue work on the Checklist—Steps 5-6.

Sample Bibliography

Caddy, John, "I-Referenced Responses to Writing," Interview at office, St. Paul, Minnesota, August 10, 1989.

Daniels, Harvey and Steven Zimmerman, *A Writing Project: Training Teachers of Composition from Kindergarten to College*, Heineman Books, Portsmouth, New Hampshire, 1985.

Ellis, Jessica O., "Cooperative Learning in English." *English Journal*, October, 1990, p. 75.

England, David, "Teaching Writing Process and Determining Grades," *Quarterly of the National Writing Project and Center for the Study of Writing*, August, 1986.

"A Guide to Surviving the Teaching of Writing," pamphlet from Wisconsin Department of Instruction, Madison, Wisconsin, 1985.

Jensen, Jean, "Career Research: Researching for Real," *English Journal*, September, 1989.

Judy, Stephen and Susan Judy, *The English Teacher's Handbook*, Scott Foresman and Company, Boston, 1983.

Manos, Keith, English Teacher, Interview at Richmond Heights High School, May 15, 1998.

Milett, Nancy, *Teaching the Writing Process*, Boston, Houghton Mifflin Company, 1986.

Rico, Gabriele, *Writing the Natural Way*, J.P. Tarcher, Inc., Los Angeles, 1983.

Scardamalia, Marlene and Carl Bereiter, "Research on Written Composition, *Handbook of Research on Teaching*," MacMillan, New York, 1986.

Wyndham, Lee, Writing for Children and Teenagers, Writers Digest Books, Cincinnati, Ohio, 1989.

• • • • • •

Do's and Don'ts:

- Do *not* number the sources.
- Do put them in *alphabetical* order.
- Do use *block* style (no indenting).

Lesson 54 NOTES AND NUMBERS— GATHERING RESEARCH

Objective: To make distinctions between quoting, paraphrasing, and summarizing (and to avoid plagiarism)

Activities:

[This lesson could last 1-5 class periods, depending on the skill level and experience of the students.]

1. **Role-Play:** Conduct an interview with an "expert" in teen romances or the school detention policy. Students must write the exact words of the quote(s) from the expert (a student volunteer or you) that they find most interesting.

   Discuss the results. Check how accurately students copied the quote(s).

2. **Identification:** Students examine newspaper and news magazine articles, if available, to locate direct quotes. Ask volunteers to read those they find interesting.

   Then ask: Why did the reporter choose to use these quotes and not just paraphrase them?

3. **Writing:** Students *examine* a page from their own textbook or *listen* to a story you tell (possibly about an event with your family or a problem at school), and then *paraphrase* what they read or heard.

   Discuss the results.

4. **Explain:** Define the Quote, Paraphrase, Summary, and Plagiarism.

   Quote = *exact* words copied from any source.

   Paraphrase = information taken from a source the researcher chooses to put into his/her own words.

   Summary = a substantial quantity of text (possibly a page) reduced to sentences; research that is condensed.

   Plagiarism = failing to document a source; this occurs when (1) the writer uses a direct quote without providing quotation marks and (2) paraphrasing information without documenting the source.

5. **Debate:** Which is best to use: a quote, paraphrase, or summary? Use **Activity 54-1.**

   [Use the direct quote when the information is expressed exceptionally well, is succinct and memorable, or is somewhat controversial. Be sure to use quotation marks.]

   [Use paraphrasing when the information is too technical or complex.

The intent here is to get the main message of research that could possess too much figurative or flowery language.]

[Use a summary when there is too much research, and it can be condensed.]

6. **Modeling:** Illustrate what research notes could look like—Distribute **Form 54-2**.

Remind students that they should not record material that is unrelated to their topic. All direct quotes must be copied accurately, including the punctuation and grammar. They would be wise to double-check references for accuracy.

7. **Lecture:** Guidelines for Researching and Documentation—Distribute **Form 54-3**.

Advise students to investigate sources like ethnic radio stations and magazines, television documentaries, videos, any workshops featuring ethnic or cultural topics, and speakers at seminars or libraries.

8. **Library:** Spend some time here during a class session to assist students in locating information.

Guide them to locate books by Author, Title, or Subject; to locate articles with Periodical Indexes and Newspaper Indexes; to locate Reference Books; and to locate any videotape material in the library.

To make sure students can gather research and create a bibliography, you might have to work closely, step by step with those students whose skill at finding sources in the library remains weak. Also, the time provided to locate all the necessary sources is crucial. For instance, some students could work diligently for two days in the library before realizing there are no sources on their topic. They can, of course, ask for permission to change topics or have more time.

Homework:

Students continue gathering research. Suggest they use other libraries, bookstores, museums, other teachers or experts, television programs, computer software, and an online information service if they have a personal computer with modem.

Name _____

To Quote or to Paraphrase—
That Is the Question

Directions: Read the following paragraphs and then answer the questions in preparation for a *debate* on which information should be quoted and which should be paraphrased.

A manual laborer digging a ditch is just as complicated as today's computer linked with an automatic milling machine. His brain, first of all, has been programmed with the techniques of using a shovel. Through the nerves, the laborer's brain instructs his muscles to exert force on the shovel, and the earth moves. Through the senses, the brain monitors how much force is necessary to move the earth, and if, for example, the shovel strikes a stone, the brain signals the necessary muscular movements to dig around or remove it.

Similarly, the computer which guides the milling machine has been programmed with the information necessary to make, for example, an aluminum part for an aircraft. Through the connecting wires (nerves), the computer tells the machine to move in the proper directions, and with the proper extended tools to make the necessary cuts and drill holes.

1. What information regarding the manual laborer digging a ditch should be quoted?

2. What information regarding the manual laborer digging a ditch should be paraphrased?

3. What other lines should be quoted? Copy them.

4. What parts of this research should be paraphrased?

Taking Notes from a Source

Bibliographic Information: (ex) Lee Wyndham, *Writing for Children and Teenagers,* Writer's Digest Books, Cincinnati, OH, 1989.

Directions: Either quote, paraphrase, or summarize the information taken from a source.

Example:

Page #	*Notes*
Pg. 6	In children's books, "slang, swearing, and bad taste are not wanted, even as horrible examples" of characters' traits. [quote]
p. 11	Urban settings are more popular currently, especially when the theme has a multi-cultural basis. [paraphrase]
	"There is fierce editorial resistance against any material that perpetuates tired, stereotypical images." [quote]
p. 16-18	Establish a writing routine and start by trying to sell a story before trying to sell a novel. [summary]
p. 20	"Keep a number of stories circulating and you will become known among editors as a producer. And that is what editors want." [quote]

Q & A Guidelines for Researching
and Documentation

1. Should the entire essay be research?

    [No. Students should insert their own insight and reactions with the research.]

2. Where should I insert my thoughts on the topic?

    [Either before or directly after important research (ex) The Secretary of Education has said, "The school year must be expanded to eleven months." This suggestion would be totally rejected by students who enjoy summer or need to work.]

3. How can I insert any thoughts on a topic I may know nothing about?

    [Adding opinions about new information is very common. The key is to respond with honesty and insight.]

4. Where should the research appear in the body of the essay?

    [Everywhere, except in the introduction and conclusion]

5. Should I use more quotes, paraphrases, or summaries?

    [It depends on the type of research. It is probably best to use an even mixture of quotes and paraphrases and only 1-2 summaries.]

6. What is plagiarism?

    [Any information in the essay that isn't common knowledge or your personal thoughts must be documented. If you get information from an outside source and do not document or credit that source in the body of the essay, you have committed plagiarism.]

7. How could a researcher commit plagiarism by accident?

    [By using a source's exact words and neglecting to apply quotation marks]

8. Why is documentation still needed for information that is either paraphrased or summarized?

    [Because it's another source's information, not yours. Whether it is information that is a direct quote or a paraphrase, it still needs to be documented. Failing to do so is plagiarism.]

Form 54-3 (*continued*)

9. What is parenthetical documentation?

   [Documentation that occurs directly after the research in the body, rather than as a footnote or endnote (ex) Poet William Butler Yeats preferred the common beggar as a usual subject for his poetry and called for other poets to "return to the simple folk, to the heroic folk" (Gogarty 69).]

10. When should I use ellipses?

    [Use the three dots . . . to indicate an *omission* within a direct quote you have used.]

11. When should I use brackets in a research essay?

    [Brackets are for the *replacement* of word(s) within a quote often for the purpose of having the direct quote make sense within a sentence or for clarification (ex) "[Lincoln] worried tremendously about his popularity outside Illinois during his campaign for President in 1860."—Instead of the actual "*He* worried . . ."]

Lesson 55   OUTLINING

Objective: To master the fundamentals of outlining

Activities:

[This lesson could take 1-2 class periods.]

1. **Group work:** On Outlining.

   A. Tell students you have a four-drawer dresser at home. They are to **identify** what is in each drawer top to bottom. Give the correct group extra points.

      [One outlining skill is to arrange and group similar items.]

   B. Groups **brainstorm** the junk food eaten by teens consistently (ex) chips, candy, etc. Then select and rank the top five.

      [Another outlining skill is organizing items by order of importance.]

   C. **Knowledge check:** Discover what students already know about outlining. Students must explain what Roman numerals and capital letters stand for in any outline.

   D. Students do **Activity 55-1**.

   E. **Board work:** Get student input to construct an outline on the board where each Major Topic is a brand name for basketball shoes (ex) Nike.

      Students then go to the board to fill in Subtopics and Supporting details.

      Check their work.

2. **Debate:** Groups examine sample outline—**Form 55-2**—first to evaluate its effectiveness and then to exchange views with opposing groups.

   ["A Visit to Cleveland" is well-arranged overall, but has details unrelated to the thesis (ex) major topic IV which is about sports; the writer should also delete the details about it being a major transportation center and expand on the restaurant section.]

3. **Explain:** Key principles of outlining—distribute **Activity 55-3** and define the Outline: It is the organization of the Prewriting, the skeleton of the essay. Hemingway said, "The outline is the architecture of writing; the words and sentences are the interior decoration."

4. **Discuss:** Where are the faults in the following sections of outlines?

Example #1   II Helping
        A. Family
        B. Friends
        C. Parents

[It's incomplete—Helping how? Also, Parents should be grouped as a supporting detail with Family.]

Example #2   V They had a winning season
        A. It was a great season
        B. Winning record
            1. Hal—All State
            2. Great defense

[Don't use sentences; subtopic A repeats the major topic; the supporting details have no connection to Winning Record and should probably be subtopics.]

5. **Modeling:** Students examine more types of outlines—**Form 55-4.**

6. **Group work:** Students do peer editing of each other's outlines.

   Check the results.

Homework:

Students read any sections in their text about outlining and review Key Points about Outlining—**Form 55-3.**

Students continue work on their research essays—Step #7.

Name _____

Organizing and Categorizing

1. Place the following methods of transportation in a proper order; (each group must define "proper order").

car	airplane	canoe	truck	subway
train	bus	horse	ship	bicycle

2. Place the following scrambled items into **categories**, each with a **heading** you must determine.

toothpick	violin	magazine	map
wig	pencil	videotape	dictionary
lipstick	oil	scissors	knife
eraser	sand	socks	bus
tissue	mug	comb	ink

3. **Revise** the following section of an outline:

   I   Basketball
      A.   Varsity
      B.   Players

Form 55-2

Sample Outline

Directions: Evaluate the effectiveness of the following outline.

Thesis: Cleveland offers many cultural attractions to visitors.

A Visit to Cleveland

I "North Coast" city
   A. On the shore of Lake Erie
      1. port city
      2. climate affected by the lake
   B. Major transportation center
      1. railroad hub
      2. Hopkins International Airport
      3. national and international visitors

II Restaurants of Cleveland
   A. Pierre's on the West Side
      1. known for its French cuisine
      2. caters to tourists
   B. The Greek Isle downtown
      1. excellent lamb
      2. waiters in white smocks
      3. belly dancer on weekends
   C. Giovanni's on the East Side
      1. spicy spaghetti
      2. extensive wine list
      3. Italian music
      4. Very expensive

III Cultural attractions in Cleveland
   A. Famous museums
      1. Museum of Modern Art
      2. Field Museum of Natural History
      3. Rock-n-Roll Hall of Fame
      4. Science Museum
   B. Performing arts
      1. Art Institute
      2. Cleveland Symphony Orchestra
      3. Karamu Theater
      4. Playhouse Square

IV Professional sports teams
   A. Indians of the American Bseball League
      1. World Series in 1995 and 1997
   B. Cavaliers of the National Basketball Association
      1. made play-offs in 1998

Outlining—Key Points

Directions: Study each of the key points about outlining and then do the checklist for your own outline.

Key point #1

Roman numerals—I, II, III, IV, etc.—indicate the **major topics** of an essay.

Q: How does a writer determine the major topics for an essay?
A: By citing 4-5 main points related to the thesis.

Example: For the thesis: Competitive sports can be harmful to pre-schoolers, the writer asks, *"How can competitive sports be harmful?"* The major topics could be:

  I   Physically
  II Socially
 III Psychologically
 IV Emotionally

Key point #2

Capital letters are used to indicate the **subtopics** for each major topic.

Q: How does a writer determine these for an outline?
A: By relating some examples to the subtopic.

Example: For Major topic I (Physically), the writer creates three subtopics:

   A. Potential injuries
   B. Growth problems
   C. Bruises

Key point #3

Supporting details are indicated by numbers 1, 2, 3, etc. They are **specific examples** that relate directly back to subtopics.

Q: How many are typically necessary for each subtopic?
A: It varies.

(ex) A. Potential injuries
       1. twisting weak ankles
       2. pressure on knees
       3. separated shoulders
       4. broken arms

Form 55-3 (*continued*)

Key point #4

For logical organization, an outline is necessary. An effective outline will help you write the composition. Major topics form the topic sentences of paragraphs of an essay. The subtopics and supporting details form the supporting sentences of the essay's paragraphs.

Key point #5

When writing an outline, avoid using just single words:

(ex) I Population of Cleveland
      A. Italians
      B. Germans
      C. Greeks

Expand these into phrases (not sentences) as often as possible.

(ex) I Ethnic diversity of Cleveland's population
      A. Italians of the East Side
         1. owners of many restaurants
         2. strong presence in the city since early 1900's
      B. German descendants on north side
         1. immigrated here in 1920's
      C. "Greek Town"
         1. famous for annual festivals
         2. strong family backgrounds
         3. prefer Greek language in business dealings

Key point #6

Review your outline after constructing it and use the following checklist: Write Yes/No as appropriate.

_____   Do the major topics reflect the main ideas of the essay?

_____   Are all subtopics directly related to their respective major topics?

_____   Are the supporting details specific examples?

_____   Is the outline arranged in a logical sequence?

_____   Is the outline detailed?

_____   Have you used phrases, not sentences?

_____   Is the *form* correct with the Roman numerals against the left margin and the subtopics and supporting details indented properly?

Types of Outlines

A CHRONOLOGY

Thesis: There were several embarrassing moments during my freshmen year at Richmond Heights High School.

I Opening of school in September
  A. Buying a textbook card
    1. not needed for classes
  B. Getting lost in the hallways
    1. late to classes
II Last football game in October
  A. Ran the wrong way
    1. scored a touchdown for Beachwood
  B. Fumbled five times
  C. Missed eight tackles
III Winter "Snow Festival Dance"
  A. Blind date
    1. never talked to me
    2. refused to dance
  B. Tried to kiss her
    1. kissed her chin
IV Spring time
  A. Only person to fail a math test
    1. felt humiliated
  B. Lost all my textbooks
    1. somewhere after gym class

- Note how each major topic follows in a time-oriented sequence (first to last).

ORDER OF IMPORTANCE

Thesis: There are several advantages to joining the Richmond Heights track team.

I Improving physical abilities
  A. Cardiovascular development
    1. better heart rate
    2. increase in blood cells
  B. Increase in lung capacity
    1. more oxygen to your system
  C. Improved muscle strength
    1. in both hamstrings
II Enjoying the competition
  A. Won 200 meters against Beachwood
  B. Defeated defending conference champion from Solon
  C. Relays
    1. first place at Columbia Relays in 200 and 400 meters

Form 55-4 (*continued*)

III Making new friends
   A. Mike Robinson
      1. shot putter
   B. Danielle Somrak
      1. 100 and 200 meters
   C. Natalie Mitchell
      1. distance runner
IV Learning a better running stride
   A. Stretching my steps
   B. Passing the baton
   C. Sprinting
   D. Leaving the starting blocks
      1. must stay alert to the starter

- Note how each major topic here is one advantage.

Lesson 56 OUTLINE TO FIRST DRAFT

Objective: To draft the research essay

Activities:

1. **Visual aid:** Draw a circle on the board and/or play a video that you play-stop-rewind. The idea is to show that writing a research essay is a *cyclical* process: they may keep going back to earlier parts of the outline or first draft to expand, delete, or move information.

2. **Math:** Tell students they have 1000 words to use in three parts—Introduction, Body, and Conclusion.

    A. How many words will you put in each part?

    B. Now, in the body, you have four parts—background, first main point, second main point, and third main point. How many words will you put in each part here?

    C. Finally, if the essay is six paragraphs, how many words should there be per paragraph?

    [Of course, answers can vary, but look for an equal number in the introduction and conclusion—(ex) one hundred words each—and equal numbers in the body paragraphs—(ex) two hundred words each.]

3. **Model:** Students examine a sample research essay in their text or from a previous student. What are its strengths and weaknesses?

4. **Lecture:** on options for the drafting process:

    A. write *everything* out in a rough form, then revise.

    B. write, revise, and polish each section at a time.

    Also, caution students against using clichés, informal language, contractions, and poor grammar. They should follow their outline as they write.

    Again, students must be prepared to "rewind" and return to an earlier section as they insert research and insights. Essays can be organized under several formats—order of importance, simple to complex, chronological, or chaos. Obviously, students are to avoid the last method.

5. **Writing:** Students write the first draft of the essay—Step #8-9. **Check** their work.

Homework:

Students should also check sample research essays in their grammar text to locate quotes, paraphrases, and summaries.

Lesson 57

PEER EDITING— RESEARCH ESSAY

Objective: To complete effective peer editing of the research essay

Activities:

[Refer to Section 13 for specific instructions on peer editing. This lesson could take 1-2 class periods.]

1. **Group work:** Students exchange first drafts.

   Before exchanging essays, writers should provide at least one prompt question to the reviewers—(ex) "What parts are the most interesting?" or "What parts are unclear?" This gives the reader a focus on the essay.

   Students should exchange essays at least twice to check for possible plagiarism, the use of formal diction, grammar and spelling, and any vagueness or confusion regarding the research.

   Students should also assist each other in determining which research is helpful and which research is off the topic or unnecessary.

   Monitor their work.

2. **Review:** Go over plagiarism.

3. **Explain: Activity 57-1**—Evaluation criteria for the final copy.

4. **Assessment:** Students offer feedback on the assignment and learning activities.

Homework:

Students complete Checklist steps #10-12.

Name _____

Research Essay Final Copy Evaluation Form

Rating: 1 (Weak); 2 (Needs improvement); 3 (Average); 4 (Nearly perfect);
(5) (Excellent work).

Points   **CRITERIA**
                                        Organization

_____   Effective thesis statement
_____   Effective introduction
_____   Effective paragraph development
_____   Paragraph unity
_____   Effective transitions between sentences (coherence)
_____   All sentences relate to the thesis
_____   Logical arrangement of main points
_____   Forceful conclusion

Content

_____   Thorough exploration of the subject
_____   Quality research (and no more than 60% of the essay)
_____   Quality insight (approximately 40%)
_____   The paper accomplishes its objective as stated in the thesis.
_____   Subject matter is presented in an interesting and informative way.
_____   No documentation problems
_____   Diction (no jargon, slang, clichés, etc.)

Bibliography

_____   Proper format—alphabetical, margins, etc.
_____   Appropriate and varied sources
_____   Bibliography page is complete
_____   Correct punctuation on the bibliography page

Grammar

_____   Correct punctuation
_____   Correct spelling
_____   Correct capitalization
_____   Proper sentence structure
_____   Usage
_____   Proofreading

Section 8 : INTERVIEWS

> "A human being is not, in any proper sense, a human being till he is educated."
>
> (*Horace Mann*)

Objectives: Introduce the benefits of interviewing
Explain the characteristics of a successful interview
Prompt students to master the use of quotation marks, the apostrophe, and ellipses
Guide students as they write an article based on an interview

Length: Ten Lessons

Introduction:

Celebrities, athletes, performers—they are the constant focus of news programs and tabloid magazines. The wise teacher can take advantage of the public's fascination with the lives of these persons to introduce interviewing. The best results for this project occur when students can produce a comprehensive list of questions, identify the guidelines for an effective interview, perform the actual interview, and finally transform the answers into an interesting article.

Successful interviewing occurs when there is effective communication, but communication must be more than talking. It also involves careful listening. The teacher needs to deal with how messages are heard and interpreted. Students need, therefore, training in effective listening which also requires an overview of non-verbal communication.

To keep students motivated the teacher has to keep class sessions active and *verbal*. Interviewing can be an enjoyable experience for students once they understand the format (question-answer; ask-listen) of the interview and the biographical style of the article where less interesting details are removed and important ones are highlighted. The interviewer can choose to focus on *one* aspect—(ex) the career, childhood, or hobbies—of the interviewee.

The final article must, of course, contain the quoted replies of the interviewee, but the reader should also be treated to the general observations of the interviewer. These comments should be inserted effectively to enhance the reader's understanding of the person and his/her background. The keys are to get the reader interested in reading about this person and to portray him/her in an honest and thorough manner.

At the end, consider creating a booklet containing all the interviews for distribution to the school administration, library, and students.

Lesson 58

CELEBRITIES, IDOLS, AND HEROES

Objective: To introduce the benefits of interviewing

Activities:

1. **Writing: Activity 58-1**—Students complete it as thoroughly as possible. **Discuss** the results.

2. On the reverse side of the paper students are to make three columns:

   America   *State Name*   *School Name*

   Under each column, they are to **write a list** of 8-10 of the most prominent people in each category.

   For example, the U.S. President, Michael Jordan, or a current top Hollywood actor could be included under America; your governor, any pro athletes, or television personalities under your state; and the principal, all conference athletes, and possibly the school valedictorian in the school column, among others.

   Discuss the results. Students compare, maybe **debate**, their responses.

3. **Freewriting**—Students circle one name from each list whom they would most like to interview and write questions they would like to ask those persons.

   Discuss the questions.

4. **Discussion:** About interviews. [Answers will vary.]
   A. What could be gained from interviewing someone? What could be learned that's important?
   B. What are some of the articles based on interviews you've read in the past?
   C. What are some magazines that frequently have articles based on interviews? Why are they so popular?
   D. What shows on television consistently deal with interviews?
   E. Why is the public so interested in *reading* interviews?
   F. Who is the most famous person you have personally met?

5. **Show pictures:** Display photos of various celebrities, taken from magazines or the newspaper, and **discuss**:

   How are their lives different from yours?

Why are we so interested in the lives of celebrities?

[Answers will vary.]

6. **Freewriting:** How could you become a celebrity?

Homework options:

A. **Identification:** Students locate a magazine article based on an interview that appeals to them and explain the focus of the article and its appeal.

B. **Research:** Students research the circulation numbers of 6-8 different magazines and make a chart documenting their findings. Have them analyze the chart for the magazines that frequently have articles based on interviews.

C. **Listing:** Students select 5-6 different popular magazines and list the special departments and kinds of feature articles (including their titles) for each. They then write 1-2 paragraphs explaining how the writers and editors appeal to their readers.

D. Students do **Activity 58-2.**

Interviewing Celebrities

1. Why do we idolize celebrities?

2. Why are we so interested in the personal lives of celebrities?

3. Who are some celebrities from the previous centuries?

4. What is the connection between fame and success?

5. Why does our society value fame (and the famous) so much?

6. How have criminal acts turned some people into celebrities?

7. Why do we feel inferior, at times, to celebrities?

8. Why is a simple signature so valuable and why do some people wait such a long time to get an autograph?

9. Why are the personal lives of celebrities so fascinating to many people?

10. How has television affected the celebrity status of some people?

Name _____

Magazines and Interviews

Directions: For each category below, list the person (the interviewee) most likely to provide the best information about it and the magazine in which that interview would most likely appear.

	Subject	Person	Magazine
1.	Travel	_____	_____
2.	Astronomy	_____	_____
3.	Engineering	_____	_____
4.	Gardening	_____	_____
5.	Homes	_____	_____
6.	Inventions	_____	_____
7.	Football	_____	_____
8.	Baseball	_____	_____
9.	Basketball	_____	_____
10.	Cosmetics	_____	_____
11.	Camping	_____	_____
12.	Politics	_____	_____
13.	Literature	_____	_____
14.	Theater	_____	_____
15.	Music	_____	_____
16.	Photography	_____	_____
17.	Television	_____	_____
18.	Cooking	_____	_____
19.	Medicine	_____	_____
20.	Education	_____	_____

Lesson 59   SUCCESSFUL INTERVIEWS

Objective: To create an effective relationship between the interviewer and the interviewee

Activities:

1. **Prompts**:

   A. **Videotape:** Play a tape of an interview. Students assess the effectiveness of the interviewer.

   B. **Show a picture:** Display a photo of two people talking. Students guess the focus of the conversation and explain their rationale.

   C. **Role-play:** Students conduct an interview and have the rest of the class critique both the interviewer, (effective questions?) and the interviewee, (sincere, detailed answers?).

   D. **Freewriting**: Students list questions asked at a job interview (many might have first-hand knowledge). Also, students should analyze how a job interview could be less stressful.

   Discuss the results.

2. **Compare**: Put on the board the following headings. Students list what should be expected of both:

Interviewer	*Interviewee*
(ex) Must prepare questions	Must give honest answers
Research subject's past	Should be sincere
Listen closely	Thorough answers
Be polite and listen	Provide the time
Etc.	Etc.

3. **Explain:** Distribute **Form 59-1**—the Guidelines for Successful Interviewing.

4. **Lecture:** On Listening Skills

   - Give yourself adequate time to hear what the interviewee wants to say.

   - Focus intently on what the interviewee says.

   - Repeat the message as you understand it and see if your understanding is correct—for example, "What I hear you saying is . . .".

   - Don't interrupt the interviewee.

   - Hold back any emotional response.

- Active listening, as opposed to passive, silent listening, involves interacting with the interviewee by providing him/her with confirmation that you understand.

- Promote effective communication by emphasizing the importance of good verbal skills, paying attention, and being conscious of non-verbal cues.

5. **Practice:** Students interview the teacher as a class. Each student can ask 1-2 questions.

Homework:

Students transform their interview with the teacher into a 1-2 page article (to be placed eventually in their portfolio).

Guidelines for Successful Interviewing

1. Make an appointment with the interviewee and honor the time limits you agree on.

2. Prepare 12-15 questions beforehand that are focused on *one* area of the interviewee's life.

    (ex) his or her occupation

3. Be ready to ask a follow-up question based on an answer from the interviewee.

    (ex) "You just said you were fired from your first job. Why?"

4. Put your questions in a proper order—Introductory first, Open-ended at the end.

5. Call the day before to confirm the interview.

6. Come prepared—notebook, clipboard, possibly a tape recorder, pen—to the interview.

7. Stay calm during the interview and ask the interviewee to repeat something if you are uncertain. Politely ask for clarification.

8. Jot down key words and phrases—later write the complete sentence. Use quotation marks with exact words.

9. Let the interviewee talk freely. Don't interrupt to get to your next question.

10. Remember: The best interview is a pleasant conversation between two friendly people.

11. Write a thank-you note afterwards.

12. Organize the answers into a detailed article.

13. Consider interviewing others who can give more information about your interviewee.

Lesson 60   TYPE OF INTERVIEW QUESTIONS

Objective: To explain the qualities of effective interview questions

Activities:

1. **Discuss**: Fantasy interviews.

   A. If the principal walked into the room right now, what question would you ask?

   B. If the President of the United States walked in, what would you ask?

   C. If your favorite performer or professional athlete walked in, what would you ask?

2. **Freewriting:** Students write the questions they'd ask any famous individual in history (ex) George Washington—What did it feel like being the first President?

   Discuss the responses.

3. [**Read**: Study if possible, sections from Studs Terkel's book *Working*. Ask students to identify the types of questions Terkel asked these persons.]

4. **Summarize:** The fundamental basis of all learning is asking questions. For example, we ask questions from our doctor, our car mechanic, our travel agent, etc.

5. **Discuss:**

   A. How can you tell a good question from a bad question?

   [A good question leads to a detailed explanation.]

   B. When is a question *too* personal?

   [Anything to do with an interviewee's personal relationships]

   C. What questions might be considered aggressive type questions?

   [When the interviewer asks about religious or political views, questions about morals]

   D. What are some easy subjects to ask about?

   [Family, work, vacations, leisure activities]

6. **Identification:** Students locate direct quotes in magazine or newspaper articles and try to determine the question that might have prompted that quoted statement.

7. **Analysis: Activity 60-1**—the Types of Interview Questions. After each

example question, students should write *one* of their own.

Discuss the results.

8. **Freewrite:** Assign one type of question to different groups of students who then write a list of sample questions based on that type.

Discuss the results.

9. **Discuss: Activity 60-2**—a sample interview. Ask students to identify types of questions used here.

10. **Inquisition.** Here, you need a student who works, a student with siblings, and an athlete. Role-play an inquisition where the inquisitor demands a confession.

Scenario #1:   An employer wants to fire an employee.

Scenario #2:   The older sibling wants to find some missing item.

Scenario #3:   The coach wants to motivate the athlete.

Homework options:

A. Students clip an article written by a syndicated columnist and brainstorm a list of questions they would like to ask him/her. They should staple the article to the page.

B. Students can select another famous person from history and make a list of comprehensive questions they would ask that individual.

C. Hand out a school newsletter or pamphlet for students to read and determine the questions to which the information provides answers.

D. Students must select a foreign city and write a list of questions they'd like to ask a teenager who lives there (the more remote the city is, the better). Direct them to an atlas.

E. Students practice interviewing family members, then write a summary of their *reactions* to being interviewed.

Types of Questions for Interviews

Example focus: Ask about the person's occupation

1. The Introductory Question

This is designed to help the interviewer and interviewee get acquainted and comfortable with each other.

(ex) How long have you been working there?

(ex)

2. The Yes/No Question

This is designed to help the interviewer obtain some basic facts about the interviewee.

(ex) Do you like your job?

(ex)

3. The Personal Question

Questions here relate primarily to the interviewee's family and social life. Interviewers should avoid asking questions that are too personal.

(ex) What jobs do other members of your family have?

(ex)

4. The Probe Question

Questions here require the interviewee to deal with issues or topics that relate to his or her values, morals, or inner beliefs. These questions usually make the interviewee reflect carefully before answering.

(ex) Why is your job important to the community?

(ex)

5. The Open-ended Question

These questions require the interviewee to come up with a theory, prediction, hypothesis, or creative thought. There is great potential here for a variety of answers.

(ex) What kind of job do you think you'll have ten years from now?

(ex)

Sample Interview

Directions: Label each of the interviewer's questions below. Are they Introductory, Yes/No, Personal, Probe, or Open-ended?

Topic: Problems during the lunch period

Q: Do you bring your lunch or buy it?

A: Buy it.

Q: When you buy it, do you notice people breaking into the lunch line?

A: Sure, it happens a lot.

Q: How do you feel about that?

A: I get angry, but I also admire their courage.

Q: Why do you admire their courage?

A: They don't care who's ahead or behind them. They want something to eat, and they want it *now*.

Q: How do you handle it?

A: I might kid around with them or tell them a teacher is watching. You have to use a little psychology.

Q: Do you think there's a way to stop this from happening?

A: No, unless they hire some security people.

Q: What else could they do?

A: I don't know. I guess everyone just accepts it now. Maybe if more people complained, something would be done.

Q: Do you think more people will complain?

A: No. Most people at this school are too nice.

Q: What do you think the lunch line will be like next year?

A: It'll get worse and worse. I can even see someone getting nasty about it and shoving somebody else out of the way. When that happens, they'll have more problems than just someone breaking into the lunch line.

Lesson 61   GUIDELINES FOR INTERVIEWS

Objective: To identify the format of an effective interview

Activities:

1. **Debate:** Challenge students to define the differences between *People* magazine and the *National Enquirer* (both use articles based on interviews). Provoke them by saying there are no differences.

2. **Discuss:** Interviewees [Answers will vary.]

   How do you know when an interviewee is lying?

   If we're just writing what someone says, does it matter if he or she is lying? Why/Why not?

   Why are politicians so often accused of lying?

   How would you encourage your interviewee to be sincere?

   How important are someone's exact statements?

   Why are direct quotes more important than paraphrasing for an article based on an interview?

3. **Lecture:** On dealing with an interviewee. Distribute **Form 61-1.**

4. **"Quickie" interview:** Students take turns briefly interviewing a partner on any one of the following topics:

   A. Favorite school subject

   B. Extra-curricular activities

   C. Recreational activities

   First, give them several minutes just to talk and get comfortable with each other. Next, allow them several minutes to devise 1-2 questions of each type. Finally, allow them time to complete their interviews.

   Assess this activity afterwards by asking students about the problems they had. Any difficulties with quotes?

John Hohenberg, writer for *The Professional Journalist*, declares, "No talking reporter ever had a good interview." Great interviewers should not be interested in showing off their wit but in obtaining the best from the person they're interviewing. Like a good referee at a good sporting event, the interviewer is doing an effective job if the audience hardly notices him.

Homework:

Students need to select an interviewee and make an appointment. Possible selections:

(1) anyone over the age of 60 about their teenage years (possibly make an arrangement with a senior citizen group to serve as interviewees)

(2) someone in a career the interviewer finds interesting

(3) a local celebrity, performer, or musician about his/her career

(4) a local politician about any current issue

(5) another teacher about his/her other occupations outside of teaching

They should also study various magazines, such as *People*, that have articles based on interviews.

"A Week with _____" Project—Students observe a person (family members are acceptable) for one week (five dated entries) and write interesting and detailed descriptions to practice preparing to describe the actual interviewee. Students can also take pictures, use a tape recorder, or create an illustration.

Name _____

Handling the Interviewee—
Ten Suggestions

1. An interview satisfies readers' curiosity: What do they really want to know about the person?

2. Bring to the surface the interviewee's most interesting traits.

3. Do background research about the interviewee *before* the interview.

4. Be sure you and the interviewee both enjoy the experience.

5. Judgmental questions could make the interviewee uneasy. They could become cautious, even defensive, wondering how you are evaluating them at the moment.

6. Don't neglect their physical mannerisms that make up non-verbal communication like head and hand movements, any gestures, and body position.

7. Check their tone of voice as they answer to pick up a cue that a question has made them uneasy.

8. It's wise to note their personal achievements. They have to know that the interviewer cares about them personally. It's also acceptable to highlight their accomplishments in the article.

9. If the interviewee speaks incorrect English you have the discretion to correct bad grammar.

10. Through the interview, ask the interviewee if he/she needs a break.

Lesson 62 TALK SHOW

Objective: To refine skills at interviewing

Activities:

[Students are in groups for each of these activities. This activity takes two class periods.]

1. **Talk Show:** Each group creates a television talk show format by portraying a real (Jay Leno, Oprah Winfrey) or imaginary host. Their guests could be actual celebrities or imaginary persons.

   Students spend one class period preparing the format of the show, the list of questions, and roles of each member.

   Be sure to approve their topics and roles.

   Each talk show has a ten minute time limit.

   The next day, call on each group to perform their talk show (with a fake microphone) and do interviews. Permit the "studio audience" (the rest of the students) to ask good questions, make appropriate comments, or assess the overall effectiveness of the interviews.

2. **Job Interview:** Each group brainstorms a list of jobs for which teenagers typically can apply (landscaper, fast food restaurant, camp counselor, etc.) and then a list of interview questions related to that job.

   Students spend one class period preparing the format of the job interview, writing the questions, and deciding the roles they will have during the interview (ex) manager, president, secretary, etc.

   Be sure to approve their job selection and roles.

   The next day, each group can select one member to volunteer to be the job applicant for another group's job.

   Interviews are conducted with the student applicants first knocking and then entering from outside the classroom.

   The remaining students critique the performance of each interviewee.

Homework:

Students can complete their evaluations of the interviewers and interviewee.

Lesson 63 — DIRECT QUOTE VS. PARAPHRASE

Objective: To master the direct quote, paraphrase, and summary

Activities:

1. **Prompts**—Choose any of the following:

    A. **Cassette tape**—Students write the dialogue or lyrics. Remind them to use quotation marks.

    B. **Identify**—Students locate direct quotes in magazine articles and note the placement of quotation marks.

    C. **Debate**—Should someone who speaks nonstandard English be quoted directly?

    D. **Copying**—Students first copy several sentences from their grammar text, word for word, and apply quotation marks correctly. Second, they must paraphrase these sentences. Third, they must write a summary of the page.

2. **Lecture:** On Quotation Marks

    • Quotation marks go outside all other marks of punctuation.

    • It is **"Sentence. Sentence."** not **"Sentence." "Sentence."** [If two sentences are used together, do not put quotation marks *between* them.]

    • Use direct quotes especially when the interviewee says something provocative or unique.

3. **Text:** Use any exercises in the grammar text to show how the quotation marks are placed in sentences.

4. **Discuss:** Direct Quotes

    A. Why use direct quotes? Why not paraphrase or summarize all of it?

    [For accuracy; if the interviewee says something very provocative or unique; quotes give the article credibility.]

    B. How important are someone's exact statements?

    [Very important; they can help refute possible denials.]

    C. What if the interviewee speaks incorrect English or makes inaccurate statements?

    [This depends; the interviewer must decide to quote the person exactly or edit grammatical errors.]

    D. What are ellipses?

        [The three dots . . . which are used to show an omission in a quote. You might not wish to include all of a single statement.]

5. **Writing:** Students practice paraphrasing/summarizing—**Activity 63-1. Discuss** the results.

6. **Review:** What problems are you having with quotation marks? In what circumstances do you want to use a direct quote? In what circumstances do you want to paraphrase?

Homework:

Students complete the prewriting for their interview and proceed with the interview.

Paraphrasing

Directions: Read the following exchange and paraphrase the comments of both speakers.

Student #1: You are stupid for writing me a note like that. Don't play with me. I don't want to talk to you because you are foolish for writing that stupid note. I am not crazy, you are the one that's crazy, and we should put you in a mental institute.

Student #2: You really want to pick a fight.

Student #1: Oh, my god, you are crazy!!

Student #2: You are the crazy one. I am not trying to pick a fight! Oh please, who do you think you are?

Your Paraphrase:

ARTICLES

Objective: To evaluate the effectiveness of articles based on interviews

Activities:

1. **Discussion:** Consider sample interviewees. [Answers will vary.]
   A. What would be a creative title for an interview with George Washington, our first President?
   B. What are the more prominent features of _____ [a selected celebrity]?
   C. What background details would you include about our President?
   D. How would you describe your favorite relative?

2. **Explain:** Discuss inserting background details—job, hobbies, history—about an interviewee. These are as important as the interviewee's quotes.

   Typical faults in articles have been too much paraphrasing and not enough direct quotes, and neglecting to organize the information and to have a concluding paragraph.

3. **Discussion:** Call on each student to offer one specific background detail about his/her interviewee. Also ask:
   A. What important things has your person done?
   B. To whom could you compare this person?
   C. What makes this person important?
   D. Who else could give you background details about your interviewee?

4. **Analysis:** Study of an article based on an interview.

   Deal with the "hook"—the catchy beginning, the type of information presented, the quotes, and the general positive and negative qualities of the article—Use **Activity 64-1**—the Marc Robinson interview.

   Discuss the results.

5. **Explain: Form 64-2**—Interview Article Checklist.

Homework:

Students complete the first draft of their article based on an interview.

Name _____

Marc Robinson—Varsity Basketball Player

Directions: Evaluate the effectiveness of the article below based on the interview of Marc Robinson.

Born May 18, 1975, Marc Robinson has grown to 6'6", 210 pounds and is the best varsity basketball player at Richmond Heights High School. In fact, he has been the best player at all of the schools he has attended and looks forward to playing in college.

Marc started playing basketball when he was fourteen because everyone else was playing. "In middle school," Marc says, "we had tryouts, and that was tough at first. But later all the guys who made the team had a lot of unity because we were friends before we were teammates."

Anfernee Hardaway is his favorite player, and Marc says he's learned a lot from watching professionals play. "I think I've learned how to break a press, run a fast break, and how to penetrate better from watching them."

His other idol is Michael Jordan (surprised?). Marc explains, "When Jordan was a sophomore he got cut from the varsity but never gave up. Now, he's a star."

Marc has also been motivated by his older sister Kim, who encouraged him to try out the first time and Coach Bernhardt, who "noticed [his] potential and took [him] to summer basketball camp."

Marc already has been named 1st Team All-Conference as a junior. This is his last year, and he hopes to bulk up and make 1st Team All-State.

Name _____

Interview Article Checklist

1. _____ Do I have a creative title and strong diction in the body?

2. _____ Do I have a catchy introduction with a thesis at its end?

3. _____ Have I avoided using the interviewee's name to begin most sentences?

4. _____ Have I included the interviewee's physical appearance?

5. _____ Have I described any gestures or mannerisms that are particular to the interviewee?

6. _____ Is the article detailed and well-organized?

7. _____ Is there a balance between paraphrasing and direct quotes? And have I selected the best quotes?

8. _____ Does the article reflect just one aspect of the interviewee's life?

9. _____ Is all the information accurate?

10. _____ Is there a strong concluding paragraph?

Lesson 65   DESCRIBING THE INTERVIEWEE

Objective: To describe the interviewee effectively with both literal and figurative language

Activities:

1. **Prompts:**
   A. **Pantomime:** Either you or volunteer students act out any specific action (ex) typing, washing hands, exercising.

      Students **write,** describing the mime's appearance and gestures.

   B. **Describe a classmate**—Students select one classmate in the room and list that person's outstanding features, without naming the person.

   C. **Identification:** Students use their literature text to locate descriptions of story characters to copy onto their paper.

   D. **Definitions:** Students define the following words related to describing human behavior and then use them in sentences to describe people they know.

contemptuous	*flippant*	*ingenuous*
obsequious	*querulous*	*taciturn*

   E. **Writing:** Students identify the personality of an interviewee. Use **Activity 65-1—Psychology and Description.**

   Discuss the results.

2. **Lecture:** Discuss describing a person. Focus especially on:
   - head and hand movements and gestures
   - style of clothes
   - hairstyle
   - tone of voice
   - attitude

Homework:

Students expand their first drafts with added description. They should also allow the interviewee to check the draft to be sure it contains accurate information and quotes.

247

Name _____

Psychology and Description

Directions: Read each statement regarding psychology and then answer each question in detail.

1. Some sports psychologists call this "burn out." Other terminology is "mental fatigue" and "getting stressed out."

   How would a coach who is experiencing this behave?

2. When we feel stress, most of us try to hide our anxiety.

   What would be the facial features of someone trying to hide his/her feelings of anxiety?

3. Typically, each day we hear someone else complain.

   What would be the head, hand, and body gestures of someone who is complaining?

4. Fear is one of our worst emotions.

   What would be the head, hand, and body gestures of someone who is experiencing fear?

5. Anger is one of our most intense emotions.

   What would be the head, hand, and body gestures of someone who is angry?

6. Meditation is one of the most common forms of relaxation.

   What would be the description of someone who is relaxing through some form of meditation?

Lesson 66

PEER EDITING AND PUBLISHING— INTERVIEW ARTICLE

Objective: To work cooperatively in editing classmates' first drafts

Activities:

[More specific activities for peer editing can be found in Section 13—Peer Editing.]

1. **Group work:** Peer Editing

    A. By turn, each student explains what he/she found most fascinating about his/her interviewee. Other group members note this information (in writing, if necessary) to see if it is highlighted in the article.

    B. Group members exchange first drafts (at least twice).

    C. Students critique each other's articles by:

        1. marking sentences that demonstrate or lack effective description of the interviewee

        2. putting question marks by any passages that remain confusing

        3. putting check marks on strong diction and underlining weak word choice

        4. circling misspelled words or punctuation errors, especially those with quotation marks

        5. commenting on the effectiveness of the introduction and conclusion

    D. Drafts are returned to writers who then can ask any questions on the marks/comments made by other group members.

    Monitor their work.

2. **Discuss:** Publishing the articles—Options:

    A. Produce a class magazine containing all the articles to distribute to the school administration, parents, community members, and student body.

    B. Publish 1-2 articles per month in the school newsletter, especially if these articles profile any members of the teaching staff or administration.

    C. Submit the articles to a community newspaper or local magazine.

    D. Submit them to the media guides of area businesses, if the articles profile any personnel associated with that company or business.

E. Create your own media guide(s), grouping articles of similar content to be distributed to any interested subscribers.

F. Include them with the thank you letter to the interviewee and ask for a response.

Homework:

Students complete the revising and editing of their first drafts and type the final copy of their article based on an interview.

Lesson 67 GUEST SPEAKER

Objective: To summarize and/or quote the comments of the guest speaker and to review all skills related to successful interviewing

Activities:

[This lesson can be done at any time during the unit.]

1. **Guest Speaker:** Invite a newspaper reporter, local radio or television broadcaster, freelance writer, and/or media publicist to speak about interviewing.

    [This could also be done in a panel discussion format where you have several speakers who offer their suggestions for completing successful interviews.]

    Students should be prepared to ask questions and take notes on the comments made by the speaker.

Homework:

Students summarize the comments and suggestions made by the guest speaker(s) and explain their reaction to the presentation.

Section 9 : THE NEWS

"Jails and prisons are the complement of schools; so many less as you have of the latter, so many more you must have of the former." *(Horace Mann)*

Objectives: Cite a definition of news

Prompt students to evaluate news sources and news writing

Identify the 5 W's and news writing formats

Explain the duties of a news editor

Explore the privacy issue related to news reporting

Make clear distinctions between facts and opinions in any news story

Guide students as they write a news article

Length: Approximately ten lessons

Introduction

What makes watching television news or reading a newspaper difficult for some students? Often, the answers are that they don't have the time, aren't interested, or find no benefit in knowing current events. To get students actively involved in the subject of news writing and news reporting, we teachers need to introduce first the importance of knowing the news and, second, the appeal of being a news reporter.

Students usually come to recognize the relevance of news when they can detect its connection to their lives or age group. Once they see the drama in every day news stories and how those events can affect their lives, they become more involved. Stimulate their interest with carefully selected news articles. Encourage their curiosity with dramatizations, field trips, and dialogues. These practical experiences give students a hands-on approach to learning the material.

This unit provides great opportunity for individualized instruction as students seek their own news events. The teacher, in turn, learns along with the students, functioning now more as an editor than as an instructor. Newspapers and news magazines, though used here in English class, can also supplement their history, geography, and science lessons. Moreover, students can be challenged to become more involved in the world outside the classroom.

Finally, publishing a class newspaper, newsletter, or news magazine leads to cooperative learning and increased awareness in the journalism process. Ultimately, both reading and writing skills improve. This class newspaper, newsletter, or news magazine can then be distributed in the school community, giving students a genuine audience for their writing.

Lesson 68   WHAT'S NEW(S) TODAY?

Objective: To introduce the importance of news articles

1. **Freewriting:** Discover what students know already about news writing with the following surveys—**Activity 68-1** and **Activity 68-2.**

    Discuss the responses.

> Although they may pay great attention to the daily sports page, the MTV newscast, or tabloid-style television shows, students are often not truly familiar with the aspects of news reporting or writing. Indeed, they may love an investigative report on a celebrity but have no idea about the actual work done by the reporter to compose that news article. It is up to the teacher to introduce this to them.

2. **Identification:** Students examine news magazines or newspapers, if available, to identify their topics and the writer's "angle" or *attitude* about the topic.

3. **Lecture:** News should be defined as "major and recent events that affect the majority of people."

    *   What is meant by *major*?

    [The news item is so important it affects the economic, political, or social well-being of the public.]

    *   What determines the *majority of people*?

    [Newspaper, radio and television companies consider the demographics of their audience and cater to their needs and interests. The "majority" for the *Akron Beacon Journal* will differ from that of the *New York Times*.]

4. **Discussion:** Talk about newspapers and news magazines.

    [Answers will vary.]

    A. How often do you read newspapers or news magazines?
    B. What are some popular news magazines and newspapers?
    C. Why are newspapers and news magazines important news sources?
    D. What sections of either one appeal to you? Why?
    E. Why do newspapers seem to focus so much on tragedies?

F. News reporters and broadcasters are sometimes said to be cynical (negative) people. Why?

G. What if news reporting and broadcasting ceased to exist?

H. Television news vs. written news—Compare and contrast these two news sources.

Homework options:

A. Students locate news articles that focus on teenagers. They clip these articles, staple/tape them to a paper, and then summarize them in a paragraph.

B. Students clip ten headlines from newspapers or news magazines to evaluate—Do they attract the reader's attention? Are they part of an effective lead? How do they announce the news event? Then students can create their own news headlines.

C. Students research the front pages of various local and national newspapers and analyze the content of their articles in general.

D. Students examine any section of a newspaper, news magazine, or news broadcast and chart the stories: use a summary of the content, number of words or minutes, level of interest, etc.

E. Students make a chart and beneath each of the following headings they list the headlines of the articles related to that heading that appear in any newspaper or news magazine they choose. The categories are Politics, Economy, Celebrities, Sports, and Education.

F. Students do a poll of family, friends, other teachers, etc.—What are their favorite magazines and newspapers? Then students analyze the results of the poll in 1-2 paragraphs.

Name _____

What Do You Know About News?

Directions: Answer each question in detail.

1. Who determines what is published or broadcast as news?

2. What are the most popular news magazines?

3. Who are the most popular news broadcasters?

4. What are some current news topics?

5. What were the major news topics six months ago?

6. What might you anticipate being the major news topic six months in the future?

7. Where would you find an article about a teenage shoplifter?

8. Where would you find an article about a teenage chess master?

9. Why are newspapers arranged into sections?

10. How can we be certain the news we receive is accurate?

11. List from the most common to the least common, the ways people learn the news.

12. How would you define *news*?

Name _____

Headlines

Directions: Rate the following headlines from Most Important to Least Important
(1–10)

_____ **8 treated in school bus crash**

_____ **Madison teen wins spelling bee with 'wapentake'**

_____ **Bombing suspect confesses**

_____ **Gretzky scores hat trick in playoffs**

_____ **Legislators delay road work bill**

_____ **Man gets six months in jail for making bombs**

_____ **Condo development planned for inner city**

_____ **President vetoes welfare bill**

_____ **Polish WW II vet recalls comrades**

_____ **Storm socks East Coast**

Objective: To identify and define the five W's

Activities:

1.   **Surveys:** A.   What are the five W's of news writing?

   [WHO = Who is the news story about?
   WHAT = What happened to them?
   WHERE = Where did the event happen?
   WHEN = When did the event happen?
   WHY = Why is this event important or Why did it happen?]

   B.   Rank them in order of importance.

   [Answers will vary]

   C.   Which one is the most difficult for the news writer to learn?

   [Why]

   D.   Which one is most often missing from news articles in general?

   [Why]

   E.   Where can the reader expect to find the 5 W's in a typical news story?

   [First paragraph, opening comments]

   Discuss the responses.

2.   **Identification:** Students locate the five W's in various newspaper and news magazine articles.

3.   **Explain:** Present the format and structure of a typical news article.

   Consider it as an inverted pyramid.

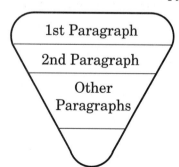

1st Paragraph	- Who, What, Where, When
2nd Paragraph	- Why
Other Paragraphs	- Quotes from authorities, background details

- Names (people) first

- The "Lead" = opening sentence = five W's

- Followed by a description of the news event

- Any direct quotes from authorities?

- Brevity very important—avoiding wordiness (inches on a newspaper or in a news magazine article)

4. **Analysis:** Sample news article—Ask: What are the five W's? Use **Activity 69-1.**

5. **Discuss:** News writing

   A. What is the function of a headline?

   [To identify article content; generate an interest in the article]

   B. How are news stories unlike fictional stories in terms of format?

   [Fiction does not follow the five W's format; these stories can resemble each other, however, sometimes in feature articles.]

   C. Why do reporters in straight news articles avoid using first person references?

   [It is not standard procedure or part of news writing style.]

6. **Write:** Revise a poorly written news article—**Activity 69-2.**

   Check the results. Possibly do **oral reading** of the better revised articles.

Homework options:

   A. Students locate a typical news article, clip it and staple it to a paper, and analyze it for the five W's.

   B. Students compare and contrast their school newspaper with the local newspaper in terms of news content and structure.

   C. Students make a chart of the articles that appear in any news magazine or newspaper to document the articles that appear under the following headings: Straight news, Feature articles, Editorials, and Business.

Identifying the Five W's

Directions: Read the following actual news articles and then identify the five W's for each.

**Rocket launcher found
in school locker**

SHEFFIELD: A Brookside High School freshmen is on suspension after school officials found a rocket launcher in his locker.

The 66-millimeter rocket launcher, a military anti-tank weapon was discovered Monday, according to asst. principal Charles Krepop.

Krepop said he is waiting for a report from Sheffield police on whether or not the weapon is operable before deciding if he'll recommend the student be suspended.

Who _____

_____

What _____

_____

When _____

_____

Where _____

_____

Why _____

_____

Bad perm nets $837

LONGVIEW: A woman was awarded $837.29 for a bad perm she got at a local hair salon. Laura Boyer sued Regis Hairstylists for $2500, citing the cost of buying conditioners and other products to tame her frizzy locks for the next two years. A small claims court judge ruled in her favor last week.

"I sued for $2500, and he gave me $837," Boyer said. "I don't think he realizes how much a girl's hair means to her. I look like a bad poodle."

Who _____

_____

What _____

_____

When _____

_____

Where _____

_____

Why _____

_____

Directions: Evaluate the following news article and then rewrite it following the correct format.

Storms Assault Southwest

There were a lot of tornadoes in several states like Texas, Arkansas, and Oklahoma. A high school gym roof was blown off after 100 mph winds hit it. I don't think they had high school the next day.

Three people were killed when a tornado hit a place called Fordyce, Arkansas. It's really sad when that happens. Another town in Arkansas called Neosho had a lot of property damage that some said would cost about one million dollars to fix.

Back in Texas, mobile homes did not have a chance. Power lines fell. Utility poles also fell. Then crews had to go out and clean everything up. It must have taken them a long time to do it.

By the way, four eighteen wheel trucks were hurled on top of a building in Oklahoma.

Your version:

Lesson 70   FACTS VS. OPINIONS IN THE NEWS

Objective: To distinguish between facts and opinions in news reporting

Activities:

1. **Prompts:**
   A. **Visual aid:** Show a videotape of any typical 6:00 PM news broadcast and ask students to point out any examples of the broadcasters expressing an opinion. Be sure to observe facial expressions as well. Have 1-2 students chart the frequency.
   B. **Survey:** Poll students—Who thinks news reporters—whether from newspapers, magazines, radio stations, or television stations—should never express their opinions as reporters? Why?
   C. **Knowledge check:** On facts and opinions. Students **write** on the following:
      1. Define Fact
      2. Cite two facts
      3. Define Opinion
      4. Make two opinions
      5. Explain: Between the two facts and the two opinions, which one do you find to be most meaningful or important? Why?
   D. **Write:** Do facts lead to opinions or do opinions lead to facts? Explain this relationship.
   E. **Debate:** Which are more important—facts or opinions? We hardly deal with facts, but express opinions all day—why is that? Between facts and opinions, which are more meaningful?
   F. **Role-play:** Two students have a real conversation where neither one of them is permitted to express an opinion.

   Discuss the results of any of the options.
2. **Lecture:** On Facts and Opinions.
   - Fact = something that actually happened; reality. These can be proven true or false.
   - Opinion = a belief not based on actual knowledge or certainty.
   - There is nothing wrong with opinions. There *is* something wrong with opinions that are not supported by facts or a reliable source.

3. **Identification:** Students examine selected news articles for statements that are the reporter's opinions.

4. **Discuss:** Opinions in news reporting.

   A. How should we evaluate news reporter's opinions?

   [Check how authoritative the source is. Is this person an expert on the subject? Is it supported by clear evidence?]

   B. How could opinions, which are based on fact, cause harm to someone?

   [Consider politicians being voted out of office; pro athletes getting cut or traded; the effect on some school finances; etc.]

   C. How can the public respond to an opinion expressed in a newspaper or news broadcast?

   [Letter to the editor; call in; speak at neighborhood meetings, etc.]

   D. What kind of news writing has *no* opinions expressed?

   [Straight news articles (ex) crimes; box scores in the sports section; school board meetings; etc.]

   E. What kind of news writing has *many* opinions expressed?

   [Feature articles, editorials, reviews of movies and theater, op-ed pieces, etc.]

Homework options:

A. Students become investigative reporters who locate the abuse of opinions in news reporting. Clip and analyze selected articles.

B. Students videotape several television news programs to document the anchorpersons expressing opinions.

C. Students analyze the textbooks used in their other classes for opinions being expressed by the editors and authors, especially in history textbooks.

D. Students chart their conversations over a one day period to cite the number of opinions they hear over that period.

Lesson 71   OUR RIGHT TO PRIVACY

Objective: To determine a person's right to privacy vs. rights of news reporter

1. **Freewriting:** On celebrities—**Activity 71-1** and the privacy issue—**Activity 71-2.**

    Discuss the results.

2. **Review:** Facts vs. Opinions in the news. [Answers will vary.]

    A. How do tabloids violate celebrities' privacy?

    B. How can we distinguish between accuracy and falsehood in a tabloid article about a celebrity?

    C. What are the differences between facts and opinions?

    D. What have been some major news articles involving celebrities?

    E. How would you feel about being the focus of an article in a tabloid?

    F. How could a news (newspaper, radio, or television) reporter's failure to distinguish between a fact and an opinion cause harm to someone else?

3. **Explain:** Libel and Slander.

    Libel = any false written or printed statement that seriously damages a person's reputation or exposes a person to public ridicule.

    Slander = false oral comments that seriously damage a person's reputation or expose a person to public ridicule.

4. **Writing:** Students react to the results of libel cases on **Activity 71-3— Libel Cases.**

    Discuss the reactions.

5. **Discussion:** How would you react to a statement—either written or oral—that harmed either directly or indirectly your reputation or status?

6. **Identification:** Students examine selected news articles for statements that are the reporter's opinions. **Check** their work.

Homework options:

A. Students research the term *sensationalism*, introduced to news reporting by tabloids and newspapers in the late 19th century and continued through the 1930s. They should locate and describe several examples of "Yellow Journalism" which sensationalized crimes, disasters, and scandals.

B. Students evaluate one day's news: What is the top story? How do several news sources treat it? What are the facts and opinions mentioned about it?

C. Students research one news event from history (ex) the bombing of Pearl Harbor. How did several news sources treat it? What were the facts and opinions about it?

D. Students do a survey, polling at least fifty persons on their preferences for facts or opinions in the news. They should create a chart and do an analysis of the data.

E. Students study tabloids, both written and televised. How do they excite and arouse the interest of the audience in terms of their news subjects, language, and techniques?

Privacy and the Press

Directions: Complete the following survey.

1. List those persons either by name or title who deserve to be in the news regularly (ex) the President.

2. List ways these celebrities could protect their privacy.

3. What aspects of a person's life should *not* be in the news?

4. How could a news article harm a celebrity?

5. What could make you suddenly the focus of a news article?

6. How can we be certain the published news about a celebrity is accurate?

Quotes on Privacy

Directions: Evaluate each of the following quotes from non-celebrities dealing with the issue of privacy. Write your response below each quote.

1. "People should have a right to privacy. If they don't want it known, it shouldn't be told."

2. "The press should mind their own business and not everyone's personal life where it could affect the person for life."

3. "It's your fault for being in the news—it's a risk you have to take."

4. "People have a right to privacy no matter what. It is given to us in the Constitution. What is done behind closed doors is that person's business unless it affects society and the citizens of the United States as a whole."

5. "People deserve limited privacy. News should be printed only if it is important, not just to make news."

6. "The public has the right to know what the government is doing to us."

7. "We all have a right to privacy unless it affects the majority of the people."

8. "Everybody should have a right to privacy because it is one of our main human rights. News should publish facts about a person only if he allows them to do so."

Name _____

Libel Cases

1. Actress Carol Burnett sued the *National Enquirer* and won $1.6 million (she wanted $10 million) in 1981 after the tabloid claimed she was drunk and "boisterous" in a restaurant. The editor knew the source was unreliable but printed it anyway.

   Why do you think the editor did this?

2. In 1987, Jerry Falwell, minister and leader of the Moral Majority, sued *Hustler* magazine for its cartoon depicting him having sex with his mother in an outhouse. He won $200,000 for "emotional distress" in a lower court but the U.S. Supreme Court eventually ruled in favor of Larry Flynt, publisher of *Hustler*.

   Whom do you think deserved to win this case? Why?

3. Oprah Winfrey filed a $300 million libel suit in a U.S. District Court in Chicago against the tabloid *News Extra* which claimed her then fiancee had sex with a male cousin.

   Why do you think Ms. Winfrey sued for so much money?

4. Convicted serial killer Randy Kraft filed a $60 million lawsuit against Warner Books and author Dennis McDougal, arguing that McDougal's book *Angel of Darkness* defamed him when it called him a "sick, twisted man." He was on death row for the torture and murder of 16 men.

   How should the court treat a case like this?

Lesson 72   GUEST SPEAKER

Objective: To learn the craft of news writing and reporting in greater depth

Activities:

1. **Guest Speaker:** Invite a local newspaper reporter, freelance writer, radio newscaster, or television news broadcaster to address the class.

2. **Discussion:** Students should come to class with a list of questions about news reporting and/or news writing. They might also inquire about the speaker's background.

Homework:

Students summarize the comments made by the guest speaker.

Lesson 73   DRAFTING THE NEWS ARTICLE

Objective: To draft the news article

Activities:

1. **Writing:** Students work on their own news articles, choosing to write a straight news article, a feature article, or an editorial.

   [Teacher should write an article as well.]

2. **Explain:** Discuss the articles. Articles should be 4–6 paragraphs (8–14 sentences each), and approximately 100 words; they should also be about current news events.

   Conference: Confer with students to monitor their work.

3. **Discuss:** Examine each section—sports, local, business, etc. in preparation for grouping the students' news articles together into a class newspaper.

4. **Modeling:** Use some straight news, features, and editorials from various newspapers and news magazines for students to examine as they write.

Homework:

Students complete the writing of their news article.

Lesson 74

PEER EDITING—NEWS ARTICLE

Objective: To engage in successful peer editing

Activities:

[More detailed information about peer editing is in Section 13.]

1. **Group work**: Students as editors—warm-up activities:

   A. Students examine actual, current news articles—straight news, features, and editorials—taken from a local newspaper, to make comparisons to their own.

   B. Students review the sections of a newspaper and decide where each article from their classmates belongs.

   C. Groups examine and revise headlines written on the board:

      GAME IS WON IN LAST MINUTE

      MEETING OF THE STUDENT COUNCIL

      THERE ARE TEN NEW STUDENTS IN __name__ SCHOOL.

      [Note: headlines should be specific, have active verbs, omit punctuation end marks, and leave out articles and conjunctions. See below:

      GIRLS' BASKETBALL TEAM WINS IN LAST MINUTE

      STUDENT COUNCIL MEETS

      TEN NEW STUDENTS ENROLL]

   D. Students exchange articles and begin editing.

      Articles are exchanged at least twice for group members to proofread and edit, especially for wordiness and the five W's.

      Group members ensure that each article has a good headline. (These normally have no articles or conjunctions).

      Groups discuss each article in turn, offering other suggestions for improvement. (Did the article follow the inverted pyramid format? Did it use any quotes from authorities? Is the article complete?)

Homework:

Students make revisions in their news articles to produce a typed final copy.

Lesson 75   CLASS NEWSPAPER

Objective: To organize a class newspaper or news magazine and review all aspects of news writing

Activities:

1. **Survey:** Discover how many students in the class would be interested in organizing and publishing a class newspaper, newsletter, or news magazine. Decide which of these formats to use if the majority of the class shows interest. If students show no interest, proceed to activity #3.

2. **Discussion:** Talk about publishing a class news magazine or newspaper (possibly arrange student committees).

   A.   Once published, how could we distribute it in our school and town?

   [Sell and distribute during lunch periods; distribute through city hall, possibly local stores]

   B.   Marketing the publication? Selling price?

   [Advertising—posters in hallway, flyers, announce it in high school newsletter, set up a stand in lobby for before school; use school public address or announce in homerooms]

   [Cost? Fifty cents/Twenty-five cents—The first one could be free to encourage more response; it could be a possible fund raiser; volunteer(s) might work with school treasurer]

   C.   How could we arrange for subscriptions?

   [Market it by word of mouth; give it to relatives, talk to other students about it; subscriptions could be ordered from a form stapled inside the magazine; put order form in school newsletter; sign up people for subscriptions]

   D.   What about pictures, ClipArt, graphics?

   [Responses will vary.]

   E.   Types of articles? Any limits on subject matter?

   [Responses will vary.]

   F.   Its title?

   [Brainstorm titles and put them on the blackboard; then students vote to decide the title.]

   G.   Due date for submissions?

   [Determine a reasonable due date.]

    H.   Present to principal, superintendent, and Board of Education?

        [Seek volunteers to give copies to these administrators and to local businesses that support the schools.]

    I.   What supplies do we need?

        [Paper, possible computer-generated graphics, etc.]

    J.   Typing of articles?

        [Seek student volunteers to type during study hall or class time.]

    K.   What can be gained from this experience?

        [Accomplishment, satisfaction, getting published, and contributing a publication to the school]

    L.   How would you feel about being published?

        [Answers will vary.]

3. **Write:** Which is the most accurate summary of today's news? Students react to the journalists' definitions—**Activity 75-1.**

    Discuss the responses.

4. **Read:** Have students read **Form 75-2—News Trivia.** Then ask students to respond. What did they find most interesting?

5. **Discuss:** Today's students and the news. [Answers will vary.]

    A.   One study reveals that Americans ages 18-29 care less about the news than any generation in the past fifty years. Why is that?

    B.   How important is it for students (and the public) to monitor the news?

    C.   How can reading the newspaper benefit you in your education?

    D.   How can reading the newspaper benefit you in your career?

    E.   How can reading the newspaper benefit you if you are an athlete?

    F.   The population segment that favored newspapers most consistently was the age group of married people over the age of 65. Why is that?

    G.   How could newspapers and news magazines be helpful in all school subjects?

6. **Debate:** What is the most important news story this week?

7. **Summary:** Review news reporting and writing.

- News reporters and editors are always making choices about the news story they want to publish.

- Presenting the news in a clear, factual way is their most important duty as they focus on the five W's.

- Some reporters and publications, like tabloids, at times abuse the use of opinions or false information in the news.

- Newspapers, news magazines, and news broadcasters will always try to appeal to the interests and needs of their audience.

- In a democracy, it is very important to stay informed about public affairs, especially by using news sources of all types.

- Reading newspapers and news magazines can be very beneficial to a person's educational and recreational interests.

Homework:

Students select one assignment to show their mastery of news writing and reporting.

Students begin work on making their own class newspaper.

Name _____

What Is News?

Directions: The following definitions have been written by professionals in the field. Write a reaction to each one.

1. "News is the honest and unbiased and complete accounts of events of interest and concern to the public."

2. "News is not what happened. It's what someone says has happened."

3. "News is not reality, but a sampling of the portrayal of reality by sources."

4. "News is an institutional method of making information available to consumers."

5. "News is not what some journalists think, but what sources say."

News Trivia

1. The first woman reporter—**Margaret Fuller** in 1840 for the *New York Tribune*
2. Words most commonly used in headlines: *cop, kill, judge, death, Wall Street, no, slay, U.S., Soviet, court*
3. **President Warren G. Harding** was first publisher of the *Marion Star.*
4. Senator (later President) **Lyndon Johnson** threatened young reporter **Dan Rather** in 1955 right before a news conference, calling him a "rude pissant."
5. **John Chancellor**, an NBC reporter, was arrested on camera at the 1964 Republican National Convention.
6. In 1986 the Soviet KGB arrested American reporter **Nicholas Daniloff** of the *U.S. News and World Report* and charged him with spying.
7. *New York World* publisher **Joseph Pulitzer** was forced to hide out at sea on his yacht in fear of being arrested by government agents sent by **President Theodore Roosevelt.**
8. *Publick Occurences Both Forreign and Domestick*—first newspaper (1690) to appear in the American colonies. The *Boston News Letter* (1700's) was the first newspaper printed in a major metropolitan area in the colonies. The *News Letter* was usually six months to one year behind in its news stories.
9. "Blackout"—This term is used to describe the news media's refusal to publish or broadcast a story. Some prominent examples:

    A. **John F. Kennedy's** adultery with **Marilyn Monroe**
    B. Televangelist **Jim Baker's** adultery with **Jessica Hahn** (It took three years before the story became public.)
    C. America's secret spy plane flights over the Soviet Union (The *New York Times* knew about it but chose not to print it until one plane was shot down in 1960.)
    D. **Martin Luther King's** adulteries
    E. Congressman **Wilbur Mills'** alcoholism and affairs

10. Famous news reporters—past and present: **Walter Winchell, Edgar Allan Poe, Walter Cronkite, Ronald Reagan, H.L. Mencken, Dick Van Dyke, David Hartman, Mariette Hartley, Florence Henderson, Mike Wallace, Dan Rather, David Brinkley, Chet Huntley, Barbara Walters**
11. **Walter Winchell** continually described **Adolph Hitler** in his 1930's news reports as a homosexual.
12. **Nellie Bly (Elizabeth Cochran)** was assigned to travel around the world by the *New York World* in eighty days in 1889 (in an imitation of Jules Verne's novel). She did it in seventy-two, which was termed "lightning travel."
13. The first newspaper interview in the United States was with a prostitute. It appeared in 1836 in **James Gordon Bennett's** *New York World.*
14. In 1835, the *New York Sun* reported the existence of life on the moon.
15. In 1980 people urged CBS news anchor **Walter Cronkite** to run for President.
16. Famous publishers—past and present:

    E.W. Scripps (founded newspapers in Chicago and in Philadelphia), **Adolph Ochs** *(New York Times)*, **Frank Munsey** (major publisher in New York City),

Frank Gannett (owner of a giant newspaper chain), **Joseph Pulitzer** *(New York World* in late 1800's), **William Randolph Hearst** *(New York Journal in* 1890's), **Rupert Murdoch** *(London Sun),* **Horace Greeley** *(New York Tribune),* **Benjamin Franklin** *(Pennsylvania Gazette)*

17. **Merriman Smith** of the United Press International had a fist fight with **Jack Bell** of the Associated Press for the use of a car phone right after the assassination of **President Kennedy. Smith** got the phone and won a **Pulitzer Prize** for his story.

18. A 1941 *Chicago Tribune* editorial declared: "Japan cannot attack us. This is a military impossibility. Even our base at Hawaii is beyond the striking power of her fleet."

19. In the 1700's a normal gift from a man to a woman he was courting was a newspaper.

20. **Dan Rather** experimented with heroin and marijuana in order to develop a story on drug use.

21. As of 1986 *Rolling Stone* and the *Los Angeles Herald* drug test their writers.

22. Studies of television news audiences say most people are interested in **flames, blood, and sex.**

23. The country's major news services are the **Associated Press, United Press International, Knight News Service.** The country's top newspapers: *Washington Post, New York Times, USA Today, Chicago Tribune, National Enquirer.*

24. Researchers at the University of California at Berkeley discovered that 51% of the people interviewed directly after a newscast could not remember a single story.

25. First President to appear on television: **Franklin D. Roosevelt;** First President to distribute press releases: **William McKinley** (1897-1901); First President to allow television cameras at a news conference: **Dwight Eisenhower** (1953); First President to allow live broadcast of a news conference: **John F. Kennedy** (1961); First President to meet with reporters in groups: **Grover Cleveland** (1885)

26. Coverage of an antiwar protest in October, 1967 was described as follows:

Washington Post	50,000 protesters
Time	35,000 protesters
Wall Street Journal	2500 protesters

27. New York newspapers through the years:

New York American	*New York Daily News*
New York Daily Times	*New York Evening Mail*
New York Evening Post	*New York Evening World*
New York Graphic	*New York Herald*
New York Herald Tribune	*New York Journal*
New York Journal American	*New York Journal of Commerce*
New York Mercury	*New York Morning Telegraph*
New York Post	*New York Review*
New York Star	*New York Sun*
New York Times	*New York Tribune*
New York Weekly Journal	*New York World*
New York World Telegram	*New York World Journal Tribune*

28. **George Washington** became publisher of a newspaper in New Jersey in order to get news to the people about his troops' victories during the Revolutionary War.

Section 10 : LETTER WRITING

"Letters should be easy and natural, and convey to the persons to whom we send just what we would say if we were there with them."
(Lord Chesterfield)

Objectives: Affirm the importance of letters today

Define the types and parts of letters

Encourage students to appreciate letter writing

Enlighten students on the U.S. Postal Service

Review the types of diction expected in letters

Length: Ten lessons

Introduction:

Establishing a formal, business relationship with someone outside the school is difficult for most students. Because they have more informal interactions with others than formal, students often are unclear about communicating and corresponding in the business community. Whether they are seeking employment or requesting information about a product, they are unfamiliar about the correct, professional approach. Phone call? Letter? Resumé?

This unit eliminates this confusion and introduces students to the importance of letters. Even though the electronic age is upon us, a business letter still remains that primary method for official correspondence. Through letter writing, students can debate with a politician, negotiate to replace a defective product, or praise their favorite celebrity. With letters, everyone benefits, especially students.

The goals here are to generate genuine reasons for students to write letters, and to instruct them in the types of letters and their formats. Letter writing has the added rewards of the satisfaction of first completing the correspondence and, second, of getting a response from the recipient.

Lesson 76   WHY WRITE LETTERS?

Objective: To recognize the importance and variety of letters

Activities:

1. Tell students they have just been kidnapped and they have to write the ransom note to their parents.

    Or: Have students write *telegrams* to each other, with two students serving as mail carriers. No talking is allowed as students write their messages, fold their notes, address the blank side, and raise their hand for the mail carrier to deliver the *telegram*.

    Discuss the results. Have volunteers read their letters.

2. **Writing:** Check the students' background with letter writing—**Survey on Letter Writing—Activity 76-1**.

    Discuss the results. Answers are as follows:

    #1   Answers will vary.

    #2   Answers will vary.

    #3   Pen pal = a correspondent who lives very far away and with whom one rarely, if ever, meets.

    #4   Business, personal, letter-to-the-editor, fan mail, newsletter, invitation, memorandum.

    #5   A letter has a heading, inside address, closing, salutation, and signature.

    #6   Amount of postage; no envelope for post card; there is often a picture on one side for post card; post card is usually from someone on a trip; etc.

    #7   Letters are permanent correspondence—they can be saved; letters are more official and more formal. They remain expected modes of communication for businesses.

    #8   Letters are still regarded as the more official way of doing business.

    #9   500-600 million.

    #10 Answers will vary.

3. **Discussion:** Talk about letters. [Answers will vary with most responses.]

    A.   How could a letter affect a couple's romance?

280

    B. How could a letter affect a murder investigation?

    C. What could be the benefits of having an international pen pal?

    D. How could a letter influence a politician?

    E. What are mailing lists? How does someone get on one?

    F. What was the content of the best letter you have ever received?

    G. Why write letters?

    [More economical; can be copied; more likely to prompt action; more detailed form of communication; serve as a permanent record; etc.]

4. **Read:** Interesting facts about letters. Distribute **Form 76-2—Letter Trivia.**

5. **Discuss:** Letters, the school, and students.

    A. What letters from the school have arrived at your house?

    B. What letters have you ever sent to the school or a teacher?

    C. How have you felt about these letters?

6. **Analysis:** Students respond to the questions after reading **A Senior's Letter—Activity 76-3.** Then **discuss** students' responses.

7. **Summary:** Letters play an important part in our daily lives. We receive letters every day, and they can affect our social lives, education, careers, and families. Letters can also be enjoyable and rewarding.

Homework options:

A. Students locate and bring to class two different letters (junk mail, business letters, etc.). They should be prepared to identify the parts of these letters.

B. Students write a detailed letter to an anonymous student in the elementary school or to any student who will be entering their school in the fall in order to pass on what they think these younger students should know about the school—the key points about succeeding at the secondary level. The salutations should simply be: *Dear Elementary Student* or *Dear Middle School Student.*

C. Advanced students can research the origin of the U.S. Postal Service and the position and duties of the Postmaster General.

D. Students could research the following: Differences between Express Mail and Priority Mail; a Telegram and a Mailgram; and Certified Mail and Registered Mail?

Name _____

Survey on Letter Writing #1

Directions: Answer the following questions in detail.

1. Name the person(s) who last wrote you a letter:

2. Name the person(s) to whom you last wrote a letter:

3. What is a pen pal?

4. What are some types of letters?

5. What separates a letter from other types of writing?

6. What are the differences between a post card and a letter?

7. How could a letter influence someone's career more than a phone call could?

8. Even though we can communicate faster over long distances with computers, why do letters still remain important?

9. How many letters do you think are mailed each day across the United States?

10. What would you like to learn about letter writing?

Letter Trivia

1. Some of the world's greatest romances—Poet Robert Browning and writer Elizabeth Barrett; Sigmund Freud and his wife, his "treasured princess"; Napoleon and Josephine; the 2nd President John Adams and his wife Abigail—have been documented on letters.

2. Over one thousand letters to the parole board of the Ohio Department of Correction and Rehabilitation argued against and stopped the parole for a man convicted for the 1974 murder of a 17-year-old girl.

3. "Dear Abby" receives nearly five hundred letters a day.

4. Terry Anderson, as a hostage in Lebanon for nearly five years (1985-1990), received nearly 7000 Christmas cards each year from persons across the world although there was no certainty he would ever get them.

5. A 13-year-old girl in Chelsea, Oklahoma wrote to the President about unsafe railroad crossings. Her letter was forwarded to the National Transportation Safety Board which prompted Oklahoma state highway officials and the Burlington-Northern Railroad company to correct the problems. The federal government, the Chelsea city council, the railroad company, and the NTSB united their funds and personnel to construct a new crossing gate, repair all flashing lights, and tear down a depot.

6. Stamp collectors (philatelists) collected some 31 million James Dean stamps in 1996, 47 million Marilyn Monroe stamps in 1995, and 124 million Elvis Presley stamps in 1993.

7. United States Congressmen and Senators have *free* access to mail services; i.e., they can send letters without paying postage.

8. Zip codes are organized based on the post offices across the country. Post offices that begin with the numerals 0 or 1 are near the East Coast while post offices that begin with 9 are in California—(ex) "Beverly Hills 90210." Ohio post offices, for instance, begin with #4 while Colorado post offices start with #8.

9. The United States Postal Service delivers mail under four classifications:

1st Class	regular mail	2nd Class	magazines and newspapers
3rd Class	junk mail	4th Class	large packages and parcels

10. The Postal Inspection Service can investigate mail fraud complaints without use of warrants. Their primary objectives are to uncover any evidence of mail fraud or false advertising, to stop theft in post offices, and to investigate the transportation of illegal items by the mail (drugs, weapons, explosives, etc.). The U.S. Postal Inspection Service was created by the Mail Fraud Statute in 1872, making it the federal government's oldest law enforcement agency.

Name _____

Directions: Read the following letter and then answer the questions that follow.

Letter from a Senior

Dear Mom,

The end of my senior year is approaching quickly and it is easy for me to sit back and make foolish judgments about the year. However, it is necessary when forming views to always keep the future in mind and remember that everything we did during the year was based on some positive purpose.

In many classes, we are required to deal with material that is quite boring. "King Lear," for instance, made me to go to sleep. Exercises involving vocabulary, paragraph development, and parts of speech seemed to be a completely useless waste of time.

But things like group work, going to the library, and seeing filmstrips made the class less monotonous. Now that the school year is nearly over, I can look back at every seemingly useless exercise we did in English class with a feeling of accomplishment. I am extremely glad we had to work hard in English because I now feel that I am much better prepared for college.

Your son,

Questions

1. Why do you think this senior wrote this letter?

2. What attitudes toward English are expressed here?

3. How do you think the parents felt about receiving this letter?

4. What would *you* say in a letter to your parents about your schooling?

Lesson 77   LETTERS AND HISTORY

Objective: To recognize the historical value of letters

Activities:

1. **Discussion:** According to Theodore R. Sizer, former dean of Harvard Graduate School of Education, "Many adolescents complete high school unprepared for what follows in their lives; they are marginally literate, uninspired . . . and imbued with a narrow view of the world."

    A. If you were to write Mr. Sizer a letter what would you say?

    B. How could a letter from you prove him to be wrong?

2. **Read:** Famous letters in history—**Form 77-1.**

    Discuss them. Ask: What prompted Marie Antoinette and President Lincoln to write these letters? What do you think was the reaction of the recipients?

3. **Discussion:** What could have been some famous letters that were *never* written?—(ex) President Truman surrendering to the Emperor Hirohito and the Japanese.

4. **Read:** Go over selected pages in their text about letter writing.

5. **Lecture:** Historical overview of postal services—Distribute **Form 80-2**.

6. **Freewriting:** Students predict the future of the postal service (the technology, delivery systems, post offices, etc.). Prompt: What do you think the postal service will be like fifty or one hundred years from now?

    Discuss the predictions.

Homework options:

A. Students write a fictional letter from one famous person—(ex) General Patton—to another individual—(ex) General Eisenhower—in the same time period that, if actually written, could have changed history in some way.

B. Students focus on one event in the history of the postal service and write a research report about it.

C. Students write an editorial offering critical or positive commentary about the U.S. Postal Service.

Famous Letters

- **From Marie Antoinette to her sister**

October 16, 1793

My dearest sister,

I am writing to you for the very last time. I have just been condemned to a death that is in no way shameful—since a shameful death is a fate reserved for criminals—but I am going on a journey to meet your brother once again. I hope I will show the same fortitude as he in my last moments.

I am calm, as one always is when one's conscience is clear. I am deeply saddened to abandon my children; you know that I have lived for them alone, as well as for you, my dear and gentle sister, who through your friendship have given everything to be with me. May my son never forget the dying words of his father, which I have expressly repeated to him: "Never seek to avenge our death."

Farewell, my dear sister; may this letter find its way to you! Think always of me; I embrace you with all my heart, you and my poor, dear children—my God, it is heart-wrenching to leave them forever! Farewell, farewell! I now give myself up to my spiritual preparation.

Marie

- **From Pres. Lincoln to a mother of five dead soldiers**

Washington
Nov. 21, 1864

Dear Madam,

I have been shown in the files of the War Department a statement that you are the mother of five sons who have died gloriously on the field of battle. I feel how weak and fruitless must be any word of mine which should attempt to beguile you from the grief of a loss so overwhelming. But I cannot refrain from tendering you the consolation that may be found in the thanks of the republic they died to serve. I pray that our Heavenly Father may assuage the anguish of your bereavement, and leave you only the cherished memory of the loved and lost, and the solemn pride that must be yours to have laid so costly a sacrifice upon the altar of freedom.

Yours very sincerely and respectfully,

A. Lincoln

History of the Postal Service

1516 First successful postal system is established between Vienna and Berlin.

1683 London Penny Post began operation in England.

1775 Benjamin Franklin is appointed first Postmaster General by George Washington and the Continental Congress to get word to colonists about the victories of the Revolutionary Army.

1789 Samual Osgood becomes first Postmaster General under the official U.S. Constitution; he begins with 75 post offices.

1840 Great Britain introduces the first postage stamps.

1847 United States issues postage stamps.

1860 The Pony Express service is established with riders carrying mail in the western frontier, going from St. Joseph, Missouri to Sacramento, California in 14 days.

1864 Mail trains slowly phased out the Pony Express, but they had to deal with bandits who would block the tracks and steal mail packages looking for money.

1869 Austria becomes the first country to use post cards.

1874 Universal Postal Union is formed to assist in delivering mail between countries.

1913 Parcel post, postal insurance, and C.O.D. services are offered for the first time.

1918 First mail delivery by airplane begins between New York and Washington, D.C.

1963 Zoning Improvement Plan codes (five digit zip codes) are initiated to help speed the sorting and delivery of the mail.

1971 U.S. Postal Service, an independent agency, replaces the Post Office Department.

1977 Railway delivery of mail ends.

1980s FedEx, UPS, etc. become popular delivery services.

Lesson 78 — PARTS OF A LETTER

Objective: To identify and define all parts of a letter

Activities:

1. **Survey:** Check students' knowledge and background with letters—**Activity 78-1.**

    Discuss the answers:

    #1 It is a letter sent to a magazine or newspaper editor about a recent article or current issue—(ex) an election.

    #2 C.O.D. stands for Cash on Delivery and is used to prevent money from getting lost or stolen in the mail.

    #3 Other options include: *Respectfully, With appreciation, Cordially, Yours truly.*

    #4 It is out-dated; it shows the writer has no certainty about the destination of his/her letter; it is too informal.

    #5 They are sent to the Mid-Atlantic Dead Letter Office in Philadelphia and its 30 or more employees who try to identify the destination of nearly 74 million mangled, unaddressed, or incorrectly addressed letters each year; (1.1 million lost packages end up here also).

    They also end up with letters to Santa Claus and to the IRS, along with burned letters from plane crashes.

    About 30% are finally sent to the correct receiver.

    #6 Junk mail consists of advertisements sent in the mail to all residents or boxholders.

    #7 The date proves when the letter was written and can affect a first-come, first-serve situation.

    #8 Pencil can be erased.

    #9 Enclosure refers to additional items sent in the envelope.

    #10 Their staff, secretary, or agents do. They may even have a stamp of their signature to be used for any return correspondence.

2. **Lecture:** Discuss the general Guidelines for Writing Letters. Distribute **Form 78-2**.

3. **Discussion:** Talk about letter writing.

    A. Why should a letter be filed and saved?

[It could prove to be a valuable future reference.]

B. If a letter is sent to a business, it can be read by several people. Why is this acceptable?

[An official letter sent to a company, though it may be addressed to a single person, has the potential to be read by multiple executives or office staff.]

C. Why is formal diction expected in a business letter?

[This is standard business practice.]

D. "To whom it may concern" is no longer acceptable as a salutation. Why?

[It demonstrates an old-fashioned way of communicating and seems to indicate the writer has done no research about the recipient.]

E. In any typical letter, how much should be written in the body?

[Two to four paragraphs is plenty; stick to one page.]

4. **Identification:** Examine sample business letters either distributed by the teacher or brought in by students. On each, have students label the following:

Heading—Sender's address

Date—The day and year the letter was written

Salutation—The greeting—(ex) Dear President Jones

Inside Address—The receiver's name, title, business, and address

Body—The letter's message

Closing—The end of the letter—(ex) Sincerely

Signature—Verifies the authenticity of the letter writer

5. **Explain:** Elaborate on the inside address. It consists usually of five lines:

Name*	Irene Beville
Title	Principal
Business/Organization	Richmond Heights High School
Street Address	447 Richmond Road
City, State Zip	Richmond Heights, OH 44143

* If the name isn't known, then begin with the title.

For practice, have students create an inside address for another person, possibly another administrator.

6. **Analysis:** William Armore letter—**Activity 78-3**. Students analyze it

for its faults.

Check or **Discuss** the analysis.

7. **Modeling:** Study the sample business letter following the standard and professional format—**Form 78-4**.

8. **Preview:** Present the homework assignment. Ask: Who do you know deserves a letter of appreciation? A parent? Friend? Neighbor? Employer?

Homework options:

A. Students can write a letter of appreciation for someone else's kindness, generosity, or assistance. Remind students that these letters will be mailed. A business letter format is preferred.

B. Advanced students can research how to write to a famous writer.

C. Students can write to an author they have just read (the teacher should provide the inside address—usually the publishing company) describing their reaction to his/her book.

D. Students can write to the local chamber of commerce requesting that it consider teenagers more in its plans for the city (the letters might possibly advocate increased awareness of teens as consumers).

Name _____

Survey on Letter Writing #2

1. What is a letter-to-the-editor?

2. What is C.O.D.? Why is it used?

3. What are some other types of closings other than *sincerely?*

4. Why is the salutation "Dear Sir or Madam" no longer considered appropriate in standard business letters?

5. What do you think the Postal Service does with letters that are incorrectly addressed and lack a return address on the envelope?

6. What is junk mail?

7. Why is a date so important on a business letter?

8. Why must a business letter be typed or in ink?

9. What does *enclosure* refer to when written at the bottom of a business letter?

10. Politicians, actors, and celebrities receive hundreds of letters each week. If they don't read them, who does?

Guidelines for Letter Writing

1. Be sure to type the correct date between the heading and the salutation.

2. The salutation should be *Dear* Mr./Ms. Last Name (Dear Mr. Jones); Dear Title and Name—(ex) Dear Governor Voinovich; or *Dear* Title if the name of the recipient is not known—(ex) Dear Manager, if the letter is a business letter.

3. The salutation should be *Dear* First Name—(ex) Dear Joe, if the letter is a personal letter.

4. Acceptable closings are *Sincerely, Respectfully*, and *Cordially* in business letters.

5. *Yours truly, Love,* and *Sincerely* are some acceptable closings for personal letters.

6. Be sure the letter is correctly punctuated.

7. Keep the body (the message) detailed, courteous (even if it is a complaint), and brief (one page).

8. State the intent of the letter immediately—(ex) I am interested in the secretarial position advertised in the newspaper. No introduction is necessary.

9. Use no abbreviations, except for *Inc.*

10. Write or type on one side of the paper only and have equal margins top and bottom, left and right.

11. The letter should be neatly written and error free.

12. Avoid awkward (wordy), insensitive, or sexist language—(ex) You are hereby advised (I'm writing to inform you)—(ex) Indian (Native American).

13. Be sure you have the correct postage for the envelope.

14. Proofread the letter for accuracy and proper grammar.

15. Fold the letter no more than twice.

William Armore Letter #1

Directions: Examine the letter of application below and mark its faults.

31325 Drake Dr.
Bay Village, Oh 44140

May 2, 1998

Mr. William Armore
Personnel Man
Cityside Bank
Clevland, Oh

Dear Will,

I've worked with the public before, and I type really well. I also want to learn new things, so I think I'd like to work for your bank. I saw the ad that said you needed a teller, so I'd like to start as soon as I can.

Before, I was working at this dead-end job as an office manager, but now I want new challenges and more money. I was wasting my time there. And nothing else really appeals to me.

Because I'm gone alot, there's usually no one home to answer my phone. But that's okay since I've got an answering machine. If you want to talk to me directly you better call around 3:30 PM sharp because that's when I get home usually, unless my friends come over and ask me to go out with them.

I really want to come in for an interview. After we hang out for a bit I'm sure you'll want to hire me.

Talk to you soon.

Later,

Hank

William Armore Letter #2

31325 Drake Drive
Bay Village, OH 44140

May 2, 1998

Mr. William Armore
Personnel Manager
Cityside Bank of Cleveland
3451 Euclid Avenue
Cleveland, OH 44117

Dear Mr. Armore:

I am interested in applying for the position of bank manager that was advertised in the newspaper. After working with the public as a loan officer and teller, I am seeking new challenges. Working for the Cityside Bank of Cleveland would be the perfect opportunity to utilize my professional skills and take on an exciting new career.

Previously, I worked at Third Federal Bank first as a teller and then a loan officer, and for a mortgage company as an office manager. I appreciate those experiences as important to my professional growth in the banking industry. If hired I would bring fifteen valuable years of experience to Cityside Bank. A more detailed resume is enclosed.

I look forward to an interview. I can be reached during the day at 216-555-7472.

Sincerely,

Henry Thomas

Lesson 79   CONSUMER MAIL

Objective: To recognize a letter's value in eliciting action from businesses

Activities:

1. **Preview:** Everyone at times has a problem with purchases—(ex) a new fishing rod breaks, potato chips are stale, the stitching on a sweater comes loose. Ask students:

   What problems have you had?

2. **Group work:** Focus on consumer letters.

   A. Give each group a collection of empty packages and boxes—(ex) an empty Nabisco crackers box, the label from a Campbell's soup can, the plastic wrap for some paper towels, etc. Have them locate the name and address of the company.

   B. One member writes the complete name and address for each product and package.

   C. Each group then selects one company to whom to write a letter that describes a real or fictitious complaint. This letter must follow standard business letter format.

   Check the results.

   D. Each group then decides on their own company name and address—(ex) The People's Popcorn Company—and creates their own letterhead.

   E. Each group member takes on a fictitious position in the company—(ex) President, Vice-President, CEO, etc.

   F. Each group writes a standard business letter that announces their entry into the market place.

   G. Groups exchange business letters and edit for possible improvements.

   Check the results.

3. **Lecture:** Speak about consumer-oriented letters.

   • Businesses, especially national ones, want to hear from consumers, even if they're complaints.

   • Look for the company's address on the merchandise, package, or warranty paper first.

- If the address is uncertain, ask the retailer from whom the product was purchased.

- Direct the letter to a *specific* person—(ex) Consumer Affairs Manager or Public Relations Director.

- Be sure the letter has all the facts and is easy to read.

Homework:

Students select any company or business to receive their consumer letter. This letter must reflect a genuine concern or issue (criticism or praise) for their product or service. It will be mailed.

Lesson 80   DICTION IN LETTERS

Objective: To identify the appropriate diction various types of letters

Activities:

1. **Freewriting:** Create the first sentence for each of the following types of letters.

   A. In a letter from your grandfather to your grandmother the day after they met for the first time (personal letter)

   B. In a letter to your favorite performer (fan mail)

   C. In a letter to a student presently in another class (personal letter)

   D. In a letter to an employer asking for a job or for a promotion or a raise (business letter)

   E. In a letter to a company about one of their products or services perhaps a compliment or complaint (consumer business letter).

   Discuss the results.

2. **Discuss:** Consider sentences from other letters. (Put these on the blackboard). Ask: What's wrong with the following?

   A. A management position is something I'm interested in.

   [It isn't written in the active voice. It should be: I am interested in a management position.]

   B. I'm interested in working for you right away.

   [It's too direct and does not identify the position. It should be: I am interested in the position of bank manager.]

   C. Your product stinks.

   [It's too aggressive; it lacks courtesy, and they may not respond favorably.]

   D. You're one in a million.

   [It's a cliché and lacks enthusiasm.]

3. **Explain:** Go over the standard format of a business letter.

   • 1st Paragraph   State the specific intent.

   • 2nd Paragraph   Clarify reasons.

   • 3rd Paragraph   Provide background details, if needed.

   • 4th Paragraph   Closure—(ex) I look forward . . .

4. **Writing:** Students select one of the letters above and complete the body, heading, and closing, following the standard format.

   Check the results.

5. **Discussion:** Talk about special types of letters. Answers can vary.

   A. What do businesses try to accomplish with junk mail if so many of us just throw it away?

   B. What is some typical language in junk mail?

   C. What is the intent of fan mail?

   D. Since celebrities receive so much fan mail, how could one letter stand out from the next?

   E. What kind of language was in the most unusual letter you ever received?

   F. How can you encourage the recipient to write back?

   [Ask questions; tell the recipient how much you enjoy his/her letters; tell yours and then ask for his/her opinion on an issue; include a self-addressed, stamped envelope; etc.]

6. **Read:** Copy letters from Ted Nancy's book *Letters from a Nut.* They are very entertaining.

Homework:

Students gather several examples of junk mail and study the language used by the companies.

Students research the diction in school newsletters, analyzing how the school administration tries to appeal to parents and community members.

Lesson 81 LETTER TO THE EDITOR

Objective: To complete a letter-to-the-editor

Activities:

1. **Discuss:** Why would anyone write to an editor? What could they hope to accomplish?

    [Answers will vary, but most writers just want to be heard. They may want to praise or protest an article. There could be an issue that concerns them.]

2. **Modeling:** Students examine magazines and newspapers, if available, for their letters-to-the-editor. Ask students to summarize in one word the attitude expressed by the writer—(ex) anger, frustration, gratitude—and in one sentence the intent of the letter.

3. **Read:** Study any pages in their text about letters-to-the-editor.

4. **Discuss:** Letters sent to editors. [Answers will vary.]

    A. How could your letter stand out from the hundreds of others?

    B. How could your letter make a positive impression?

    C. What kind of diction is appropriate?

    D. Why should the letter be grammatically correct, clean, and attractive?

    E. Why must it be typed?

    F. What makes you qualified to write such a letter?

5. **Freewriting:** Students take on any school-related issue—(ex) the dress code—and write a letter-to-the-editor of the school newspaper or school newsletter.

    Or: Students can write to the editor of *Teen* magazine or to Dear Abby about a specific teen issue or problem—(ex) dealing with peer pressure to use drugs/alcohol.

    Check the results. Have students exchange letters.

Homework:

Students develop a genuine concern about an issue or previous article of a favorite magazine or newspaper to send their own letter-to-the editor. This letter will be mailed.

Lesson 82   LETTER OF APPLICATION

Objective: To recognize the correct format of a letter of application

Activities:

1. **Discuss:** Today's technology vs. letters—Knowledge check.

   A. What is E-mail?

      [Letters that appear on a computer screen sent via wires]

   B. How does a fax work?

      [Written information is coded electronically and transmitted through the phone lines from one fax machine to another.]

   C. What makes a better impression—E-mail or standard mail (in an employment inquiry)?

      [Standard business letters are always more appropriate since they are usually cleaner, more legible copies.]

   D. How does one get on the internet?

      [Answers will vary.]

   E. What typical business practices can currently be done on the internet?

      [Banking, buying/selling stocks, gambling, purchasing products, etc.]

2. **Lecture:** Speak on today's technology vs. letters.

   • Business letters are cheaper to transmit than E-mail and faxes, in some cases.

   • Letters are more confidential.

   • Letters have more of a personal touch; it makes a better impression.

   • A letter is permanent.

   • A letter has more impact, (it took more time to compose and send).

3. **Modeling:** Format of a typical letter of application—

1st Paragraph	Declares the job being sought
2nd Paragraph	Provides applicant's background (education, work experience, and age)
3rd Paragraph	Reveals applicant's reasons for his/her interest in the position
4th Paragraph	Asks for an interview

Review **Form 78-4**—Henry Thomas letter to William Armore.

[Note: The salutations *Dear Sir* and *Gentlemen* have been retired because they are too generic and too sexist.]

4. **Review:** Block and Semi-block style.

   Block = all items directly against the left margin. This is the style currently favored in standard business letters.

   Semi-block = date and closing are placed at mid-center of letter. This is the style still used in many personal and informal letters.

5. **Debate:** Discuss issues related to letter format and employment.

   • If an applicant submits an application and resumé, is a letter even necessary?

   [Yes—It is more formal; the letter establishes the date and intent of correspondence, and can provide additional information]

   [No—It may bog down the personnel director or manager; one can sometimes phone for interview; the company might prefer a more informal approach; etc.]

   • The resumé is more important than the letter of application.

   [Responses will vary.]

   • An applicant's qualifications and personality are more noticeable in a letter than the application.

   [Responses will vary.]

6. **Reading:** Have students read any pages in text on letters of application. Perhaps work on 1-2 exercises.

Homework:

Students research or survey how executives and other business leaders feel about business letters vs. E-mail and faxes.

Students select any company or business and write a standard business letter requesting employment such as a summer job or career information.

Lesson 83 PERSONAL LETTERS

Objective: To review the qualities and format of personal letters

To work at improving students' social skills

Activities:

1. **Write:** Answer questions about post cards and personal letters—**Activity 83-1.**

    Discuss the answers:

    #1 [Use a number-coded list of greetings; use a special vocabulary; make the message very generic; etc.]

    #2 [Comments on the weather; expressions of friendship; requests for money; etc.]

    #3 [A joke; a poem; political news; menu descriptions; some foreign phrases; a map or diagram; a cartoon; a creative story; etc.]

    #4 [It could be a complaint, an accusation, a problem.]

    #5 [Pen pal; love letter; invitations; to relatives; special announcements or anniversaries (ex) wedding; apologies; reminders; etc.]

    [Questions #6-8 give great opportunity to deal with *social skills*, which many students lack.]

    #6 [Begin by complimenting the person; state how you value the friendship and the relationship; explain what you want to have happen in the relationship; give some reasons; thank the person.]

    #7 [Begin with a compliment; remind your friend how you value the friendship; warn him/her about the possible consequences for stealing; explain why it is wrong; ask him/her to consider the feelings of the store owner and yourself; suggest other solutions—(ex) I can lend you the money.]

    #8 [Make a positive comment about the person—(ex) You have always been a good student; state your intent—(ex) I don't want you to . . . or It would be wrong for you to . . .; explain why; state that you wouldn't do it; suggest something else for the person to do.]

2. **Discuss:** What are the values of such letters? How open would you be to receiving such a letter? [Answers will vary.]

3. **Explain:** Discuss the format of a personal (also termed, friendly) letter.

- Expected salutation—Dear First Name
- Expected closings—Sincerely, Love, Yours truly
- Body is conversational in tone, and informal in its diction
- A heading is required, but not an inside address

4. **Discuss:** What kind of typical details do recipients expect to see in the body of a personal letter?

   [Answers will vary. Usually, personal letters discuss recent events in the writer's life; they're conversational in tone and may also pose questions.]

5. **Compare:** Contrast personal letters and business letters. What parts are different? What about the bodies? Format? Stationery?

Homework:

Students read any pages in their text about writing personal letters.

Students write a personal letter to a classmate, friend, or relative dealing with a social skill.

Advanced students can interview someone who deals frequently with mail—a secretary, local politician, business executive, school administrator, etc. on his/her approach to receiving and sending letters.

What Do You Know About Personal Letters?

Directions: Answer each question in detail.

1. How can you send a message on a post card to a close friend without anyone else understanding the message?

2. What are some traditional messages on post cards?

3. What could be some unusual comments on a post card or in a personal letter?

4. How could a personal letter not be a friendly letter?

5. What are the various types of personal letters?

6. What would you write in the first sentence of a letter where you break up with someone?

7. What would you write in a letter to stop a friend from stealing or shoplifting?

8. What would you write in a letter to help someone resist peer pressure?

Lesson 84 LETTER WRITING PROJECTS AND PEER EDITING

Objective: To work on letter writing projects

Activities:

1. **Review:** Go over diction in business letters vs. personal letters.
2. **Writing:** Students work in class on letter writing projects—**Activity 84-1**.

   Addresses can be found in the yellow pages of the telephone book or possibly in the guidance office.

   Also, use the following reference books for locating addresses:
   - *Celebrity Directory* by Axiom Information Resources
   - *Star Guide* by Axiom Information Resources
   - *The Address Book* by Michael Levine
3. **Peer Editing:** Students exchange letters with classmates at least twice for proofreading and editing.

   Students confer with teacher as necessary.

Homework:

Students continue work on letter writing projects to completion.

Students complete **Activity 84-2—Review questions on Letter Writing**.

Letter Writing Projects

Objectives:　1.　To demonstrate competence at writing complete and coherent business letters

Materials:　1.　Typewriter or word processor and paper
　　　　　　　2.　Envelopes and stamps

Projects:　Select any _____ of the following assignments.

1. Write to a politician who can respond to a genuine concern you have about our local, state, or federal government.

   (ex) to a city council person about bad pavement on your neighborhood street

2. Write to a company or business, requesting employment or career information.

3. Write to an organization or agency, requesting information about membership, its background, policies, agenda, and/or meetings.

   (ex) to the United Way regarding its policy on the monies that they distribute to various charities.

4. Write to a professional sports team, requesting information about its schedule or team pictures, or an individual player, and his/her background.

   (ex) to Michael Jordan about his decision to turn pro before graduating from college.

5. Write to an agency regarding their policies, background, and/or agenda.

   (ex) to a local organization that helps the mentally handicapped, or the Special Olympics, requesting information about volunteering.

6. Write a consumer letter to any business or company.

   (ex) to a cosmetics company about a product you use.

7. Write a fan letter to a celebrity (actor, singer, performer, etc)

8. Write to a college requesting information about admissions, housing, tuition, etc.

9. Write to any governmental agency, requesting information.

Review Questions on Letter Writing

1. What is an inside address? Define this term associated with letters.

2. What is a letter's heading? Define this term.

3. What is the appropriate salutation in a business letter, when a writer doesn't know the recipient's name?

4. What are several useful closings in a standard business letter?

5. What are several useful closings in a personal letter?

6. Why is a signature necessary on a letter?

7. Why should a business letter be formal in its structure and diction?

8. What should the recipient of a business letter do with it after reading it?

9. What should be the structure and diction of a personal letter?

10. What is the difference between block and semiblock format in letters?

11. Why should a letter be filed and saved?

12. How might an employer detect an applicant's skills in a letter?

13. What are some types of business letters?

14. Why are letters still more useful than E-mail and faxes?

15. What are some types of personal letters?

16. What are some punctuation rules associated specifically with letter writing?

17. What is the general purpose of a newsletter?

18. What makes a letter more useful than a phone conversation?

19. How many classes of mail does the U.S. Postal Service have?

20. What special capitalization rules relate to letter writing?

Section 11 : SHORT FICTION

"It is better to fail in originality, than to succeed in imitation."
(*Herman Melville*)

Objectives: Teach students to make distinctions between fiction and nonfiction

Introduce the writing of short fiction

Explain types of narration

Provide definitions for literary terms

Improve students' reading skills

Cite aspects of characterization in fiction

Lead students in identifying a story's structure

Length: Approximately eight lessons

Introduction:

Story telling has been a part of human culture since communication began. In fact, we are born story tellers. We *love* story telling. More importantly, we love hearing stories. Good ones, especially. Gossip, if need be.

And what is a story?

Most often, it is an invention of words. *The Old Man and the Sea* is Ernest Hemingway's award-winning creation about a poor fisherman named Santiago and a huge marlin. *The Adventures of Huckleberry Finn* is Mark Twain's amusing tale about a mischievous boy and a superstitious slave's journey down the Mississippi River. When we read these wonderful novels we know we're reading a falsehood, that the events depicted didn't really happen, and that the author presents characters and scenes in order to enlighten and entertain us.

When teaching how to write fiction, a teacher must first deal with creativity. To accomplish this, the teacher has to provide creative lessons (activities) and positive feedback (evaluations). Perhaps the essence of teaching someone to write fiction is helping them recognize a weak story, diagnose the difficulty (the main character, for example, needs more characterization), and suggest a better way of telling the tale (try adding more dialogue, for instance).

There are several ways to introduce fiction writing to students, (ways that appeal to all learning styles) when guiding their efforts towards composing a story. Whatever your approach, focus on students being creative and descriptive.

STORIES BEGIN WITH CHARACTERS

Objective: To make distinctions between fiction and nonfiction

Activities:

1. **Brainstorm:** Create a character, an imaginary person. What does this person look like? His/her personality? Family? Habits?

2. **Campaign:** Each student reads the details of his/her character, hoping the other students will find him/her (or it) to be interesting and unique.

   Write the names of each character on the board as they are read.

3. **Vote:** Students vote for the character they find most appealing. Have two rounds of voting. In the first round students can vote as many times as they want. From that, select the top 5-6 vote-getters.

   Before the second round, have those 5-6 students read their character profiles again. In the 2nd round, students can vote only once. In short, all characters, except one, "die."

   Discuss the results. Ask: Why do you think _____ won the vote (got to live)? This could be a **debate** about the merits of one character over another.

4. **Visual aid:** View interesting or unusual-looking people (either in magazine ads, on a transparency, or on pictures on the bulletin board). Ask: What kind of backgrounds do you think they have? What is interesting about them?

5. **Analysis:** Use old yearbooks for students to examine and predict the characteristics of some of the interesting faces they observe in them.

6. **Summarize:** The best stories have the best characters, those who are the most interesting, the most unusual, the most dynamic, etc. We are intrigued by people who aren't just like us.

7. **Preview:** Go over the homework options.

Homework options:

A. Students write one page describing a character, possibly from the class list, and placing him/her/it in a particular setting (a place).

B. Students write a one-page description of the most unusual or interesting character they've ever read—(ex) Huckleberry Finn.

C. Students research types of stories—short story, novella, novel, tome. Students define these terms, give examples of each, and explain their appeal. As part of this research, students can also explain the various types of literary *genre*.

D. Students write an editorial explaining which author they think is the best story-teller.

Lesson 86 FICTION IS LYING

Objective: To recognize the value of creative lying

Activities:

1. **Discuss**: Stories as imagination. Begin by narrating a story about an event in your past—(ex) an athletic contest—that either did or did not happen, then ask:

   A. How do you know when a story, whether written or verbal, is true?

   [It can be checked to other sources. Several people might narrate the same story. Fiction comes in one narration (ex) there is only one *Gone with the Wind* or *The Adventures of Tom Sawyer.*]

   B. What is fiction [knowledge check]?

   [A narration whose events or characters are imaginary]

   C. Where do writers get their ideas for stories?

   [Answers will vary.]

   D. How do authors make stories *real*?

   [Through their descriptions, possibly making reference to actual people or events, in the dialogue, etc.]

   E. What stories have you enjoyed reading in the past? Why?

   [Answers will vary.]

2. **Debate:** Oral vs. written stories. Which are better? Why?

3. **Identification:** Students examine the titles of the stories (fiction) in their literature text. Ask: What do you think each story is about?

   Discuss: How important are titles to a story?

   [Very important. Consider why the Ford Motor Company named their sports car Mustang and not Donkey.]

4. **Freewriting: Activity 86-1.** Students work here at developing creativity. **Discuss** the responses. Ask other students to decipher the lies and/or the more interesting responses.

5. **Lecture:** Much of fiction is exploration, emotion, and experimentation.

   • Exploration = Coming up with a variety of characteristics about an imaginary character or setting.

   • Emotion = Describing the character's tensions and emotions.

- Experimentation = Analyzing what works and what doesn't for readers of fiction. Will they accept my imagination?

6. **Freewriting: Activity 86-2**—Play *What if?* to show Exploration and Experimentation

   Check the results.

Homework options:

A. Students research types of fiction—(ex) Historical Fiction—and then pretend to be the editor of a magazine (think of a title) that features fiction for teenagers. They must write the criteria explaining the kinds of fiction that their magazine will publish.

B. Students select one event in their life and **write** 1-2 paragraphs about it, changing *one* element.

C. Students explain the difference between science fiction and regular fiction, citing examples.

D. Students select a short story with an interesting title to read. They should return prepared to discuss the story.

Playing with the Truth

Directions: Answer each question below creatively (use some imagination).

1. What will you be doing ten years from now?

2. What really makes you cry?

3. What really makes you laugh?

4. What scares you?

5. What is the most unusual event you've ever seen on a bus?

6. What is the worst mistake you've seen someone make (including yourself)?

7. Where were you once when you got lost?

8. What do you do every Friday night?

9. What happened when you got injured?

Name _____

What If?

Directions: Answer each of the following *What if* questions in detail.

1.   What if the sun were to shine only two hours every day?

2.   What if new born babies could talk immediately?

3.   What if the airplane had been invented before the Civil War?

4.   What if cars could also fly?

5.   What if there were no more gasoline?

6.   What if there were only three known colors—blue, green, and red?

7.   What if there were no more schools?

8.   What if people were never allowed to leave their hometowns?

Lesson 87   CHARACTERS AND PLOTS

Objective: To identify how to create characters and plots

1. **Group work:** Consider characters and plots.

    A.   Describe a superhero of your own invention that you would want defending our city (no Superman or Batman). Each group member must come up with different characteristics of this superhero.

    B.   What is the danger that faces the city that brings the superhero into action? The group creates one problem.

    C.   What eventually happens? The group decides 1-2 possible outcomes.

    Check the results.

2. **Lecture:** Talk about character types in a story—Distribute **Form 87-1.**

3. **Group work:** Class works on plot (the events in a story). The instructor may wish to reward the group that devises the most creative plot events with extra points.

    A.   What happens to the person who suddenly wins the lottery?

    B.   What do you think happens in the story titled "Ship of Fools" by Katherine Anne Porter?

    C.   What happens in a politician's (or pick another profession) life that finally causes him/her to admit he/she has a problem with alcohol and go to Alcoholics Anonymous?

    D.   What happens when the elementary school students get lost at the chocolate factory?

    E.   What makes a good mystery story?

    Discuss the results.

4. **Music:** Play the lyrics of any song. Based on those lyrics, what could be the premise of a story's plot? Each group **brainstorms** plot events.

5. **Timeline:** Put a timeline on the blackboard. It could be structured 8 AM to Midnight; Monday—Friday; September—June. Groups write the important events—imagined or real—in chronological order on the timeline.

6. **Summary:** Plotting depends directly on the actions and behavior of the characters, especially the main character. Most plots are arranged in chronological order as the characters move from one situation to another.

Homework options:

A. Students make a chart where they list all the types of characters. For each type, they describe one person: his/her physical characteristics, personality traits, background, and vocation.

B. Students write a detailed essay, explaining a character's—one from literature or one they make up—humorous behavior and actions. What is his/her view of the world?

C. Students list moral values (at least 10)—(ex) honesty. For each value, they cite one character they have read in other literature who has that value (with an explanation).

D. Students create a character and write a one-page narrative that reveals that character's positive and negative traits.

E. Students select any story and create a timeline of the key plot events in that story.

Types of Characters

Protagonist = the main character; the character who occupies the majority of the story and whose struggle is the most important element of the conflict and plot.

> (ex) Huckleberry Finn, King Lear, Robinson Crusoe

- This character may not necessarily be heroic or positive

> (ex) the narrator in Poe's "The Tell-Tale Heart"

Antagonist = the obstacle or enemy to the main character; the second most important character who influences the plot.

> (ex) Lear's daughters, Bob Ewell in "To Kill a Mockingbird," Curley in "Of Mice and Men"

- This obstacle/enemy may not be another *person*.

> (ex) the dinosaurs in "Jurassic Park" or Henry Fleming's cowardice in the "Red Badge of Courage"

Flat Characters = minor characters who help advance the plot but who are not truly important; they may lack detailed characterization.

> (ex) Lord Montague in "Romeo and Juliet" and Aunt Sally in "The Adventures of Huckleberry Finn"

Foils = minor or lesser characters opposite the main characters who do not serve as obstacles but who do influence the plot.

> (ex) Tom Sawyer in "The Adventures of Huckleberry Finn" and Huckleberry Finn in "The Adventures of Tom Sawyer"

Stereotypes = "typical" characters whose traits are easily recognizable.

> (ex) politicians, pro athletes, teachers

Lesson 88

CONFLICT, CLIMAX, AND RESOLUTION

Objective: To identify conflict, climax, and resolution in a variety of situations related to fiction

1. **Write:** Students read the first half of "**Morgan's Revenge** "—**Activity 88-1**—and identify the conflict and the next significant event (climax).

   Discuss their responses.

2. **Read:** Study the second half of "Morgan's Revenge" and answer the remaining questions. Then **discuss** their reactions.

3. **Explain:** Discuss the importance of *conflict* in fiction.

   Conflict = what generates the actions of the protagonist.

   This is his/her obstacle or problem. It determines the plot.

   Distribute **Activity 88-2—Types of Conflicts.** Then students **write** their own examples, either from imagination or other literary works.

   Check their responses.

4. **Visual aid:** Show videotape of a tense scene from any non-comedic movie (possibly one with suspense). Students must discern the conflict(s). **Discuss** their responses.

5. **Explain:** Climax and resolution.

   Climax = the highest point of action in a story.

   Resolution = how the conflict is resolved.

6. **Quiz:** Students explain, in writing, a personal conflict they experienced—why it was an obstacle, the event that was the climax, and how it was resolved. Evaluation is based on the thoroughness of the explanation.

   Or: Students explain the type of conflict and resolution that occurred in a book, a news article, or movie.

Homework:

Advanced students can research an important historical event—(ex) the Depression, soldiers returning from Vietnam, the San Francisco earthquake—and describe some real or imaginary conflicts and outcomes based on that event.

Students read a selected short story from their literature text that has an interesting conflict and many plot events.

"Morgan's Revenge"

Directions: Read only the first page of the following story. Then add its ending (climax and resolution).

The room was empty when Morgan entered. He smiled, happy that he was alone. He walked quickly to the window where the long, blue velvet curtains hung. He stepped behind them to hide. He loved those curtains—their warmth, their softness, the darkness. "Yes," he thought. "I'll hide here and wait for her. She'll feel sorry when I'm through with her!"

Suddenly, he heard her steps, the click of her heels on the hard wood floor. He smelled her perfume and listened to her soft humming as she dusted the furniture.

He hated her. His body stiffened. Soon she would be close enough. The humming grew louder, and he peeked through the drapes. Her back was now only inches away from his hands. That's when he opened the curtains and . . .

What is the conflict here?

What happens next? Write the climax:

"Morgan's Revenge" continued

she turned around. "Morgan," his mother said, "what are you doing there?"

"Playing . . ." His small voice trailed off.

"Playing?"

"Playing . . . army," Morgan said weakly.

"And what does a six-year-old know about playing army?" She sat on the sofa and pulled him into her lap, hugging him close to her. "My little boy, my sweet, precious, little boy."

Morgan relaxed, suddenly enjoying her smile, her warmth, the softness of her sweater. His mother kissed him and tickled his sides, making him giggle and push at her hands.

"What were you doing behind the curtains, Morgan?" she asked again.

Morgan searched his six-year-old mind, but he couldn't remember. Maybe it was something about cookies he couldn't have or a toy she didn't buy for him, but he just didn't know anymore. All he did know was his mother's sweet perfume and gentle arms around his body.

What was the climax (the highest point of action)?

How is the conflict resolved?

Name _____

Types of Conflicts

Part I

Directions: Write a real or imaginary example for each type of conflict below.

1. ***Protagonist vs. Another Character***
   (ex) Lennie vs. Curley in "Of Mice and Men"
   Your example:

2. ***Protagonist vs. Nature***
   (ex) The scientists vs. the dinosaurs in *Jurassic Park* or the old man vs. the marlin in *The Old Man and the Sea*
   Your example:

3. ***Protagonist vs. the Supernatural***
   (ex) Dorothy vs. the witch in the *Wizard of Oz* or the plots of most of Stephen King's books
   Your example:

4. ***Protagonist vs. Self***
   (ex) Henry Fleming vs. his fear of being a coward in *Red Badge of Courage*
   Your example:

5. ***Protagonist vs. Society***
   (ex) The Joad family vs. the banks in *The Grapes of Wrath*
   Your example:

6. ***Protagonist vs. Fate***
   (ex) Romeo and Juliet vs. "the stars"
   Your example:

Part II

Directions: Answer each question below in detail.

1. What could be some potential conflicts in the life of a professional athlete?

2. What are the potential conflicts for someone who has a drinking problem? How could this affect other people? Explain these conflicts and some potential outcomes.

3. How could self-esteem serve as a potential creator of conflict?

4. What have been some conflicts from other stories or novels that you have enjoyed? Why?

5. What are some other examples of the *Protagonist vs. Self* conflict?

Lesson 89   WHAT DOES A STORY LOOK LIKE?

Objective: To identify the form of a story

Activities:

> **Teachers should consider flexible guidelines when alternatives for writing fiction are presented to students. Emphasize quality, creativity, and description.**

1. **Lecture:** Consider the forms a writer could use for narrating a story:
   - a journal or diary entry
   - a myth
   - an anecdote
   - a fable
   - a personal narrative

2. **Contest:** Consider how writers *begin* their narratives. Who can write the best first sentence for a story . . .
   A. where the main character can see into the future?
   B. where astronauts are stranded on the moon?
   C. about traveling in a time machine?
   D. about a school taken over by the students.
   E. where the main character is lost in the woods?

   Discuss the results. The teacher or a panel of students should judge the contest.

3. **Modeling:** Examine stories in their literature text—their titles, first paragraphs and overall structure. If possible, also look at the works of Mark Twain, Raymond Chandler, John Grisham, and Ernest Hemingway.

4. **Explain:** Present the paragraph to paragraph plotting of a story.

   Ask: If I'm reading a chemistry book and I come to a section labeled "Strong Acid Reactions" what might I anticipate the next section being about? ["Weak Acid Reactions"]

   Fiction is similar. Events should follow each other logically and chronologically.

5. **Freewriting: What happens next?—Activity 89-1.**

   Discuss the results.

6. **Discuss:** What is the function and importance of a story's title? What are some interesting titles?

7. **Summarize:** Stories need to have a chronological and logical progression of plot events. The beginning should introduce the main character, conflict, and setting in a way that catches the reader's attention and encourages him/her to continue reading. To continue the plot, the writer could play a *what if* game.

Homework options:

A. Advanced students locate 1-2 stories by winners of the Pulitzer Prize for Literature. Students should study their beginnings, characters, and plots as well as the different structures those authors used.

B. Students compare various famous American literature—(ex) works by Mark Twain, William Faulkner, John Steinbeck, Richard Wright—to recognize the variety in fiction that crosses over ethnic and regional boundaries.

C. Students compare and contrast the events depicted in a book and the movie based on the book (ex) *Ordinary People, The Shining, Gone with the Wind,* etc.

D. Students decide the premise or basis for the story they plan to write.

Name _____

What Happens Next?

Directions: Answer each of the following in detail.

1. A dog barks, growling and snarling. Glass is heard shattering. What happens next?

2. A puff of smoke appears by the school. What happens next?

3. A scientist throws his hands up in horror and then collapses to the floor. What happens next?

4. The ground opens up and two long tentacles encircle a young girl. What happens next?

5. A blinding, flashing light illuminates the sky. What happens next?

6. There is a long piercing scream, followed by three quick taps on the wall. What happens next?

7. The fist came straight at me. What happened next?

Lesson 90 SETTING

Objective: To discover the importance of setting and mood to fiction

1. **Prompts:**
   A. **"Real Estate" writing:** Each student must have a different advertisement from the Real Estate section of the newspaper stapled to a piece of paper for them to examine. After studying the ad, they should list the characteristics of the people they believe would buy that house (or live there).

   (ex) for a $350,000 suburban home—professional husband and wife, three children, belong to a country club, own a boat, enjoy golfing, college educated.

   B. **Writing:** Students describe any room in their house—(ex) the basement—in two different paragraphs: first, as a pleasant, relaxing place and second, as an uncomfortable or dangerous place.

   C. **Analysis:** What is the setting (time and place of a story) for the following: "Once upon a time . . ." Why isn't the writer more specific? Explain.

   D. **Listing:** Students list the settings seen in stories or dramas they have read. Give brief descriptive details.

   E. **Illustration:** Students draw, illustrate, or make a collage of the setting of a story they've heard or read.

   Check the results.

2. **Visual aid:** Students examine pictures of exotic locales found in magazines, their text, or on a video. Have them **list** the descriptive details about these settings and the people who might inhabit them.

   Ask: What mood (feeling)—(ex) happiness, anger—do you get from the picture?

3. **Read:** Study a selected short story found in their text and focus on its setting.

   Ask: How does the setting influence your understanding of the story? What is the mood—(ex) gloom and sorrow in a Poe story—the author creates in the story?

4. **Closure activities:**
   A. **Illustration:** Students write a description of the school grounds, as if for a brochure to present to the principal. They should pinpoint

key events in certain areas (ex) Library—Researching for English; Football field—Winning the conference title; etc.

Check the results. [This activity helps students better visualize the significance of setting to a story.]

B.   **Activity 90-1—"The Journey"**—Students complete the narrative. **Discuss** the results.

C.   **Discussion:** Explore setting.

1.   How could the seasons affect a story's setting?

2.   How could your neighborhood serve as a good story setting?

3.   As settings, compare the frontier of the West with the frontier of Space.

4.   What geographical location—(ex) the Andes Mountains—would be an interesting setting?

Homework options:

A.   Students take any scene from a novel or story and rewrite it, inserting new details into the setting. Students must be descriptive, yet retain the original scene.

B.   Students describe, in one page, the most unusual setting for a story they have read or seen.

C.   Students examine an atlas or map and find 3-4 unusual names of towns or cities. For each selection, they write 1-2 descriptive paragraphs about it, explaining why that would be a good place for a story's setting.

Name _____

The Journey

Directions: Read and complete the following narrative.

The heat from the sun made the air thick. So thick and heavy it was difficult to breathe, and the puffy, white clouds that floated lazily overhead barely lessened the sun's blinding rays.

George tasted his own sweat and felt it sting his eyes as his tongue became swollen with thirst. He lay in the raft, using his arm to shield his eyes from the sun's glare.

His brother Nick rested opposite him in the raft's stern. Nick stared across the water as the raft tossed calmly in the ocean's waves. "How much longer, do you think?" he asked.

George sensed his fear. "A day, maybe two . . ." He raised his voice. "They'll find us, don't worry."

Nick turned again to stare across the water. Only miles and miles of ocean water stared back, and beyond their voices the only sound was the lapping of the water against the hull of the raft. There weren't any other ships, not even a bird could be seen.

Nick rubbed his hot face and blinked. "Oh, no," he said suddenly.

George lifted his arm off his forehead and peered across the water. "It can't be . . ." he said, and then . . .

Lesson 91   DIALOGUE

Objective: To relate the importance of dialogue to good characterization (and fiction writing)

1. **Survey:** Use **Activity 91-1** on spoken words.

   Discuss the results.

2. **Role play:** Have a conversation with a student (or two volunteer students converse together) about any topic. The rest of the students critique: What dialogue was important? What was unnecessary (or boring)?

3. **Videotape:** Show a videotape of a selected movie scene where the actors use intense dialogue. **Discuss** how the dialogue moves the plot or adds to characterization.

4. **Modeling:** Examine the dialogue found in selected short stories in the literature text, quotes from magazine articles, or the script from a play.

   Ask: What do you find interesting? What does the dialogue reveal about the person saying it?

5. **Explain:** Present using stems and quotation marks with dialogue in a story.

- Stem = who said the quote (ex) he said, she shouted, Joe exclaimed, Joan whispered, etc. If it is clear who is speaking for the reader, then the stem does not have to be used.

- Quotations = punctuation mark indicating spoken words of characters— " ". Be sure they are used accurately.

6. **Writing:** Students work with the issue of dialect in dialogue—**Activity 91-2.**

   Check the results.

7. **Lecture** on the need for dialogue to be natural, that it should be important to the story, not extraneous, that it should reveal something crucial about the character

   Using dialogue in a story is important. Dialogue can reveal characterization, advance the plot, and reflect all the characters' dialects or speech patterns.

Homework options:

A. Students script the dialogue they have with family and friends in a single day.

B. Students write one page of dialogue between two imaginary characters.

C. Advanced students can research and compare the dialogue used in the narratives of two different authors.

D. Students list 20-25 of the most frequently used expressions by friends, family, classmates, and/or teammates.

E. Students write an editorial arguing either *for* or *against* the use of slang, profanity, and "street talk" in stories for young adults.

Name _____

What Did They Say?

Directions: For each situation below, provide the first words that come to mind.

1. What are the first ten words of an infant? Why those words?

2. What are the words students say on the bus as they ride it home after school?

3. What are some words you've heard or read from politicians?

4. What are some of the more interesting words you've heard or read in some popular advertisements?

5. What is the most interesting dialogue you've heard an actor say in a movie?

6. What is the most interesting dialogue you've read in a story or novel?

7. What are some typical phrases or words you hear from your parents?

Name _____

Dialogue and Dialect

Directions: Rewrite each of the following bits of dialogue taken from famous novels. Use modern language.

From *Red Badge of Courage* by Stephen Crane

1. "We're goin' t' move t'morrah—sure. We're goin' 'way up the river, cut across, an' come in behint 'em."

   Your version:

2. "An' take good care of yerself in this here fightin' business—you watch out, an' take good care of yerself. Don't go a-thinkin' you can lick the hull rebel army at the start because yeh can't."

   Your version:

3. "That's all true, I s'pose, but I'm not going to skeddaddle."

   Your version:

From *The Adventures of Huckleberry Finn* by Mark Twain

4. "Yo 'old father doan' know yit what he's a-gwyne to do. Sometimes he spec he'll go 'way, en den ag'in he spec he'll stay. De bes' way is to res' easy en let de ole man take his own way."

   Your version:

5. "You gwyne to have considable trouble in yo life, en considable joy. Sometimes you gwyne to git hurt, en sometimes gwyne to git sick; but every time you's gwyne to git well agin."

   Your version:

Lesson 92 GUEST SPEAKER

Objective: To improve students' understanding of the craft of writing fiction.

Activities:

[This activity can be done at any time during the unit.]

1. **Guest Speaker:** Ask a fiction writer, librarian, or another teacher to discuss the craft of writing short fiction.

   Potential topics:

   A. Author vs. Narrator vs. Main character

   B. How to begin and end a story

   C. What to read to improve our skill as writers

   D. Censorship and the fiction writer

   E. How does a story writer get published?

2. **Discussion:** Students ask questions of the guest speaker.

Homework options:

A. Students summarize the comments of the guest speaker.

B. Students pretend to be story reviewers, (like Siskel and Ebert) and critique a self-selected story.

C. Students analyze the following statement from Ralph Waldo Emerson: "Talent alone cannot make a writer. There must be a man behind the book."

Lesson 93 FROM START TO FINISH

Objective: To continue work at plotting

To write the first draft of a short story

1. **Discuss:** Starting and ending a story. [Answers will vary.]

    A. What makes for a successful story beginning?

    B. What do most readers expect to see at the beginning of a story?

    C. Should stories end optimistically or pessimistically? Why?

    D. How does a writer create suspense?

2. **Freewriting:** Each student begins a story, writing only the first sentence. Students pass their papers around the classroom, allowing each new reader to add one additional sentence to the story. Pass the papers 8–10 times.

    Discuss the results.

3. **Analysis:** Study some children's books—(ex) Dr. Seuss—for their conflict, climax, and resolution. Students should write their information in their notebooks. **Check** the results.

4. **Explain:** Discuss how the short stories will be evaluated.

John Bonstingl, international education consultant, proposes that "grades as assessment symbols [need] to be rethought. If nothing succeeds like success, why do we seem to structure schooling for boredom, apathy, and marginal student involvement, rather than structuring the work that teachers and students do together for ultimate success?" Accordingly, you might base this evaluation on the thoroughness of the writing, the creativity in description, and the proper grammar.

---

5. **Writing:** Students work on the outlining/drafting of their short stories.

6. **Conferences**: Spend 2-4 minutes with each student talking about his/ her writing. Conferences enable the teacher to assist if there are difficulties, and monitor progress (to promote success, not necessarily to document failure).

    Discussions could focus, for example, on the story's title, the first paragraph, the most interesting character (Why is this person appealing?), or effective descriptions. This can help students analyze their story—

characters, events or setting—at various stages. Typical questions to ask:

A. What shows the suspense? The humor?

B. Why did you choose this setting?

C. Let's read the dialogue out loud. Does it seem natural?

D. What are the differences between these characters?

E. What do you hope to accomplish?

F. How does it compare to other items in your portfolio?

> **The teacher's role here is crucial to the students' enjoyment of writing fiction. You should use literary terminology, but only for the purpose for initiating discussions about their writing. It is especially important to be alert if a student writes a story that may be deemed controversial by the school board or community members. You should learn your school administration's policies or standards regarding this and prepare for any complaints that could come later.**

Homework:

Students complete the writing of their short story.

Lesson 94   PEER EDITING—FICTION

Objective: To complete peer editing and assist with publication

1. **Debate:**   The Pulitzer Prize is an annual award given to authors and other artists each April for work done the preceding year. The $500 award was initiated in 1911 by Joseph Pulitzer, a wealthy newspaper publisher. The prize for literature (novels) is selected by an advisory board and distributed by trustees from Columbia University.

    If you were on the advisory board, what story writer would win the Pulitzer Prize? Why?

2. **Explain:** Remind students to avoid passive reading where their eyes just skim over the words. They should engage in a silent dialogue with the material: What ideas or facts am I looking for? What details seem important? What is an interesting scene or characterization?

3. **Explain:** Use **Form 94-1** to assist with the peer editing of short fiction in a writing workshop format.

4. **Review:** Remind the students what to look for.

    A. Structure—What is the plot? The setting?

    B. Characterization—How fully developed are the main characters? Why do you think the character acted that way?

    C. Interest level—What makes the story interesting or different? Which story is better? Why? Would this be suitable for all readers?

> **With literature, students should respond intellectually and emotionally to what they read. Students may read a story first for the pleasure it may bring, but they're also developing their skills as a critical reader each time they determine its aesthetic appeal and consider its meaning. Certainly, reading itself should be a pleasurable experience, but there is no harm in making it challenging as well. The readers should have questions about the story, engage competently in discussions that determine the relevance of the work, and exchange interpretations.**

---

5. **Group work:** Students exchange with group members the first drafts of their stories, providing a brief summary of the story. Group members critique it and offer suggestion on characterization, setting, dialogue, plotting, grammar, etc.

337

Students complete peer editing by discussing each story and exchanging views about the material.

If time remains, each group selects one story that they feel is the best story from that group. They write a paragraph advertisement/review to interest the other groups in adopting their point of view. In this way, students can come to see themselves as authoritative readers.

6. **Summarize:** Students should expect to do continuous revising and editing of their work, especially fiction—(ex) Tolstoy revised *War and Peace* ten times.

Homework:

Students make revisions of their stories based on the comments and markings from their classmates and the teacher.

Students can submit their stories for publication. Use **Form 94-2**.

Form 94-1

Peer Editing—Fiction

Directions: Follow the steps below to critique fiction.

1. Read as far as you can in the allotted time. When told to stop, write down what you have found to be most interesting in the story to that point.

   Maybe it is a character, an interesting description, a scene, or even the author's vocabulary. Be sure to explain in detail why you have selected that aspect of the story as most interesting.

   If you find *nothing* interesting, then write an explanation of what is lacking in the story.

2. Continue reading to completion. At the end of the allotted time for silent reading, stop and offer commentary on the paper, (in the margins, above or beneath a sentence) on the characterization, dialogue, setting, plot, grammar, etc.

4. Pass the story to the next person in the group. Repeat the procedure beginning with Step #1.

5. After 3-4 passes, finish the activity by discussing each story. Consider writing styles, creativity, and content.

6. Review all aspects of story writing with other group members. Create some typical test questions—(ex) Where can an author get an idea for a story?

Submitting Fiction for Publication

1. Creative Arts Institute
   8021 Kennedy Road
   Blacklick, OH 43004

   Notes: Five dollars entry fee; publication and cash awards

2. Ohio PreK-8 WRITING AWARDS
   1291 Fairgreen Avenue
   Lima, OH 45805
   419-991-4723

   Notes: U.S. Savings Bond awards; submissions according to school enrollment

3. Fiction Contest
   Department of English
   Mercyhurst College
   Erie, PA 16546
   814-824-2461

   Notes: Cash awards

4. 21st Century Magazine
   Box 30
   Newton, MA 02161
   1-800-363-1986
   Fax# 617-964-1940

   Notes: Publication; students must write a statement declaring the essay is an original

5. Scholastic Art and Writing Awards
   555 Broadway
   New York, NY 10012
   212-343-6931

   Notes: Publication; $5000 scholarship and cash awards; different categories

6. American Council for International Studies
   800-888-2247

   Notes: $1000 scholarship

7. Check "The Market Guide for Young Writers" by Kathy Henderson (Writer's Digest Books, 1996).

Section 12 : POETRY

"I have never started a poem yet whose end I knew. Writing a poem is discovering."   (*Robert Frost*)

Objectives: Inspire an appreciation of poetry

                  Explain poetry terms and technique

                  Encourage students to experiment with language

                  Establish a criteria for effective poems

Length: Approximately ten lessons

Introduction:

Poetry has been a part of our history since ancient peoples began devising entertainment. The first songs were poems; the first stories were written as poems; some literary critics believe the first signs of culture were poems.

We have come to expect poems to bring enlightenment and entertainment, humor and history, and romance and realism to the reader. Robert Frost identifies the great spectrum of poetry when he says, "A poem begins in delight and ends in wisdom."

Because poetry is an art form where often the unexpected is to be expected, and responses are so varied, teachers face a serious challenge when explaining how to write a poem. Poetry is also, of course, very personal.

The best approach is to make the student's encounter with poetry as simple as possible by dealing with only one skill at a time. Be sure to introduce poetry by appealing to all learning styles, by evaluating student's own poems carefully, and by selecting appropriate poems as models.

Students may approach poetry at first for the pleasure it may bring to their lives. Teachers need to create a classroom environment that encourages students' active participation with poetry, promotes critical reading of poems, and makes accessible a variety of poems. Once students accept poetry as a craft, they become more open, as poet James Dickey said, "to [understanding] the world as it interacts with us, as it can be re-created by words, by rhythms and by images."

Lesson 95   THE POPULARITY OF POETRY

Objective: To introduce an appreciation for poetry

Activities:

1. **Survey #1:** What do you think was the first forms of entertainment used by ancient humans? List them in order.

    [(1) Stories told orally; (2) stories told as poems; (3) paintings on cave walls; (4) music by chants and percussion.]

2. **Survey #2:** Should poems entertain or teach the reader?

    [Generally, poems should do both, yet many reasons can be found for doing either one.]

3. **Discuss:** Why have the following poems remained so popular for decades and decades?

Roses are red,	Twinkle, twinkle, little star
Violets are blue.	How I wonder what you are.
Sugar is sweet	Up above the world so high
And so are you.	Like a diamond in the sky.

    [They're short, sweet, simple; they rhyme; they're about romance, love, affection, friendship, appreciation, etc.]

4. **Debate #1:** Poetry is more popular now than ever before.

    [Statistics from editors, universities, and teachers say more people are writing and submitting poems now than ever before; more poetry books are being published in a single year than there have been in some past decades; poetry readings are now very popular in coffee houses, libraries, and universities.]

5. **Debate #2:** Poetry is more difficult to read than a story.

    [Obviously, it depends. With time, all poems can be understood and enjoyed.]

6. **Discuss:**   Poets and Poems.

    A.   Who are some poets?

    [Prove the popularity of poetry. Students could name a famous poet or their own sister.]

    B.   Where can we find poems?

[Literature text, anthologies, in songs, some radio advertisements, magazines, some speeches, the Bible, billboards, Hallmark cards, etc.]

C. Why is there such a strong connection (think of Hallmark cards) between poetry and romance?

[Answers will vary.]

7. **Freewriting: Activity 95-1**—Answer questions about the popularity of poetry.

   Discuss the results.

8. **Music:** Play songs from popular performing artists whose lyrics are understandable and appropriate. Ask: How do these lyrics constitute poetry?

9. **Assessment:** Ask students: What do you want to learn about poetry? Put their answers on the blackboard.

Homework options:

A. Students locate a poem that appeals to them to bring to class and share with classmates.

B. Students pretend to be the editor of a poetry magazine (devise a name) and list the criteria they will follow for publishing poems submitted.

C. Students create a definition for poetry, then select a poem that matches the definition closely. They must also explain their reasoning.

D. Students respond to quotes about poetry—**Activity 95-2.**

E. Students bring in the written song lyrics that are poetic and interesting in terms of word choice.

Name _____

The Popularity of Poetry

1. What holidays or special days are often marked by people as appropriate for delivering or receiving poems?

2. What are some typical topics or themes found in poems?

3. What are some influences on poets for their ideas?

4. What poems (or kinds of poems) have you enjoyed reading in the past?

5. What are the qualities of poetry that appeal to you? What makes a good poem?

Name _____

Quotes About Poetry

Directions: Read each quote and write a reaction to it, explaining why you agree or
disagree with it.

1. "Poetry is the devil's wine."   (St. Augustine)

2. "All poetry is difficult to read."   (Robert Browning)

3. "Writing free verse is like playing tennis with the net down."   (Robert Frost)

4. "A poem is the very image of life expressed in its eternal truth."   (Percy Bysshe
   Shelley)

5. "Poetry is nothing but healthy speech."   (Henry David Thoreau)

6. "Poetry is the spontaneous overflow of powerful feelings."   (William Wordsworth)

7. "All men are poets at heart."   (Ralph Waldo Emerson)

8. "Poetry is simply the most beautiful, impressive, and widely effective mode of
   saying things."   (Matthew Arnold)

9. "All poets are mad."   (Robert Burton)

10. "Every man is a poet when he is in love."   (Plato)

Lesson 96   BENEFITS OF POETRY

Objective: To expand on the appeal of poetry

Activities:

1. **Oral reading:** Students read favorite poems. (Give extra points for any special demonstration of drama or theatrics). Be sure you read a favorite poem, too.

2. **Lecture:** Explain the benefits of poetry.
   - Lets the writer show emotion in an intense way
   - Prompts the use of imagination (creativity)
   - Allows the writer to work with words in new ways
   - Helps improve the thinking skills of analysis, synthesis, and creativity
   - Can guide a writer through self-analysis

3. **Videotape:** Show a video of poets discussing the craft of poetry or poems being dramatized.

4. **Discuss:** Speak about various aspects and attributes of poetry.

   A. Experts say babies in the womb benefit from hearing rhythmic poems and song lyrics. How and why might this occur?

   [They're soothing, can prompt relaxation, enjoyable melodies, etc.]

   B. What are some nursery rhymes? Why is it that these poems stay with us?

   [Answers will vary.]

   C. Why is it said that poetry is the form of writing that is most pleasing to the ear?

   [Poets arrange words in rhyme, use alliteration (repeating consonant sounds) or assonance (repeating vowel sounds) to create a musical quality, etc.]

   D. Poems seem to say a lot in few words. How is this accomplished?

   [Answers will vary, but be sure to deal with economy in writing, how poets emphasize *more* with *less*.]

   E. What is our country's most patriotic poem?

   ["Star Spangled Banner"]

5. **Explain:** Talk about how poetry can teach us history. Distribute and **discuss Form 96-1.** Perhaps have students look up the location of Middlesex, MA, show them a lantern, or play a videotape of western movie bandits robbing a train.

6. **Writing:** Students write paragraph(s) on how poetry has appealed to them, pointing out what they like and those elements of poems—(ex) rhyme—that they enjoy.

   Discuss or **check** the results.

Homework options:

A. Students write a one page comparison explaining the differences between the lyrics of country and western, rap, and heavy metal music. Be sure they focus on the lyrics, not the music.

B. Students research and make a chart or time-line of famous poets that includes the decades in which they wrote, the awards they won, and the general topics of their poems.

C. Students write an editorial that declares the importance (or unimportance) of poetry for students today.

D. Students select a poem that they think is important, or has true literary merit and include a copy of it with a letter to a friend or relative.

E. Artistic students can create a collage of illustrations and pictures on poster board that features a favorite poem—(ex) winter scenes for Frost's "Stopping by Woods on a Snowy Evening".

Poetry and History

Directions: The following excerpts are from poems that involve elements of history. Beneath each poem explain the time period of history it reflects and the attitude the poem takes toward the subject.

1.   *"Paul Revere's Ride"*

Listen my children and you shall hear
Of the midnight ride of Paul Revere,
On the eighteenth of April, in Seventy-five
Hardly a man is now alive
Who remembers that famous day and year.

He said to his friend, "If the British march
By land or sea from the town tonight,
Hang a lantern aloft in the belfry arch
Of the North Church tower as a signal light.
One if by land, two if by sea;
And I on the opposite shore will be,
Ready to ride and spread the alarm
Through every Middlesex village and farm,
For the country folk to be up and arm."

(by Henry Wadsworth Longfellow)

2.   *"Jesse James"*

Jesse James was a two-gun man,
Strong-arm chief of an outlaw clan.
He twirled an old Colt forty-five;
They never took Jesse James alive.

Jesse James was King of the Wes';
He'd a di'mon' heart in his left breas';
He'd a fire in his heart no hurt could stifle,
Lion eyes an' a Winchester rifle.

Jesse rode through a sleepin' town,
Looked the moonlit street both up an' down;
Crack-crack-crack, the street ran flames,
An' a great voice cried, "I'm Jesse James!"

Jesse's heart was as sof' as a woman;
Fer guts an' strength he was sooper human;
He could put six shots through a woodpecker's eye
And take in one swaller a gallon o' rye.

Jesse James was a Hercules.
When he went through the woods he tore up the trees.

(by William Rose Benet)

Lesson 97   POETIC LANGUAGE

Objective: To identify the variety and vividness of poetic language

Activities:

1. **Survey:** What is one way a poem differs from other types of writing? [Most students will identify how poets use words in different or unusual ways. Survey results will vary.]

2. **Discuss:** Talk about word choice in poems.

    A. What are the connotations of the following colors: red, blue, yellow?

        [Red implies blood, anger, debt, violence; blue can mean cold, sadness, water; yellow suggests cowardice, heat, happiness.]

    B. If love and death remain such common topics for poems, how do poets show creativity?

        [By dealing with them in new ways—their own unique poetic structure and choice of words]

    C. How do poets create rhythm in a poem?

        [With meter in a line, syllables per line]

3. **Analysis:** Students examine magazine articles and advertisements for poetic language. Note how writers try to be poetic in other formats (essay, ads, etc.)

4. **Read:** Have students read a selected poem(s) from the literature text that shows vividness, experimentation, and creativity in use of language.

5. **Explain:** Discuss strong and weak lines.

    • Strong lines = lines that have strong diction, unique phrase(s), a detailed image, or figurative language

    Distribute **Form 97-1**—Poems that have strong lines.

    • Weak lines = one-word lines; clichés; dull phrases; no figurative language

6. **Contest:** Who can create the strongest lines of poetry? Students write single lines that show creativity and vividness with word choice. A panel of students could be judges.

7. **Write:** Explain that clichés in poems show poor language skills. Clichés are to be avoided. Distribute **Activity 97-2—Clichés—What do they mean?**

    Discuss the results.

Homework options:

A. Advanced students could locate two poems from different centuries (15th-20th), copy them, and write a comparison/contrast essay detailing how poetic structures have changed in the time between the two poems.

B. Students locate a poem that has strong lines and vivid language to share with classmates.

C. Students take a common topic—(ex) friendship—and write a 6, 8, or 10 line poem that has strong lines and unique phrases about it.

D. Students take any poem and transform its lines into complete sentences and its stanzas into coherent paragraphs (i.e., working backwards). This activity affirms how poets play with language and grammar to structure their poems.

Strong Lines

Directions: Note the poets' unique wording and strong lines.

"Instruction"

The coach has taught her how to swing,
run bases, slide, how to throw
to second, flip off her mask for fouls.

Now, on her own, she studies
how to knock the dirt out of her cleats,
hitch up her pants, miss her shoulder
with a stream of spit, bump
her fist into her catcher's mitt,
and stare incredulously at the ump.

by Conrad Hilberry
(Reprinted by permission of Conrad Hilberry)

"Little Leaguers"

No national anthem introduces them,
these little leaguers in hardware store uniforms
whom no one calls Babe or Campy or Catfish or Doc.
Their field of dirt, grass, and heat sits flat
in the city park, a dusty oasis on June evenings
for ballpark groupies and sweaty parents.
When slick smooth wood strikes white tight leather,
the crack creates standing room only for moms and dads
on the splintered bleachers, the warm air
full of their slaps, screams, and cheers
for the little Giant, Tiger, or Yankee,
desperately sprinting for first base and beyond.
No refereed whistle stops the play,
only three outs or a setting sun.
And strikeouts, stolen bases, homeruns
soon fade, like smoke, in the summer haze,
forgotten for the ice cream sundae melting slowly down
small chins, crimson jerseys, and dirty pants.

by Keith Manos

Clichés—What Do They Mean?

Directions: For each cliché below, explain what it means in more original language.

1. At the end of my rope =

2. Back against the wall =

3. At the drop of a hat =

4. Between a rock and a hard place =

5. Bite the bullet =

6. Boys will be boys =

7. It's a breeze =

8. Bury the hatchet =

9. Chip off the old block =

10. Clear as a bell =

11. Dead tired =

12. Dog-eat-dog =

13. Down in the dumps =

14. Elbow room =

15. Flipped his lid =

16. Fed up =

17. Fits like a glove =

18. High off the hog =

19. Head over heels =

20. Have a ball =

21. Hit me like a ton of bricks =

22. King of the hill =

23. Like a bat out of hell =

24. Like a herd of elephants =

25. Needle in a haystack =

26. On the tip of the tongue =

27. Over the hill =

28. Safe and sound =

29. Saved by the bell =

30. Run like a deer =

31. Shake a leg =

32. Slept like a log =

33. Smart as a whip =

34. Like taking candy from a baby =

35. Walking on air =

36. Time flies =

37. Throw in the towel =

38. Through thick and thin =

39. Worked her fingers to the bone =

40. Like two peas in a pod =

Lesson 98 RHYME AND RHYTHM

Objective: To work at writing rhyming poems

Activities:

1. **Music:** Play a song in class that has an easy beat and an even tempo [that one, two, three . . . one, two, three kind of beat—(ex) "The Wanderer" by Dion]. Students may start swaying or moving to the music.

    Then stop the music and ask a volunteer (hopefully a musician) to explain the rhythm.

    [**Or: Sing** Emily Dickinson's poem "Because Death Could Not Stop for Me," if available, to the tune of "Gilligan's Island." Then ask: How do poets establish a rhythm?]

2. **Lecture:** Rhyme and free verse are opposites. There are some traditional rhyme patterns. Distribute and explain **Form 98-1**.

3. **Discuss:** Consider the appeal of rhyme and rhythm in poetry. [Answers will vary.]

    A. Why is rhyme so appealing to readers, especially young children?

    B. What are some nursery rhymes?

    C. What are some other examples of poems that show the use of rhyme?

    D. How does rhyme influence the meaning or message of a poem?

    E. What is the relationship between rhyme and humor in poetry (consider limericks)?

    F. Why do you think some of the earliest poems were in rhyme?

    G. What are some rhymes you've noticed in song lyrics?

    H. What makes a successful rhyming poem?

4. **Identification:** Students locate and read rhyming poems in their literature text or personal anthology.

5. **Freewriting:** Students write rhyming poems on a class or individually selected topic.

    Check the results.

6. **Assessment:** Ask students to respond orally which they prefer—rhyme or free verse? Why?

Homework options:

A. Advanced students can research types of meter and make a chart where they list each type, its definition, and an example for each.

B. Students locate 4-8 rhyming poems and analyze their rhyme schemes.

C. Students write a detailed essay explaining why most rhyming poems are considered light verse and entertaining.

D. Students make a chart of the three common rhyme schemes ABAB, ABBA, AABB—of poems with four-line stanzas. For each scheme, students provide an example of two poems that match it. They should include an explanation about the effect of the rhyme on the poem's meaning.

E. Students write a persuasive editorial that promotes a preference for either free verse or rhyme. Students must take a position on which type of verse is better, even if they see the value of each.

F. Students write a persuasive editorial which supports or challenges an argument that rhyming poems are always optimistic and entertaining in theme and content.

Rhyme and Rhythm in Poetry

Single End Rhyme

- Occurs at the end of the line with a single syllable word

  (ex) There was an obliging young *snail*,
  Who wished to deliver the *mail*;
  And he said that though *slow*
  He was sure he could *go*
  Once a week to each house without *fail*.

Double End Rhyme

- Occurs at the end of a line with a double syllable word

  (ex) Mike Tyson liked fighting,
  too bad he started biting.

Triple End Rhyme

- Occurs at the end of a line with a triple syllable word

  (ex) To them it was glorious
  To come home victorious.

Internal Rhyme

- Occurs when the rhyming words appear on the same line

  (ex) The thunder crashed, the lightning flashed.

Lesson 99   GIMMICK POEMS

Objective: To practice writing a variety of poems

Activities:

1. **Group work:** Explore creating poems.

    A. **Contest #1**—Which group can list the most rhyming words for *tall*? [Give two minutes and remind them to consider 2–3 syllable words, too.]

        Contest #2—Which group can list the most rhyming words for *feet*? [Give two minutes]

        Writing: Students use words from either or both lists to create a 4,6, or 8 line poem.

    B. **Dictionary Poem**—Each group member skims a dictionary until he/she finds a phrase(s) that seems interesting. These phrases are then combined into an interesting poem.

    C. **ABC Poems**—Each group writes the alphabet down the left side of the paper and then begins a line of a poem that begins with that letter.

        (ex)   **A**ll the day

                Butterflies hover

                Cautiously, **D**ancing near the

                Evergreen

                Forest, etc.

        See which group can get the farthest in 6–8 minutes.

    D. **Memory Poem:** Each group member writes 1–3 phrases about a childhood memory—(ex) laughing at clowns at a carnival, wearing a pink and frilly dress at my birthday party, etc. Students then combine their phrases into one coherent and comprehensive poem.

    E. **Share and Compare** song lyrics of favorite songs.

    F. **Assessment:** Each group lists questions about poetry, as if they were creating a test.

    Check their work.

Homework:

Students do **Activity 99-1—Formula Poems**.

Name _____

Formula Poems

Directions: Have fun playing with words and creating a variety of poems.

1. Review slogans and phrases from advertisements and pick several to create a poem with a title.

    (ex)   *"Teenage Times"* (add the source if you wish)

    The new and improved (detergent)
    Generation Next (Pepsi)
    who just do it (Nike)
    during the Irish spring (soap)
    because they are solid—like a rock (Chevy)
    to be all they can be. (U.S. Army)

    Yours:

2. Create a NAME (or acrostic) poem. This is formed by using the letters of your first or last name to begin each line of the poem.

    (ex)   *F*riendly to all.
    *R*ighteous and
    *E*ntertaining
    *D*ude.

    Yours:

3. Create an original 4, 6, or 8 line poem using the following words: chandelier, photograph, Italian, sizzle, hazy, and a sixth word, chosen from the dictionary.

4. Telephone Poem—Write your telephone number down the left side and create a poem where the syllables in each line match the digit. Ignore zeroes.

    (ex) 3 Inch by inch

          9 my puppy snuggles into my lap

          3 to settle

          2 his head

          7 with soft fur and wet whiskers,

          4 giving warmth and

          1 love.

    Yours:

    ___

    ___

    ___

    ___

    ___

    ___

    ___

Lesson 100   IMAGERY

Objective: To discover the importance of imagery in poems

Activities:

1. **Brainstorm:** Students list descriptive words and phrases related to the most beautiful place they have ever visited.

   Check the results.

2. **Board work:** Now, pairs of students go to the board and combine their phrases to create 4-6 line poems.

   Discuss the results, pointing out effective description.

3. **Explain:** Imagery in poetry refers to the sensory words the poet uses to create an *image* or *picture* for readers.

4. **Modeling:** Use **Activity 100-1**—Locating imagery in poetry.

5. **Identification:** Find several poems in the literature text that demonstrate effective imagery.

6. **Freewriting options:** The goal is to create imagery in a poem.

   A. **Word Association**: Students complete a poem, line by line, as you announce concrete words at random—(ex) dawn, musty, sparrow, headlights. The result should be a study on imagery.

   B. **Poem Pass:** Each student begins a poem about a specific place—(ex) gymnasium—object—(ex) a pencil—or scene—(ex) a fire. They write one line of effective imagery before passing it to another student who adds a second line, and so on. Pass 5–6 times.

   C. **Visual aid:** Students observe a picture, drawing, transparency, or poster to use as the focus of a poem showing vivid imagery.

   Discuss the results—students read their poems.

8. **Summary:** Poetry is often based on observations poets make about their world—(ex) flowers in a field, highway traffic, children playing. Poems that have strong imagery emerge from the poets using concrete and sensory words.

Homework options:

A. Students choose a poem from an anthology or literary magazine that has dramatic imagery to present to the class. They can use visual, technical, or musical aids to highlight the imagery in that poem.

B. Students write another poem, using concrete and sensory language, to describe a certain locale, object, or scene.

C. Students read and analyze a selected poem that they find in their literature text that contains imagery.

D. Artistic students can illustrate or paint any scene and then create a poem of imagery that relates to it. For extra points, they could also include a published poem that relates to the scene.

Name _____

Imagery in Poetry

Directions: For each poem below, locate the sensory language and explain the imagery in the right margin.

1.

Birch Tree

My backyard birch tree,
So slender and white
Waving to the midnight sky,
Like a shivering ghost,
Dancing in the darkness.

by Keith Manos

2.

The Delicatessen

Sometimes strolling late at night
I stop before a closed delicatessen,
where a single light splits the darkness
and flashes across the butcher's blades.
The owner's apron hangs on a hook,
meat stains smeared into a map,
near a wooden slab where bones
are broken, scraped clean, ready to feed me.

by Keith Manos

3.

The Spider

Its black shoe polish coat
shines evenly as it inches on
the silky web with thick hairy legs
towards the tender center.
Dew hangs like miniature diamonds
on lacy threads beneath this
black beauty and silent danger.

by Keith Manos

4.

The Sea

Sputtering, foaming, frothing
the sea rushes hard to the muddy shore,
and eats greedily the salty sand
before slipping and sliding back,
with its great billows of foam
smashed against rocky ledges
on its way to the purple horizon
and the always pale moon.

by Keith Manos

Lesson 101   FIGURATIVE LANGUAGE

Objective: To work at using figurative language in poems

Activities:

1. **Sounds:** Students write the words that match up to the sounds the teacher (or student volunteer) makes.

    A. Drink a glass of water sloppily   [slurp, splash]

    B. Drop Alka-Seltzer in a glass of water   [fizz]

    C. Touch two glasses together   [clink]

    D. Drop a book on a desk or on the floor   [thud, bang, thump]

    E. Howl like a coyote   [howl]

    F. Moo like a cow   [moo]

    G. Crumple a piece of paper   [crackle]

    H. Exhale with your teeth close together   [hiss, whiz]

2. **Lecture:** Speak on onomatopoeia and onomatopoeic words which can be useful in poetry. They can add to a poem's tone and meaning.

3. **Writing:** Work on more examples of figurative language. Use **Activity 101-1.**

    Check the results. Point out creative examples of figurative language and word choice (vocabulary).

4. **Identify:** Have students read selected poems from their literature text where various examples of figurative language can be found.

5. **Summary:** Using figurative language in any type of writing, especially poetry, demonstrates maturity as a writer. Figurative language should not be overused, or dominate a poem; however, when used judiciously, metaphors, alliteration, etc. can add power to a poem.

Homework:

Students write two poems—one whose topic is selected by the class (nominations and vote) and one whose topic is selected individually.

Advanced students can investigate and cite examples of conceits, hyperbole, assonance, and repetition in poetry.

Name _____

Figurative Language and Poetry

1. Complete the following poem using words that begin with "t"

   The terrible t_____

   t_____ until it was

   t_____ and

   t_____.

2. **Define** alliteration:

3. Complete the following poem (similes)

   Every Friday, I act like _____. (animal)

   Every Monday, I feel like _____. (object)

4. **Define** simile (and give an example):

5. **Identify** the similes in the following poem:

   She runs like a deer, swift and sure,
   She screeches like a crow when she's mad;
   She yelps like a puppy when she bruises her knee,
   My daughter coos like a dove when she's glad.

6. **Explain**: What two dissimilar things are being compared in the following poem?

   My eggs stared back with sick yellow eyes.

7. **Define** personification (and give an example):

8. **Define** metaphor (and give an example):

9. **Write** your own 6–8 line poem using figurative language.

Lesson 102   GUEST SPEAKER

Objective: To learn more about the craft of poetry

Activities:

[This lesson can be done at any time during the unit.]

1. **Guest speaker:** Ask a well-known local poet to speak to the students. Some possible topics for his/her presentation include:

    A. How to begin and end a poem

    B. How to analyze a poem

    C. Submitting poems to literary magazines

    D. Revising/editing a poem

    E. Diction and grammar in poems

2. **Discussion:** Allow students the opportunity to ask questions of the guest speaker.

3. **Lecture:** Speak on the subject of *poet vs. narrator* in a poem.

Homework:

Students summarize the speaker's comments in a reaction paper.

Students write 2–4 new poems on self-selected topics.

Lesson 103 PEER EDITING—POETRY

Objective: To engage students in peer editing of poetry

Activities:

[Examine Section 13 for more particular guidelines about peer editing. This lesson could take 1–3 class periods. Poetry workshop can be done several times during the unit.]

1. **Explain:** Go over the guidelines for effective poetry workshop.

   A. Avoid passive reading where your eyes just skim over words and lines. Look carefully for strong and weak lines.

   B. Engage in a silent dialogue with the poem: What do I like? What details seem important? Where is some figurative language?

   C. Write comments or questions about the poem.

   D. Dialogue with the poet (and other group members) about the poem.

   E. Thank the poet (and your editors).

2. **Group work:** Students should be in groups of 5–6 to promote a wider interchange of interpretations and reactions to each poem. **Monitor** their work.

3. **Discuss:** Publication options. Students can choose any of the following:

   A. Perform poetry readings to another English class or to elementary school student.

   B. Invite guests—other students, parents, principals, administrators, school board members, and the media to a formal poetry reading in the school auditorium

   C. Post poems on a hallway bulletin board or in a display case

   D. Mail poems to other students, friends, parents, media personalities, relatives, or school board members

   E. Submit their poems to a local, regional, or national publication (See **Form 103-1**)

   F. Produce a class poetry magazine (or anthology) to distribute to other students and teachers, parents, friends, school board members, and administrators

Homework:

Students revise their poems in preparation for submitting them for publication (Refer to publication options).

Submitting Poetry for Publication

1. High School Poetry Anthology
   McGregor Publishing
   118 S. Westshore Blvd.
   Tampa, Florida 33609

2. Creative Arts Institute
   8021 Kennedy Road
   Blacklick, OH 43004

3. Ohio PreK-8 Writing Awards
   1291 Fairgreen Avenue
   Lima, OH 45805
   419-991-4723

4. Poets' League of Greater Cleveland
   P.O. Box 91801
   Cleveland, OH 44101
   216-932-8444

5. High School Poetry Contest
   Gannon University English Department
   109 University Square
   Erie, PA 16541-0001
   814-871-7725

6. *21st Century* Magazine
   Box 30
   Newton, MA 02161
   1-800-363-1986
   Fax# 617-964-1940

7. Teacher's Selections: Anthology of Eleventh Grade Poetry
   Anthology of Poetry, Inc.
   P.O. Box 698
   Asheboro, NC 27204-0698
   910-626-7762

8. Scholastic Art and Writing Awards
   555 Broadway
   New York, NY 10012
   212-343-6931

Form 103-1 (*continued*)

9. CSU Poetry Contest
   Department of English
   1815 Rhodes Tower
   Cleveland State University
   1983 East 24th Street
   Cleveland, OH
   216-687-3986

10. *American Poetry Review*
    401 South Broad Street
    Philadelphia, Pennsylvania 19147

11. Merlin's Pen (grades 7–10)
    98 Main Street
    East Greenwich, Rhode Island 02818

12. Poetry Society of America
    15 Grammercy Park
    New York, NY 10003

13. *Youth* Magazine
    Room 1203
    1505 Race Street
    Philadelphia, Pennsylvania 19102

14. *English Journal*
    Spring Poetry Festival
    Box 112
    East Lansing, Michigan 48223

15. *Scholastic* Magazine
    50 West 44th Street
    New York, NY 10036

16. Check *The Market Guide for Young Writers* by Kathy Henderson (Writer's Digest
    Books, 1996).

Lesson 104   SPECIAL POEMS

Objective: To examine Couplets, Haiku, and Limericks

Activities:

1. **Debate:** Free verse (lines without rhyme or meter) is better to read and easier to write than rhyme.

2. **Writing:** Work on Couplets, Haiku, and Limericks. Use **Activity 104-1**. **Discuss** the results.

3. **Discuss:** Couplets, Haiku, and Limericks.

   A. What inspires these types of poems?

      [rhyme, nature scenes, humorous events, etc.]

   B. How could season inspire haiku? What images or scenes could be the focus of a haiku poem?

      [Answers will vary. They're based on observations.]

   C. Why do many people favor these types of poems?

      [They're short, the humor, people may appreciate nature, etc.]

   D. Why are these types of poems more common to cultures outside the United States—(ex) haiku from Japan, and limericks from Britain?

      [Answers will vary.]

4. **Freewriting:** Students write poems as follows:

   A. A haiku that reflects in some way the color red

   B. A couplet where the final word in the first line is *star*

   C. A limerick that may or may not be humorous

   Use **conferences** to assist students.

Homework:

Advanced students can research and cite examples of Italian and Shakespearean sonnets and poems that are ballads and odes.

Students research and cite examples of the following varieties of verse: Triplet, Quatrain, Quintet, Sestet, Septet, and Octave.

Couplets, Haiku, and Limericks

I   Couplets

= two lines that rhyme (Heroic couplet = two successive rhyming lines that express one idea or image)

(ex)   I always wanted to be a student hero,
but on my test there was a zero.

Your couplet:

II   Haiku

= a form of Japanese poetry that has three lines, where the first line has five syllables, the second has seven, and the third has five; traditionally focuses on nature.

(ex)   Behind me the moon
brushes shadows of pine trees
lightly on the floor.

(ex)   Goldfish in a bowl
darting, circling, hurrying
without arriving.

Your haiku:

III   Limerick

= verse that follows an AABBA rhyme scheme to convey most often a humorous tone or image

(ex)   There was a young lady from Niger,
Who smiled as she rode on a tiger.
They came back from the ride
With the lady inside,
And the smile on the face of the tiger.

Your limerick:

Lesson 105　　　POETRY TECHNIQUES

Objective:　　To review the techniques for creating poems

Activities:

1. **Survey:** Students do **Activity 105-1**—the true/false survey.

   Discuss the results: [1-F; 2-F; 3-F; 4-T; 5-T; 6-F;7-F; 8-T; 9-F; 10-T; 11-T; 12-F; 13-T; 14-F; 15-T; 16-F; 17-F; 18-F]

2. **Discuss:** Literary quality.

   A. What are the most common structures used in poetry?

   [Stanzas, rhyme, special kinds of verse]

   B. What makes a successful poem? Why?

   [Answers will vary.]

   C. Why do some poets make deliberate mistakes with punctuation or capitalization?

   [Answers will vary.]

   D. How could a social issue—(ex) peer pressure—be the subject of a poem? Examples?

   [Answers will vary.]

   E. What emotions are commonly portrayed in poetry?

   [love, romance, remorse, sadness, etc.]

   F. Why do most professional poets keep a journal?

   [Used for sorting ideas, playing with word choice, recording observations, listing feelings and any experience, etc.]

3. **Debate:** Between metaphors and similes, which is the stronger literary expression?

4. **Vote:** Which of the following is the most important technique to use when writing a poem? Explain your selection.

   • Figurative language

   • Economy in word choice

   • Imagery and sensory language

   • The type of verse (free verse, rhyme, couplet, etc.)

5. **Freewriting:** Use various poetry techniques.

A. Assign each student a different consonant. Students then demonstrate alliteration with their assigned consonant.

B. Assign each student a different image—(ex) a tree, flowers, a hamburger, rain, etc.—to use in a 2–4 line poem.

C. Students write the first paragraph of a letter to an imaginary parent who has complained that poems about death are not suitable for teenagers to read.

Discuss or **check** the results.

6. **Knowledge check:** Ask questions on poetry.

A. What is a stanza? [A grouping of lines in a poem]

B. How can a stanza be organized? [Rhyme, free verse, special types of verse]

C. What are some typical rhyme schemes in a four line stanza? [ABAB, AABB, ABBA]

7. **Poem Sale:** Students select one poem they consider worthy to "sell" to their classmates. They must write a detailed review of that poem. **Check** the results.

Homework options:

A. Students research a specific poet. Here, they must connect biographical events with images or themes in his/her poems. [Keep a file card of poets, a catalog that is accessible for future students to examine.]

B. Students write or locate a poem and pair it with a drawing or illustration they make.

C. Students write a letter to a favorite poet (living or dead) telling him/her what they think about their poems. They must cite at least one poem to support their points.

D. Students write a poem that focuses on hope, success, fame, or death using an extended metaphor.

E. Students write a letter to a teacher, parent, or published poet that describes their development as a young poet. In this correspondence they should explain what has inspired them.

Poetry—True/False Survey

1. _____   Professional poets seldom revise their works.

2. _____   Stories, but not poems, should have themes.

3. _____   Poems must have titles.

4. _____   Poems must have a beginning, middle, and end.

5. _____   Poetry writing often requires the poet to "play" with the language.

6. _____   Most poems' stanzas are only four lines.

7. _____   Blank verse and free verse are the same thing.

8. _____   Shakespeare's plays are based on poetic language.

9. _____   Poetry, since it is often based on feelings, need not be revised.

10. _____   Meter in poetry refers to the number of "beats" per line.

11. _____   Rhyme is based on syllables and sounds.

12. _____   Alliteration deals with the use of vowels and consonants.

13. _____   There are many variations in poetic rhyme.

14. _____   Song lyrics cannot truly be considered poetry.

15. _____   A poem's stanzas have a strong influence on its themes.

16. _____   A poem written in free verse has limitations on line length.

17. _____   Poetry is a dying art form.

18. _____   Figurative language is the same as literal language.

Section 13 : PEER EDITING

"I believe the writer . . . should always be the final judge. I have always held to that position and have sometimes seen books hurt thereby, but at least as often helped. The book belongs to the author."
(Maxwell Perkins)

Introduction

Research indicates that many students experience difficulty revising their writing simply because they do not know what revising requires. They falter when asked to be objective; they struggle when told to make improvements; and they often challenge the need to clarify ideas when what they have written already makes perfect sense to them. For some students, it is not that they are unwilling to edit, it is that they either lack the skills or motivation to undertake it.

Although most secondary students comprehend proofreading and might even have a system for performing it, the *editing* process remains a mysterious activity. Some students interpret editing as accepting failure—the writing isn't good enough. Others just aren't willing to test a variety of writing strategies before submitting a final copy.

The teacher's goal then is to turn student writers into critical editors and to expose them to the revision stage that goes beyond surface proofreading. Here are ten strategies to achieve this goal:

(1) Model peer editing with your own work.

(2) Provide enough time for the sharing of drafts and follow-up discussion.

(3) Be sure that each student receives a variety of comments that are both positive and constructive.

(4) Stress rereading to both the student editor and student writer.

(5) Use a checklist, if necessary (samples included).

(6) Encourage (and reward) the writing of multiple drafts.

(7) Study the revision process of professional writers.

(8) Have students compare revision strategies.

(9) Remind students that editing is about writing, not the personality of the writer.

(10) Reward careful editing.

Typical peer editing involves students in groups, but it could be pairs or even the entire class, if an opaque projector is available. Students should be able to face each other and have easy access to any materials or papers.

Peer editing can be done at any stage of the writing process, although it is especially appropriate during the drafting and revising stages. Successful peer editing occurs when students recognize their two main obligations:

(1)   To contribute a piece of writing for others to edit

(2)   To offer constructive and creative suggestions to classmates that would help them improve their written work

You should try to give a specific goal for each peer editing session—(ex) work on thesis statements. Each student must understand and accept his/her responsibility in that session. This leads to individual and group accountability.

You can maximize group heterogeneity by including students with high, average, and low abilities. Typical group numbers are 3-4, but more students could be included (for a total of 6) if more time is available. Change the make-up of these groups several times so students receive a variety of opinions.

Observe student interaction closely and if necessary, remind them to stay on task. Intervene when any breakdowns occur. Promote cooperation and collaboration by first allowing group members to learn something substantial about their fellow editors. For example, use any warm-up activities that promote speaking and listening.

Explain, especially to less-mature students, how to deal with differences in opinion and responses that might contradict each other. Be prepared to mediate varied opinions by getting students to explore the reasons behind them. Keep the Peer Editing Guidelines—**Form 106-1**—available and praise earnestly active peer editing as often as possible.

Lesson 106 FIVE MINUTE PROMPTS (ENERGIZERS) FOR INTRODUCING PEER EDITING

1. **Labels:** Each group selects a name or moniker for their group—(ex) The Smurfs—and writes it on an index card. The cards are then exchanged with another group who accepts the label or suggests a new one—(ex) The Smurfettes. The group must write on the index card their reason(s) for either accepting or revising the label—(ex) Because your group is all females. Cards are then returned to the original group who can accept the revision or create a new label.

2. **Listing:** Students list the criteria necessary for successful writing—cater this to the specific assignment (ex) essay, story, poem, etc.—from most important to the least important. Students then list the comments they would make to a writer who failed on all aspects of the criteria. Have student volunteers write these on the black board.

3. **Red pen:** Students study a paragraph(s) written by a previous student. It should already have multiple marks and comments (possibly in the traditional red pen) from the teacher. Students examine the marks and comments and make revisions. This could also prompt a discussion concerning how effective it is for students to receive such markings.

4. **Role play:** Six students are given a different role to play as designated on an index card which they receive as they enter the classroom. (See below). The class is given a piece of writing to edit (**Activity 106-3**), and each member plays his part during the following discussion.

    Be sure you call upon these students during the discussion and at the end of it, the other students must guess each role.

    A. Arguer = the person who argues every other student's idea

    B. Mr./Miss Congeniality = the person who accepts every other idea or proposal without question

    C. Criticizer = the person who finds fault with every other idea but his/her own

    D. Mr./Miss Apathy = the person who offers no comment or suggestion, showing an "I don't care" attitude

    E. Interrupter = the person who spoils any discussion by interrupting other speakers

    F. Dominator = the person who tries to dominate the discussion by declaring who speaks and what ideas will be accepted

5. **Lecture:** Introduce the peer editing.

- Writing workshop = This involves students giving specific and helpful feedback to fellow members about their writing.

- The writer should initiate all discussions about his/her writing, possibly by pointing to a specific part of the writing—(ex) the thesis, the third stanza, the concluding paragraph—and asking for comments.

- Conflicts should be viewed as helping, not hindering the writer. If an argument persists, table it and move on.

- Ultimately, the writer decides the content, grammar, and style of his/her writing. It is *not* a majority rule process, although the writer needs to listen closely to the suggestions of classmates.

- The teacher monitors peer editing and offers input when requested by a writer or group.

6. **Question/answer:** Use this to prompt students to ask effective questions of the writer about his/her work.

   Students first write the most unusual questions they have ever asked or heard—(ex) If you could date anyone you wanted in the world, who would it be and why? Give extra points to the most creative questions.

   Each writer then writes 4-6 questions about his/her writing to ask his/her reviewers—(ex) What do you like about this draft? What could make it better? What do you think of the thesis?

7. **Dilemmas about writing:**

   A. Should the writing be tailored to please the teacher who, of course, is the primary evaluator?

   B. How does a writer know when his/her work has been completely improved? How much rewriting must take place?

   C. If it is important to have a unique writing style, how does a writer know if his/her writing is quality work?

8. **Debates:** Exchange ideas on issues related to writing.

   - Who can cite the best adjective and adverb to use in a descriptive essay about skateboarding?

   - What is the most important stage/step in the writing process?

   - What is the most important criterion for judging or evaluating a composition?

   - The outline is very useful when writing a short story or essay.

   - *(Pick a name of a classmate or professional writer)* writes the best introductory paragraphs.

   - Formal diction is the best type of diction for essays.

9. **Discussion:** Focus on essay writing skills. Choose any of the following.

   A. What is a thesis statement?

   B. How can an outline help a writer?

   C. What is prewriting?

   D. How can a writer achieve paragraph unity?

   E. What is the function of the introductory paragraph?

   F. Why is it important to use specific wording in an essay?

   G. Why is it necessary to revise a composition?

   H. How can a writer narrow his/her topic?

   I. What is the function of a concluding paragraph?

   J. How can a writer eliminate wordiness in an essay?

   K. If two research papers address the same topic, what could make one more persuasive or convincing than the other?

   L. What is a concrete noun? What is a vague noun? What is a strong verb? What is an example of a weak verb?

10. **Campaigns:** Groups create a campaign to convince other students to vote for their assigned type of diction—slang, informal, jargon, clichés, formal, or profanity.

11. **Comparisons:**

   A. Compare common knowledge to personal insight when writing a research essay.

   B. Compare editing to proofreading.

   C. Compare informal to formal diction.

   D. Compare webbing to clustering (as prewriting methods).

   E. Compare sources for a research essay: an interview and an encyclopedia, a reference book and a newspaper article, a magazine article and an almanac.

12. **TRUE/FALSE:** Quiz students on the parts of speech.

   A. Adjectives and adverbs have the same purpose. [T]

   B. Prepositional phrases have grammatical requirements about their length. [F]

   C. Adjectives can be changed into adverbs. [T]

   D. There are eight parts of speech. [T]

   E. Personal pronouns are antecedents to indefinite pronouns. [F]

   F. Verbs change form in regards to tense. [T]

   G. The maximum (most) number of verbs in a verb phrase is three. [F]

H. Nonstandard English is considered unacceptable by most people. [T]

I. Indefinite pronouns have unclear references. [T]

J. Prewriting refers to writing a first draft. [F]

13. **Contests:** Challenge students on descriptive writing skills.

A. Who can use 6-8 pronouns in one complete sentence without violating any grammar rules?

B. Create a more descriptive sentence by adding descriptive adjectives and adverbs and replacing the vague nouns.

Our team defeated the other team.

C. Why do we need conjunctions? Explain their purpose and usefulness.

D. Adjectives are descriptive words. Some are better than others. For example, *nice* is a poor adjective. Why?

Peer Editing Guidelines

1. Each member must exchange his/her writing with the other members of the group.

   No one talks or asks any questions of the writer during this sharing/exchange period, even if it is to have a word spelled. Any confusion regarding spelling and/or sentences is part of the editing process and should be marked accordingly.

2. Writers must not offer any commentary about the writing during this sharing/exchange period—(ex) "This isn't very good. I wrote it real fast."

3. Writers must have questions (possibly written) to ask the group members about the writing—(ex) "What would make this writing better?"

4. Peer editors must write their comments and marks related to proofreading and editing on the manuscript. Look carefully at the diction—check descriptive or concrete words; underline dull words or phrases, etc.

   Examine the writing to see if it is thorough—do any parts need more development or description? Also, note where the writer has shown a unique writing style or some interesting insights about the topic.

5. After manuscripts are returned to original writers, each writer, in turn, will examine the markings and comments and then initiate any discussion for the purpose of clarification—(ex) "What's wrong with the final stanza?"

   Writers must strive to understand completely the comments of their editors. Writers could even repeat to the group what they think they are saying to achieve clarity. But *do not* argue with the readers, and do not explain what you meant—that is, what they didn't realize. If any particular responses do not seem useful, writers can ignore it when revising.

6. Give each writer's manuscript equal time and discussion.

7. Remember to be positive and helpful. The purpose here is not to badger a writer, nor is it just to find surface mistakes in terms of spelling and punctuation. The key is to comment on those aspects of the writing that could be expanded (for clarification) or deleted (because they're unnecessary).

8. Use the peer editing checklist if requested to do so.

9. Writers can revise a part and ask immediately for feedback.

10. Turn to the teacher for assistance when the group is in disagreement.

Name _____

Name of writer _____

Title of paper _____

Peer Editing Checklist #1

Directions: Check the appropriate line after reading the manuscript.

Weak   *Strong*
____   ____   Complete sentences?

____   ____   Variety in sentence structure?

____   ____   Correct punctuation?

____   ____   Correct capitalization?

____   ____   Spelling?

____   ____   Precise verbs, nouns, and modifiers?

____   ____   Avoids clichés and dull phrases

____   ____   Demonstrates a logical organization

____   ____   Transitional words or devices?

____   ____   All sentences support the topic

____   ____   Has well-developed paragraphs

____   ____   Effective introduction

____   ____   Effective thesis

____   ____   Effective conclusion (or closure)

____   ____   Uniqueness *in* writing style

106-2B

Name _____

Name of writer _____

Title of paper _____

Peer Editing Checklist #2

Strong points about the writing:

Weaknesses:

Please expand on:

I recommend deleting:

Name _____

Peer Editing Checklist #3

Name of writer _____

Title of paper _____

To the writer:

Step #1

Write 1-2 questions at the top of the essay that you would like the others to focus on—(ex) What do you think of the sensory language I used in the second paragraph? Avoid the yes/no questions—(ex) Do you like it?—or a vague question such as—what do you think?

Step #2

Read your introduction (the beginning of the piece).

Step #3

Tell the group what you are trying to accomplish with the piece.

Step #4

Exchange your work with editor(s).

To the editor:

Step #5

Read and critique the writing, identifying both strengths and weaknesses. Respond to the writer's question(s) at the top, but also add detailed commentary on the work about the following:

1. the topic—Is it limited enough?
2. the beginning—Does it capture your interest?
3. the word choice—Any unclear phrases or shifts in the diction?
4. organization—How effectively are paragraphs organized?
5. the grammar—Any problems with sentence structure, punctuation, or spelling?

Make these comments on the manuscript.

Step #6

Verbally clarify to the writer any markings or reactions on the manuscript.

Step #7

Help the writer begin the revision process. Make suggestions for expanding or cutting the document.

Name _____

Peer Editing Model

Directions: Read and evaluate the essay below that deals with making a contribution to others.

Helping

What is helping? real helping is the willingness to do something for someone. During a typical day, a person can find themselves helping two or more people. I often find myself helping someone without knowing, like carrying a book or taking someone somewhere, you have helped that person and have been a contribution to their life. Many people feel if you do not intend to help you do not help. That is why it is important to make contributions.

I realize that every day I make a contribution to another person's life. Like Audrey Williams who has a daughter named Auriel, and she is four years old. She needed me to baby-sit her daughter so she could run errands. By spending time with Auriel I realized that enjoyed playing and watching television with her.

I beleive that doing something like babysitting showed me that I do contribute to many people every day. Even if my contribution is to my family by cleaning up the house or taking a family member somewhere. I enjoy helping others.

APPENDIX

Answer Keys

For 5-1 *The Ugly, the Bad, and the Good*

1. aint   am not/isn't
2. wanna   want to
3. gonna   going to
4. hafta   have to
5. lemme   let me
6. bursted   burst
7. brung   brought
8. oughta   ought to
9. sorta   sort of
10. theirselves   themselves
11. nowheres   nowhere
12. hisself   himself
13. kinda   kind of
14. wierdo   weird person
15. pooped   tired, exhausted
16. wimp   weak person
17. fatso   overweight person
18. alot   a lot
19. must of   must have
20. macho   masculine, manly
21. brang   brought
22. setted   set
23. chill out   relax

For 14-1 *Verb Usage Quiz*

1. Answers will vary
2. Answers will vary
3. am, are, is, was, were, be, been
4. Answers will vary (ex) is going
5. Answers will vary (ex) has been going
6. Answers will vary (ex) must have been going
7. sold
8. threw or thrown
9. stang, stung

10-15. slithered, crept, slid, glided, sauntered, plodded, jumped, leaped, skipped, sprang, skittered, slinked, etc.

16. Helping Verbs are auxiliary verbs that must be used with main verbs, the action verbs of the sentence. An example would be *have eaten*. Linking Verbs can, however, be used alone in sentences to link the subject with the predicate. Each has their own function, yet linking verbs can be used as helping verbs—(ex) *is eating*—although helping verbs can never be used as linking verbs.

For 15-2 *Sentence Combining—Prepositional Phrases*

1. Sue drew a picture of a winter scene in art class at Riverview High School.
2. The Senator from Ohio answered many questions about health care reform.
3. The guests in the lobby will be given a tour of the downtown museum.
4. Marty found a coin from the 1920's in the mud at the park.
5. Ann called her boyfriend from Iowa on the telephone during school.

For 17-1 *Conjunctions*

1. This school has a lot of options for students who should take advantage of them. These include sports, clubs, and drama. If students lack the time, they should budget their time or consider changing some non-school activities so they could participate in more sports, clubs or drama.
2. A. We love school but hate homework.
   B. Helen Gurley Brown founded and publishes *Cosmopolitan* magazine.
3. Answers will vary.
4. Using conjunctions to start sentences can add a sense of transition to writing, but it is traditionally inappropriate. Using a conjunction to start a sentence could set up a sentence fragment.
5. Answers will vary.

For 19-2 *Pronouns and You*

1. Respecting other people is necessary.
2. Being open with a friend is really important.
3. Affection and support must be evident in any relationship.
4. Listening must happen first to understand someone's feelings.
5. Meeting a partner's needs is necessary in a relationship.
6. Trusting the other person makes a relationship work.
7. Falling in love can be really rewarding.

For 27-1 *Constructing and Deconstructing Sentences*

1. A new blond, lanky, shy student entered the classroom and smiled at us.
2. The veteran third baseman reached his mitt into the air, snagged the ball, and threw it to first base.
3. The nervous seven-year-old girl tightly grasped the handlebars of her first two-wheeler bike.
4. Barb's smiling parents watched her as she stood nervously at the end of the diving board.
5. After the school bell finally rang three o'clock, we stepped quickly to our buses for the fifteen minute ride.
6. The dog perked up its ears, barked, and raced to the door when it heard the car in the driveway. The car's tires crunched the drive-way gravel. The dog knew its owner had returned with dinner. The dinner was an expensive can of dog food.

7. The Red Devils, who hadn't won a game all year, gloated after winning the football game against the Eagles. Their arch rival had been undefeated. They also were ranked first in the state before losing 24-14.
8. I always leave my cigar box hidden behind my books on the top shelf in my bedroom. In it are my spare coins. I'll eventually use the coins to buy birthday presents.

For 27-2 *"At the Foul Line"*

1. How do these paragraphs differ in terms of their sentence structure?

   The first uses short, clipped sentences to convey a sense of tension and suspense. There is an average of four words per sentence, which are all subject-verb patterns. The second paragraph has longer sentences which seem to be more descriptive and less suspenseful.

2. What mood or "tone" is established in the first paragraph?

   Tension and suspense. The reader is led moment by moment to the outcome of the basketball being shot.

3. Why does the second paragraph seem to have a better sense of coherence?

   Transitional words like *in fact* and devices like pronoun references accomplish this. Also, the use of compound and complex sentences add to the coherence.

4. Which paragraph offers more details?

   Both offer the same details, but it appears at first that the second paragraph does.

For 29-1 *Jumbled Sentences*

1. The dense fog that comes in January is a dangerous hazard for drivers.
2. Dense fog can make driving on this road hazardous.
3. Fog often occurs in low areas in the early morning.
4. Fog is a low level mass of water particles near the surface.
5. A fogbank is a dense mass of fog that remains motionless on the ground.
6. A foghorn gives warning to ships during a fog.
7. Someone who is in a fog sometimes is said to be confused.
8. Fog can sometimes be mixed with rain.
9. During a fog a fog-alarm is used on a ship to give warning, but a fogbell is used on land.

For 29-2 *Emphasis in Sentences*

1. For a hundred years, "Romeo and Juliet" was performed with the lovers still alive at the end.

   For a hundred years the lovers were still alive at the end of "Romeo and Juliet."

   The lovers were still alive at the end of performances of "Romeo and Juliet" for a hundred years.

2. Of all of Shakespeare's plays, "Romeo and Juliet" has been produced on film the most times.

    "Romeo and Juliet" has been produced on film the most times of all of Shakespeare's plays.

    Of all of Shakespeare's plays, the one that has been produced on film the most times is "Romeo and Juliet."

3. In the 18th century (two hundred years after he wrote it), Shakespeare's "Romeo and Juliet" was performed over 400 times in London.

    Shakespeare's "Romeo and Juliet" was performed over 400 times in London in the 18th century (two hundred years after he wrote it).

    In London in the 18th century (two hundred years after he wrote it), Shakespeare's "Romeo and Juliet" was performed over 400 times.

4. Shakespeare borrowed some of the plot of "Romeo and Juliet" from Chaucer and other earlier poets.

    Shakespeare borrowed from Chaucer and other earlier poets some of the plot of "Romeo and Juliet."

    Some of the plot of "Romeo and Juliet" was borrowed from Chaucer and other earlier poets by Shakespeare.

5. The play involves an ancient feud between two families in Verona, Italy called the Montagues and the Capulets.

    The play involves an ancient feud between two families called the Montagues and the Capulets in Verona, Italy.

    Two families in Verona, Italy called the Montagues and the Capulets are involved in an ancient feud in the play.

For 31-2 *Understanding Participles*

1. The embarrassed coach was trying to quiet the booing crowd.
2. The hissing goose chased the yelling boys.
3. The screaming passengers evacuated the sinking ship.
4. The trained pilot brought the disabled plane to safety.
5. We found a faded photograph in the crumbling attic.
6. The singing Boy Scouts were gathered around the blazing fire.

For 34-2 *Mastery of Sentence Structure*

1. Answers will vary.
2. Answers will vary.
3. Answers will vary.
4. Answers will vary.
5. Answers will vary.

6. Answers will vary.
7. A natural grouping of words with a subject and predicate that makes sense

8-10. Lists will vary.

11. A writer achieves sentence expansion by adding modifiers like adjectives, adverbs, and prepositional phrases to the basic sentence core. The writer could also make some parts of the sentence compound or transform a simple sentence into a compound or complex sentence.
12. We need to use a variety of sentence patterns because this demonstrates maturity as a writer and is a first step for a writer in creating a personal writing style. Variety in sentences makes the writing interesting and coherent.
13. The advantages to using compound and complex sentences in our writing are many. Using these sentences shows skill as a writer. They also are often useful for descriptions and explanations. This adds true variety to sentence writing, especially when used with simple sentences.
14. The key differences between an independent and dependent clause is that the independent clause is a complete sentence. The dependent clause cannot stand alone; it has to be connected to an independent clause to make a complex sentence.
15. Sentence fragments and run-ons are typical sentence errors that can be avoided by proofreading each sentence to be sure it has a complete subject and predicate. Writers should also be sure no dependent clauses are left as single sentences and be careful using punctuation, especially the comma, period, and semicolon.

For 44-1 *Writing a Thesis Statement*

1. Today's teenage fashions—This must be narrowed down to one type of fashion like basketball shoes or prom dresses.
2. The importance of exercise for teens—This can be narrowed possibly to one type of exercise, like weightlifting or aerobics.
3. Weight-loss treatments or programs—This topic must be narrowed to one type of treatment or program (Jenny Craig, Slimfast, daily walking) and to one group who would use it (professional body builders, senior citizens, etc.)
4. The dropout rate in urban high schools—Focus on one urban area and one school. The thesis should specify one topic related to this issue like the dropout rate's relationship to juvenile delinquency.
5. High school cliques—The thesis should focus on one type of clique, like football athletes or freshmen girls, and one issue related to cliques, like their possible conflicts with other groups or their community service work.
6. Grandparents and their values—Here, the thesis should reflect just 1-2 values, like honesty or trust, and focus on one set of grandparents, instead of making a broad generalization about all of them.
7. Divorce rate in the United States—The specific divorce rate—i.e., 54% of current marriages will end in divorce—needs to be cited in the thesis along with a one specific statement about that statistic—possibly how it affects teenagers of divorced parents.
8. Salaries of professional athletes—Which sport? What type of athlete—i.e., the starters? The substitutes? The thesis must, of course, specify this and express an attitude toward the salaries—i.e., the players do not deserve the money.

For 60-2 *Sample Interview*

Q: Do you bring your lunch or buy it? Introd.
Q: When you buy it, do you notice people breaking into the lunch line? Yes/No
Q: How do you feel about that? Probe
Q: Why do you admire their courage? Probe
Q: How do you handle it? Probe
Q: Do you think there's a way to stop this from happening? Yes/No
Q: What else could they do? Open-ended
Q: Do you think more people will complain? Yes/No
Q: What do you think the lunch line will be like next year? Open-ended

For 69-2 *Storms Assault Southwest*

Three people were killed in Fordyce, Arkansas, and four eighteen wheel trucks were hurled on top of a building in Oklahoma when tornadoes hit these states and Texas. A high school gym roof was blown off by 100 mph winds and Nesho, Arkansas had property damage authorities said would cost about one million dollars to fix.

Many homes in Texas were severely damaged. Power lines and utility poles fell, keeping emergency crews busy through the night.

For 71-3 *Libel Cases*

1. Why do you think the editor did this?

    Students may generally responed that the editor believed the article would generate enough sales and revenues to offset any potential lawsuit fine or that Burnett would be too embarrassed to sue.

2. Whom do you think deserved to win this case?

    Some students may side with Falwell who was victimized by the vulgar and pornographic depiction of him having sex with his mother in an outhouse while others may accept, as the U.S. Supreme Court did, Flynt's right to practice free speech.

3. Why do you think Ms. Winfrey sued for so much money?

    Oprah Winfrey is an internationally known public personality whose career is based on her popular reputation within the entertainment industry. Her work has enabled her to earn nearly one billion dollars, and it is very possible *News Extra*'s story could damage her reputation with other media figures and businesses. Therefore, her $300 million libel suit has some justification.

4. How should the court treat a case like this?

    Although our courts are swamped with litigation, every case must be considered independently, including Kraft's $60 million lawsuit vs. Warner Books and author Dennis McDougal. As the plaintiff, he does not have to prove terms like "sick, twisted man" are false; the defendants have to prove they're true. As a man on death row, he has nothing to lose and everything to gain. A judge and jury would have to determine the validity of his claim.

For 84-2 *Review Questions for Letter Writing*

1. The inside address is the receiver's name, title, business or organization name, street address, and city, state zip. This is expected in any business letter.
2. A letter's heading is the sender's address, usually located at the top center of a letter. It could include a phone number as well.
3. When a writer doesn't know the receiver's name in a typical business letter, the appropriate salutation is Dear Title (i.e., Dear Vice-President, Dear Manager).
4. Several useful closings in a standard business letter are *Sincerely, Cordially, Respectfully, Gratefully.*
5. Several useful closings in a personal letter are *Sincerely, Love, Thank you, With affection.*
6. A signature is necessary on a letter because it authenticates the sender's message. Unless the signature is forged, the receiver can be certain that the sender actually wrote the letter.
7. A business letter should be formal in its structure and diction because this is the expected format expected in the business world. Business people still rely on the traditional format of letters.
8. After receiving a business letter, the receiver should share the letter, if necessary, with the appropriate colleagues and then file it after reading it.
9. There are few restrictions on the structure and diction of a personal letter. Generally, these letters are informal and friendly in their diction and only need a heading, salutation, body, and closing for its structure.
10. Block style refers to all parts of the letter are against the left-hand margin while semiblock format in letters shows the date and closing against a mid-page margin.
11. A letter should be filed and saved for future reference. If anyone, especially the sender, disputes information the receiver has from the letter, the letter proves the accuracy of those details.
12. Employers can certainly detect an applicant's skills in a letter. An applicant's writing skills obviously stand out, as could his/her personality, confidence, and experience.
13. There are many types of business letters. They include letters of application, consumer letters, letters to politicians, letters between companies and/or their executives, and letters of requests.
14. Letters are more useful than E-mail and faxes because not everyone has access to a computer or fax machine. Also, E-mail messages and faxes could possibly be viewed by others while a letter remains private within its envelope. Sometimes, faxes aren't legible and E-mails may not be thorough.
15. Some types of personal letters include love letters, pen pal letters, fan mail, invitations, announcements, and thank you letters.
16. Some punctuation rules associated specifically with letter writing include placing a comma between city and state in the addresses. No punctuation belongs between the state and zip code. In a business letter, a colon belongs after the salutation

while a comma is used for it in a personal letter. A comma always belongs after any closing. Of course, all punctuation rules apply in the body of any letter.

17. The general purpose of any newsletter is to update the receivers of the newsletter about any upcoming events or important information related to the company, organization, or institution that is sending the newsletter.

18. A letter is more useful than a phone conversation because the writer can be more detailed and comprehensive. A mistake can be erased but sometimes even an apology cannot remove the harm of an incorrect verbal statement. Letters can be filed and saved; phone conversations can't. Letters generally are less expensive and more impressive (a receiver typically is pleased the sender took the time to write).

19. The U.S. Postal Service has four classes of mail: 1st = regular mail; 2nd = magazines and catalogs; 3rd = junk mail and bulk mail; 4th = packages and parcels.

20. Some special capitalization rules related to letter writing include capitalizing all words in the salutation but only the first word in the closing. Also, cities, states, street names, business names, people's names and titles, and names of the month in the date need to be capitalized. All capitalization rules should be followed in the body.

For 91-2 *Dialogue and Dialect*

From "Red Badge of Courage" by Stephen Crane

1. We're going to move tomorrow. That is for sure. We're going way up the river, cut across, and come in behind them.

2. And take good care of yourself in this war. You better watch out, and take good care of yourself. Don't think you can defeat the entire rebel army at the start because you can't.

3. That's all true, I suppose, but I'm not going to run.

From "The Adventures of Huckleberry Finn" by Mark Twain

4. Your old father doesn't know yet what he's going to do. Sometimes he believes he'll leave and then again he may decide he'll stay. The best course of action is to rest easy and let the old man decide for himself.

5. You are going to have considerable trouble in your life and considerable joy. Sometimes you're going to get hurt, and sometimes you're going to get sick; but every time you're going to get well again.

For 96-1 *Poetry and History*

"Paul Revere's Ride" by Longfellow documents the period of the American Revolution. It presents Paul Revere as a hero whose contribution as a messenger to warn the Minutemen and other rebels about the approach of British soldiers was a crucial factor in the successful rebellion against England.

"Jesse James" by Benet presents in frontier dialect a portrayal of the western frontier of the 19th century. The bandit outlaw Jesse James is glamorized (and nearly mythologized, in fact) by the poet. His exploits as a thief are seen as achievements and his behavior is seen as heroic.

For 97-2 *Clichés*

1. At the end of my rope = I'm exhausted, unable to continue.
2. Back against the wall = No other options exist, nowhere to go.
3. At the drop of a hat = Will react or respond immediately.
4. Between a rock and a hard place = A difficult choice or decision has to be made; few options exist.
5. Bite the bullet = Suffer the consequences; take the punishment.
6. Boys will be boys = A young man's immature behavior is to be expected.
7. It's a breeze = It's a task that is easily accomplished.
8. Bury the hatchet = An agreement that the conflict or disagreement will end without a grudge remaining.
9. Chip off the old block = They are very similar.
10. Clear as a bell = It is very clear or obvious.
11. Dead tired = Being very exhausted and near collapse.
12. Dog-eat-dog = An attitude that reflects ruthlessness; no sympathy or support exists.
13. Down in the dumps = Very unhappy or depressed.
14. Elbow room = A reference to body space.
15. Flipped his lid = He acted suddenly without thought; his behavior is unexpectedly irrational.
16. Fed up = A feeling of disgust and/or discouragement.
17. Fits like a glove = Very form fitting; a perfect match.
18. High off the hog = Living with many luxuries and comforts.
19. Head over heels = Passion has overruled reason.
20. Have a ball = A party atmosphere; excitement and fun are expected.
21. Hit me like a ton of bricks = I was overwhelmed and shocked.
22. King of the hill = The most important person.
23. Like a bat out of hell = Moved quickly and aggressively.
24. Like a herd of elephants = Moved noisily and clumsily.
25. Needle in a haystack = Nearly impossible to locate.
26. On the tip of the tongue = I am nearly familiar with the correct response; it's in my memory but can't be recalled right now.
27. Over the hill = Aged; no longer useful; damaged in some way.
28. Safe and sound = There's a sense of security and comfort; undamaged.
29. Saved by the bell = A nearly disastrous or uncomfortable situation has been avoided.
30. Run like a deer = Running swiftly and quietly; much agility.
31. Shake a leg = Prompt movement is required; a quick departure, for example, is necessary.
32. Slept like a log = The sleep was deep, peaceful, and uninterrupted.
33. Smart as a whip = Possessive of a quick and sharp intelligence.
34. Like taking candy from a baby = A task that is easily accomplished and without resistance.
35. Walking on air = A sense of happiness, hopefulness, or euphoria.
36. Time flies = A period of time has passed quickly.
37. Throw in the towel = To quit, somewhat disgracefully, before the task or contest has concluded.

38. Through thick and thin = To continue through every difficulty or ease.
39. Worked her fingers to the bone = She was known for her diligence and perserverance.
40. Like two peas in a pod = They are identical.

For 100-1 *Imagery in Poetry*

1. Imagery in "Birch Tree" = much sight imagery like slender and white, [branches] waving to the midnight sky, [branches] shivering, and the tree itself dancing in the darkness.
2. Imagery in "The Delicatessen" = sight references like the light splitting the darkness and flashing across the knives; meat stains smeared into a map on the butcher's apron; and white bones ("scraped clean"). Also, some taste references with "ready to feed me."
3. Imagery in "The Spider" = description of the spider's shiny black body (sight), its thick hairy legs (touch), the dew (sight), the web's "lacy threads" (touch), and silent movement (sound).
4. Imagery in "Sea Waves" = description of waves "sputtering, foaming, frothing" (sight and sound), the muddy shore (sight), the salty sand (taste and touch), the foam (sight), rocky ledges (touch), the purple horizon (sight), and pale moon (sight), along with "slipping and sliding" which are indirect references to touch imagery.

Guidelines for Writing Compositions

1. Use regular 8 x 11 inch white paper. No spiral edges.
2. All final copies must be *typed*. Use only blue or black ink for other assignments. Double space when typing. Skip lines when writing.
3. Margins: one and half inches left / right / top / bottom
   When beginning a paragraph indent five spaces when typing/ or the length of an average word when writing in ink.
4. Type or write on one side of the paper only.
5. When using a word processor or computer, do not use italics or any fonts bigger than number 12.
6. Each composition must have a title page (as follows):

Original Title

Your Name
English 9
Period ___

Date

7. Never begin sentences with numerals. For example, write a sentence like this: *Forty-two percent of the land is used for farming*. Not: *42% of the land is used for farming*.
8. Numbers one through ninety-nine should be spelled out: *seven* tapes, not 7 tapes. For dates and years, however, use the numerals: December 27, 1996.
9. Avoid using the pronouns YOU and YOUR when writing a formal essay.
10. Follow the word length requirement of the assignment. If the directions call for 500-750 words, then do not go below 475 or beyond 775 words.
11. Neatness is extremely important. Do not fold or wrinkle the composition. Use a single staple in the upper left hand corner only.
12. Create a catchy introductory paragraph that gets the reader interested in the topic and a forceful concluding paragraph that summarizes the main points.
13. Evaluation is regularly based on:
    (A) how well the composition was organized
    (B) the actual content (the originality of your ideas and thoughts)
    (C) thoroughness (Did you complete the assignment in detail?)
    (D) grammar, spelling, and usage
    (E) your improvement on the writing chart
14. To become a better writer you must want to make improvements and do revisions. Markings and comments from the teacher and peer editors are useless unless you are willing to improve on those skills through practice.

Teacher's Checklist for Writing Assignments

When creating a lesson, consider the following:

_____ Is the assignment meaningful and interesting to students personally, something in which they can take pride?

_____ Does the assignment promote cooperation?

_____ Does the assignment cater to students' individual needs and learning styles?

_____ Does the assignment offer choices?

_____ Are there easy-to-understand examples?

_____ Do I have an alternative plan if this one is unsuccessful?

_____ Does the assignment in some way relate to their personal experiences?

_____ Can I use a diagnostic test (a pretest) at the beginning of every unit to prevent reteaching material students have already mastered?

_____ Is there a good transition (a reference to the previous day's lesson or assignment)?

_____ Are big projects broken down into smaller, more manageable steps for students? Does the deadline for each step allow a reasonable period of time for completion?

_____ Can I use a panel of other students or even the writer's parent to assess the piece?

_____ Have I allowed time and opportunity for multiple revisions?

_____ Have I allowed time and opportunity for the writer to complete a self-assessment?

© 1999 by The Center for Applied Research in Education